The Unexpected Circumnavigation

Unusual Boat, Unusual People

Part 1 – San Diego to Australia

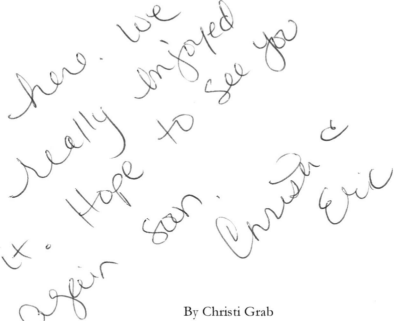

By Christi Grab

With input, help and technical editing from Eric Grab

Cover Design by Eric Grab

This book is dedicated to my high school CORE teachers. Thank you for teaching me to write, make a logical argument, and to connect the dots.

This book is also dedicated to Fred and Sonny. I wrote the blog for them, and now the blog has evolved into a book.

Photographs on the Front Cover

Top row, from left to right:

- Taiohae Bay, Nuka Hiva, Marquesas Islands, French Polynesia.

- Bay of Virgins, Fatu Hiva, Marquesas Islands, French Polynesia.

- Tahaa, Society Islands, French Polynesia.

- Manihi, Tuomotus Archipelago, French Polynesia.

Middle row, from left to right:

- *Kosmos* anchored in Anaho Bay, Nuka Hiva, Marquesas Islands, French Polynesia.

- Eric and Christi Grab in Apataki, Tuomotus Islands, French Polynesia.

Bottom row, from left to right:

- Yalobi Bay, Waya, Yasawa Islands, Fiji.

- Suwarrow Island, Cook Islands.

- Mele Cascades just outside of Port Vila, Efate, Vanuatu.

- Vava'u, Vava'u Islands, Tonga.

For more color photographs please visit the *Kosmos Travel Log* at:
http://kosmos.liveflux.net/blog

Table of Contents

We want non-boaters to enjoy our book as much as boaters, so if there are any words or abbreviations that are unfamiliar to you, please see the glossary. Also, see the diagrams and description of *Kosmos*.

Prologue

Eric and I started dating in July 1999, when I was twenty-five and he was twenty-nine. He was a software engineer, and I worked in the mortgage industry. On one of our first dates, he told me he really wanted to buy a boat. He said all his friends and family thought he was crazy since he tended to get sea sick and had a phobia of deep water. I thought he was crazy, too. But, since the boat was only a fantasy at that point, I didn't say anything.

In February 2000, Eric was offered a new job with a substantially higher salary. He accepted it and immediately bought a twenty-eight-foot sedan cruiser powerboat made by Bayliner. Had he asked me about it, I would have discouraged the purchase. I thought boats were fun, but not fun enough to justify the outrageous costs of maintaining them. I believed it was cheaper to rent a boat whenever you wanted to go out than to buy one. But, we were not serious at that point in time and he never asked my opinion.

Eric was excited about his new toy. It had a tiny kitchen and bedroom, so we could go away for the weekend on it. We learned the most basic boating skills, only enough to use our weekend cruiser. He kept the boat in San Diego, where we both lived. At first we took it out often, going to Catalina Island near Los Angeles (an eighty-nautical-mile trip) or the Los Coronado Islands near Tijuana (a ten-nm trip). Once we even traveled to the Channel Islands, near Ventura, (about 150 nm). But as time marched on, we both got busier with work and didn't have time for "long" trips. And, the truth was that we didn't like being on the boat much when it was in motion. It was loud, cold, bumpy, and uncomfortable. Eric would often turn green and not feel good. We enjoyed being on it at anchor, though. After a while we developed a routine where on Saturday evenings we would motor over to an anchorage a few miles away from our slip, spend the night, and go back home on Sunday morning. But, with our hectic work schedules, we could only manage that once a month or so.

When Eric bought the boat, he had expected it to be a rallying point for friends and family, and had envisioned hosting all kinds of get-togethers on board. The reality was, however, that the Bayliner could only hold six people comfortably, and he quickly realized that the big parties he was hoping for would never materialize with this boat. So in 2002, Eric began contemplating a new boat purchase. After doing extensive research on different models, he decided on a significantly larger thirty-six foot Carver. He selected that particular design because it accommodate ten to twelve people, allowing him to have the parties on the water he had always wanted.

At this point, we were seriously talking marriage. Fortunately, Eric was smart enough to realize that he should probably consult me before making such a huge purchase, so he took me to a boat show to see it. We walked into the show and made a beeline for the Carver. I thought the Carver was great, but a bigger boat meant more costs. The main reason we weren't using the Bayliner much was because we didn't have the time. Buying another boat, no matter how great, wasn't going to give us any more time for boating. I told him I was absolutely opposed to spending more money on something that wouldn't get used any more than what we already had. He was disappointed, but he agreed to not buy it.

Since we were already at the show, we figured we might as well look around. This particular boat show featured mostly high-end power boats. The Carver we had come to see was probably the cheapest boat there. We walked through at least a dozen gorgeous million dollar plus yachts before we came to a boat with a sign that said, "I can cross the Atlantic." I was shocked.

"You mean all these other boats can't?" I asked, pointing to the other boats around us.

Eric laughed at me. "There's no way these can cross oceans! These boats only carry enough fuel for about three hundred miles. Crossing an ocean is thousands of miles!" he said in a tone that indicated he thought I was really ignorant.

"What's the point of spending millions of dollars on a boat if you can't even cross an ocean with it?" I replied.

He didn't have an answer for that.

The ocean capable boat was forty feet long and called the Nordhavn 40. I went inside and looked around. I thought it was ugly and that the stairs were too steep. Eric peeked in and decided it was overbuilt; he never even walked around it. I took a flyer on my way out.

We never discussed that boat again. We had no idea that inconsequential moment would change the course of our lives forever.

In June 2003, Eric *finally* asked me to marry him. We immediately started planning our life together. I was twenty-nine; he was thirty-three. I told him that my dream was to take a year off work to travel around the world before I had kids, and I was determined to do it no matter what. I had always envisioned buying a round-the-world plane ticket and backpacking. To understand why I was so adamant about doing this, we have to backtrack in time.

In 2000, at Thanksgiving dinner, my mother announced she had stage four cancer and only had a few months to live. We were all stunned. People like my mother weren't supposed to get cancer. She had never smoked, always exercised, ate right, took vitamins, and did all the other things doctors say prevents cancer. She even had her own organic garden! Cancer didn't run in the family. And, she was pretty young, having just celebrated her fifty-eighth birthday a couple weeks before. My mother was incredibly bitter about her sickness. She felt like she had been robbed—she believed that since she'd done everything "right", she was entitled to a long, healthy life. She had so many hopes, dreams, and desires that had not yet been fulfilled, and now never would be. It made me realize how important it was to live for the present. She fought a brave battle, living another fourteen months before she finally passed.

About the same time my mother died, the mortgage boom started. I knew the boom couldn't last for very long, so I was working my tail off and squirreling away all my money so that when the boom ended, I could take that year off to travel.

Eric told me that he liked the idea of extensive traveling, but he didn't want to be living out of a suitcase for a year. He said he'd think about it and get back to me. A few weeks later, he came up with a proposal: how about traveling on a boat? It was a win-win-win solution. He would get the upgraded boat he wanted, we'd get to travel around the world, and we would have our house with us. I agreed it was the perfect compromise.

I thought for a minute, then asked "Where's that flyer from the boat show?"

We assumed there were zillions of powerboats that could cross oceans, and that we would find one for a reasonable price. When Eric started doing research, however, he found that there were only three brands of powerboats genuinely capable of crossing oceans, and of the three, only one brand had boats that had actually made it around the world: Nordhavn.

We didn't want to be the first ones to try taking another brand around the world, but the Nordhavn 40 cost much more money than we had in mind, and, frankly, we just didn't like it that much. We never even considered trying to build a custom powerboat. So, we started looking into sailboats. Sailboats can be much cheaper if you're willing to sacrifice "luxuries" like refrigerators, freezers, hot water, and water tanks big enough to allow you to regularly shower. Since the boat was going to be our full time home for an entire year, we decided we didn't want to skimp on the "luxuries." But to have those luxuries, we would have to spend the same amount of money as what the Nordhavn cost.

Eric did a ton of research, sure that we could find the perfect sailboat. But the more we learned about sailing, the more we realized it wasn't for us. First, in most sailboats you have to be outside on watch, even when the weather is bad. When you're outside, you're more likely to hurt yourself or fall into the water than on a powerboat, where you sit inside a protected pilothouse. Sailboats are tipped on their side while in motion, and you have to live at an angle. That may be fun for an afternoon, but not for weeks on end. And to top it all off, sailboats apparently used their motors for twenty-five to seventy-five percent of the time anyway.

Meanwhile, Eric had also been working on planning our route. He realized that we couldn't circumnavigate the world in one year on a small boat. Because of the way the weather windows work throughout the various regions of the world, we would either need to do it in six months or two years. Anything in between would mean traveling during storm seasons. If we tried to make it in six months, we wouldn't be able to spend any time on land, so that was not even a consideration. But we weren't sure that we had the money to stretch the trip to two years, especially since the boat was going to cost more money than we had originally anticipated. But, the mortgage boom was still going strong, as were the stock and housing markets, so we decided to cross our fingers that the boom would last long enough to finance an additional year of travel.

Eric chose one of the most popular conventional sailing routes that follows the trade winds, meaning the wind and seas would mostly be at our back to help push us along. From San Diego, we'd go to the South Pacific islands. Then we would travel a straight line through the South Pacific to Australia, go north to the Indian Ocean, cut through the Suez Canal to the Mediterranean, cross the Atlantic to the Caribbean, cut through the Panama Canal, and follow the coast north back to San Diego. The only bummer about this route was that the very first leg of the trip would be the very longest—a twenty-day passage from San Diego to the Marquesas Islands.

The final nail in the coffin for a sailboat came when Eric figured out the land time versus sea time ratios for our route. The average speed for a forty-foot sailboat is four and a half knots course made good, which meant that we would be spending 50 – 55% of our time at sea. A year plus of ocean time sounded terrible. However, the average speed for the Nordhavn 40 powerboat was six knots, which meant only 25 – 30% of our time at sea. We thought that was a palatable number.

About the same time we realized a sailboat wasn't an option for us, Nordhavn announced a new forty-three-foot model was coming out soon, an upgraded version of the 40. Based on the plans, Eric decided it was the right boat for us. He made an appointment for us to go to the Nordhavn sales office to see the 40 and the 47 models. The layout of the 43 was similar to the 47, Eric explained, and the size of the 43 was similar to the size of the 40.

We didn't know this at the time, but Nordhavn's typical buyers are retirement age. Most are former sailors who are switching to a powerboat because they can no longer meet the physical demands of sailing. We walked in and introduced ourselves to the salesman.

"Like, hiiiii!" I said. (I'm ashamed to admit this, but I am originally from *the* Valley and I really do talk like a Valley Girl.) "We just, like, got engaged, and we think we want to buy a boat and, like, sail around the world. We don't know anything about boating or anything. We just, like, want to check out the boats right now. Okay?"

The salesman was courteous and professional. He took us to see the boats and patiently answered all our ignorant questions. In retrospect, we're surprised that he didn't burst out laughing and tell us to hit the road.

I had my doubts about the 43. I thought the 40 was too small and couldn't imagine the 43 would feel any bigger. I loved the 47, but it was way out of our budget. Eric, however, was confident the 43 was the right boat for us. It's set up like a small apartment, so it feels like a home inside. When you first step inside, you find yourself in a small living room/dining room with an attached kitchen. You walk up four steps to the pilothouse, which has all the navigational equipment, a pilot chair and a couch. From the pilothouse, there are eight steps down to the lower level, which has two small bedrooms with attached bathrooms and a big engine room.

The boat has almost all the amenities that a house does, with normal kitchen appliances, including a large freezer and two small refrigerators that together are as big as the fridge in our house (no dishwasher, though). You can even upgrade the amenities package to include things like an air conditioner/heater and a washing machine, which are both rare luxuries on boats. We definitely would not feel like we were camping for two years on this Nordhavn.

All Nordhavns forty feet or longer boats are solidly built and capable of crossing oceans, but the 43 was truly the brand's most seaworthy. It is well refined and specifically designed for long sea passages, making it incredibly sturdy, safe, and functional. The brand of the engine is called Lugger and is a marine-ized 105 horsepower John Deere tractor engine that has been de-rated, so the engine can run nonstop for thousands of miles without problems. It has a dry exhaust system with a keel cooler, so no salt water needs to be pumped in to cool the engine. The boat is a full displacement design, making it slow but incredibly efficient. The boat pushes through the water, instead of skimming on top of it, like most powerboats. The fuel capacity is 1,200 gallons (4,500 liters) and it has a range of about 3,000 nautical miles (3,450 statute miles/5,550 km), which will safely cross the distances needed to go around the world. The boat weighs twenty-one tons with a full length weighted keel, thus the majority of the weight is under the waterline, making it unlikely to tip over if hit by an especially large wave. The hull is made of extra thick fiberglass, and at the bottom, the fiberglass is a full two inches thick (five cm), making it less likely to get a hole in the hull than most other fiberglass boats. The glass on the windows are heavy duty at twelve millimeters (almost one half inch), enabling it to withstand more force from waves than most other boats can. In short, it feels like a small ship.

We went home and talked about it for several more weeks before we agreed to put a refundable deposit on the boat. We chose hull #18, which wouldn't be delivered for another two years, because we needed the time to save money and learn more about boating.

From the beginning, Eric had been gung ho about this boat trip. He spent most of his free time doing research on the Internet and reading boating books and magazine. But now that it was real, I needed to participate in the learning. He started bookmarking sites and stories for me. We began going to forums and training seminars that were geared at cruisers.

We were in for a shock. Since almost all cruising boats are sailboats, the seminars were comprised primarily of sailors—and most of them were unsupportive of our plans. First of all, they seemed to think that we didn't have enough experience to be "entitled" to try an undertaking as huge as a circumnavigation. As far as they were concerned, the lack of hands on experience meant we were doomed to fail. We explained that we were devoting four full years to preparing for this adventure, but they didn't think that was anywhere close to enough.

When we told them which route we were planning to take, they would become even more discouraging, telling us there is absolutely no way we could do a twenty day ocean crossing for our first leg. Apparently, you're supposed to build up to long ocean passages by doing progressively longer hops. So, for example, you do an overnight trip, then a three day trip, then a five day, and so on until you build up to twenty. Starting with twenty was a no no.

When we told these sailors what boat we had chosen, most of them had the same response. "You guys are so ignorant about boating that you don't even know that it is absolutely impossible to cross an ocean on a small powerboat! See! We told you that you weren't experienced enough for this."

They all assumed the boat had no keel and would flip over in big waves. They assumed it would have a fast engine that burned a ton of fuel, more fuel than we could physically carry with us to make it across an entire ocean. They assumed the engine had many design weaknesses that would make it vulnerable to a failure, and when that inevitable failure occurred, we would be in dire straits without a sail. When we tried to tell them about the capabilities of our boat, they brushed us off as too boorish to be worth listening to. We couldn't believe how many sailors had no idea that certain powerboats are made for long sea passages, and were even more incredulous at how resistant they were to the concept.

Some of our non-boater friends, family, and co-workers were equally unsupportive. Conversations tended to go like this: "You'll probably get attacked by pirates and be killed! Don't you know how dangerous foreign countries are?" Or, "What about your careers? After a two year gap in employment, you'll never get another job." Or even, "You'll never be happy living in such a tiny space, being in motion all the time, and being together all the time! You're going to be miserable!" Fortunately, we did have some supportive people in our lives that kept us from getting discouraged.

I continued to learn boating skills. I was doing well with general sea skills, such as basic navigation, but I wasn't comprehending the mechanical aspects of boat maintenance and repair. I felt like I needed to be as good as a mechanic as Eric, and the realization that I never would made me have serious doubts.

Meanwhile, Nordhavn had been publicizing a rally in which a bunch of powerboats would cross the Atlantic together, leaving in June 2004. Nordhavn was providing a week of classes to review information about ocean crossings—both general sea skills and specific information regarding Nordhavn boats. We wanted to sign up as crew for the rally, but there was no way we could take a month off work. We could take one week off to attend the classes, but the classes weren't open to the general public, just the rally crews. We begged Nordhavn to let us take the classes in exchange for helping out with the conference, and they agreed.

We sat through every class. The mechanical classes were painful for me. Since I didn't know the names of the assorted components, I had no idea what was going on. The speaker would start the session with something like, "I'll be talking about generators. If your generator fails, first check the flooby flobber. Then check the whachamajigger. Then check the thingamabob..." I'd look around the room, play with my pen, doodle, and generally zone out until I would hear "... total catastrophe and you are in serious danger." Then I'd freak out thinking, *What did I miss? What will put us in danger?*

Since I didn't understand anything, we decided to back out of the trip. Just kidding! Actually, I did l realize one important thing during those mechanical classes-- there were no other women in attendance, just men. The vast majority of the boats were being crewed by married couples, so where were all the wives? I started talking to the women, some of whom had logged thousands of miles at sea. They all said the same thing: "My husband showed me what I need to know, and I let him worry about the rest."

If these little old ladies can do it, then I can, too, I decided. *I am as smart and competent as they are—and certainly more agile!*

Eric also got little out of the mechanical classes, but for the opposite reason. After doing a full year of research and studying, he'd already learned much of what he needed to know. It was confirmation to him that he was ready in that regard. However, we both learned a lot from the non-mechanical classes, such as "Emergencies at Sea." We also met several people who became our mentors, so the overall experience was incredibly valuable.

That same month, the first Nordhavn 43 was unveiled in Dana Point, California. We went to the showing. My doubts about the size melted away. Eric had been right--this boat was perfect. We committed to buying the boat, and our deposit became non-refundable. In May 2006—after two years of intense preparation—we took delivery of our Nordhavn 43. We named her *Kosmos*, the Greek word for world.

We tried to use *Kosmos* as much as possible before leaving on the two year journey, but we didn't get in nearly as much sea time as we had hoped. We were still working long hours and taking boating classes. Plus, we had to spend a lot of time and energy getting *Kosmos* properly outfitted, since we'd need different things for each part of the world. The hardest part, though, was getting ourselves ready to go. There are many ties that hold people to land life, and those ties are sticky and difficult to pry off. Most of our responsibilities would stand even while we were gone, and we needed to figure out how to meet those responsibilities from the middle of the ocean. Not easy.

One of the many things we needed to do was to find crew members for all of our long sea passages. It's unwise to do long passages with only two people. At sea, there's no place to stop and rest, so the boat is always moving. Someone is supposed to be awake at all times to watch for potential hazards both inside the boat (for example, making sure the engine is running properly) and on the water (for instance, looking for oncoming boats). If there are only two people on board and one person becomes incapacitated, the other needs to stand watch around the clock. And no one can go without sleep for days on end.

Eric started a web log, aka blog, as *Kosmos* was being built to help advertise for crew, and to start sharing our plans with friends and family. The *Kosmos Travel Log* started with occasional stories of our preparation and plans.

Finding the right person for our first leg was crucial. We wanted someone with a significant amount of hands-on boating experience to offset our lack of experience. We needed someone who had an iron stomach, since it was quite possible both of us would get severely seasick. The ideal candidate would understand how to run a powerboat and be able to help with troubleshooting and fixing any potential problems that might arise. And since this third person would be living with us for at least a month, we needed to be compatible.

During the two and a half years between ordering the boat and taking delivery of it, we made many trips to the Nordhavn offices. Early on, we met a man named Richard who was also in the process of buying a new 43, and subsequently became friendly with him. One day our salesperson, Jeff, told us that Richard perfectly fit our criteria and suggested that Richard join us for the Pacific crossing. Richard had always dreamed of crossing the Pacific in a small boat. He is much older than we are, and has been boating most of his life. He has logged hundreds of hours at sea—mostly in the Portland, Oregon, area, which has some of the roughest waters in the world. We knew that no matter how bad the seas got, Richard would be able to handle it. Since he owned an identical boat, he was familiar with all the systems and could run *Kosmos* as well as Eric. The three of us also have similar educations, political views, interests, and food preferences, so we thought we'd be compatible. Richard came down to San Diego and spent a weekend with us. We did indeed get along very well, so we invited him to join us for the first portion of our trip.

On April 28, 2007, we pulled away from the dock, starting what most people considered to be an overly ambitious first leg on an overly ambitious journey. They thought we were too inexperienced to accomplish the twenty-day, 2,800 nm passage across the Pacific Ocean to the island of Nuka Hiva in the Marquesas Islands of French Polynesia. After all, when we pulled out, we had only a total of 1,800 nm on *Kosmos's* odometer. The longest consecutive run Eric and I had completed was a three-day, 350-nm jaunt in coastal waters. We had never been more than ten nm from land. Plus, Eric still hadn't overcome his fear of deep water, and he had been struggling with seasickness during our practice runs.

If something went wrong on this passage, whether with us or with the boat, there was absolutely no place to stop and there would be no one help us. We were truly on our own. Many people thought that what we were doing was absolutely impossible, that we were going to our graves.

We were ninety five percent sure we would prove them wrong.

Chapter 1: The Pacific Passage

Sunday, April 29, 2007 – Day Two

Shortly after the boat pulled out yesterday, I collapsed in exhaustion. Since then I've been sleeping every minute that I'm off watch. It is to be expected. After all, I only got two hours of sleep on Friday night. There was so much to do that I literally ran non-stop all day and night–I didn't even have enough time to take a shower. I was really embarrassed when people started showing up at the boat to see us off on Saturday. Not only was I un-showered, but I also hadn't changed my clothes or brushed my hair and teeth since Friday morning.

Saturday morning was chaotic. As more and more people started showing up, I put them all to work, asking them to do chores and tasks for us around the boat, even sending people to the store to buy last minute things that we had forgotten or suddenly decided we needed. Then Eric and I ignored our guests while we went through all our bills and wrote checks, giving the mail to Eric's parents to stamp and send off for us. Around 1115 (11:15 a.m. in naval/international time) we finally checked the last "must-do" item off our list. There was tons more we had intended to do, but earlier in the day we had realized that we couldn't get to everything, so we compiled a list of vital things that we couldn't live without. We were simply going to have to make do without the rest.

With our list finished, we finally started paying attention to our guests, giving tours of the boat, and saying our good-byes. I was surprised that approximately forty people came to see us off. We felt so much love. We knew everybody there was rooting for us to succeed and were trying to be supportive, despite their fears for our safety (and sanity). I think having Richard along helped reassure them that we would actually make it to the other side.

A few minutes before 1200, Eric gave a speech about how hard we had worked to get to this point. "It's been a real adventure so far," said Eric, "and we haven't even left the dock." He talked about how we had to jump some huge hurdles to make it to this point, and confessed that we still can't believe we were able to overcome such daunting obstacles. We can't claim all the credit, though. We did have help from a handful of supportive people. But, we also had a couple of nay say-ers who tried to sabotage our plans, and dealing with them was not fun. Even if our trip winds up being a failure, we are proud of ourselves for making it this far. It wasn't easy.

Then we untied and pulled out of the slip. Our friends and family waved frantically as we slowly motored away. Some of them even walked over to the tip of the peninsula that the slip is sheltered behind and continued to wave to us as we headed toward the ocean.

When we first pulled away, Eric, Richard, and I were all overjoyed. *Wow, we had really done it. We started the adventure of a lifetime! It was really happening!* We talked about how incredibly relieved we were to finally be done with preparations and on our way. No more trips to the store or running around trying to take care of this and that. No more worrying about what we might forget. Life in San Diego is as wrapped up as it could be, and now we can focus on the adventure ahead. We called some friends and relatives that hadn't made it to the *Bon Voyage* on our cell phones to say goodbye.

Once we were out of cell phone range and the initial euphoria wore off, tiredness finally got the best of me and I crashed. I was more than just physically tired, I was also—and still am--emotionally and mentally tired. I haven't gotten much sleep for the past couple weeks because we've had so much to do. In fact, for months I've been so stressed out from all the preparation that I've been pulling out my hair, leaving a small bald spot on my head.

All has gone okay so far. We've covered a total of 140 nm since leaving yesterday and the boat has run smoothly. The sky has been overcast. Winds have been steady at five knots from the starboard bow. The swells are five feet, coming from the same direction as the wind. The wave period is about nine to ten seconds. When the waves crash into the front of the boat, it is called head seas. Eric and I think head seas suck. Eric has been sick, and I have been feeling green. Richard, on the other hand, thought the seas were just great. "They're calm compared to what I'm used to up in the Oregon area," he said.

God, I thought, I'd hate to see what the seas are like up there!

We've been doing four-hour watch rotations. Eric has been on duty from 0200-0600, I've been on from 0600-1000, Richard from 1000-1400, and then it repeats. We each do an engine room check at the start of our watch. We go into the engine room to look for leaks, sniff for abnormal smells, check equipment temperatures, etc. Eric and Richard both had a hard time staying awake on their night watch. But I got to sleep a normal night, so I think the watch schedule is fabulous!

Tuesday, May 1 – Day Four

We've logged 417 miles—the longest Eric and I have ever been at sea. Everything was pretty much the same today as far as sea conditions go, and it is still gloomy and overcast. Eric has been suffering from internet withdraw—not being able to hop online has been surprisingly hard on him. He wishes he could pass time reading the news and looking up assorted information, but has been making do with playing video games and watching movies, instead. He hasn't said anything, but I sense he is worried that he forgot something important that will prove detrimental, or that something might go wrong that we aren't prepared for. Richard has been passing the time reading and watching the horizon. He seems to love being at sea and happy as a clam. I have still been spending most of my free time sleeping. Eric and I have both gotten over our seasickness, for the most part, anyway. We still have queasy moments now and then, but the queasiness seems to dissipate as soon as we eat.

Both yesterday and today, we saw dolphins. Small pods of them came in groups, played for a while at the bow, and then took off. They are such graceful creatures.

Out here the air is really fresh. Despite the cloud cover, the sapphire blue of the ocean is startling. The passage so far has felt both peaceful and adventurous. We've often wondered how it would feel to be isolated in the middle of nowhere. Honestly, it feels fine. We don't mind being in a small space.

Thanks to our satellite phone, we still feel somewhat connected to civilization. We have talked to our families a few times. Even though the satellite service can't give us a "real" Internet connection, we can at least send and receive small text-only email, and checking email is the highlight of the day for us. We have been emailing regular blog updates to a friend at home, who is posting them for us. We know seeing these updates give our friends and family tremendous peace of mind.

We've also been talking about how hard this journey would have been in the days before GPS, when sailors calculated their position using a magnetic compass and a sextant. With the overcast skies, there would be no way we could do a sun or star sighting—in effect, no way to determine our position. Without GPS, we could drift off course and never know it!

If we were heading to a continent, we'd still find land, even if it wasn't the exact spot we were aiming for. But, islands are easily missed if calculations are off by even a degree or two.

We're eager to get to the South Pacific. It is the least densely populated place on earth with only two percent of the world population on all the islands combined. There are several hundred islands spread over several thousand miles, and most islands have tiny populations--some in the double digits! We like that our first destination will be so starkly different from home. We need the change of pace.

Wednesday, May 2 – Day Five

We are up to 549 nautical miles. The wind has shifted around to our aft and picked up to fifteen knots, which means we have finally hit the Trade Winds. The swells changed direction, coming from our aft, and increased to six feet at ten to twelve seconds. There were one to two foot wind waves on top of the swells. Swells are long-wavelength waves that often travel thousands of miles until they hit land and break. They generally have fairly consistent motion, making big troughs and peaks that the boat rides up and down. Wind waves are shorter length waves formed from the motion of the wind pushing the water. These are generally more volatile, often breaking on themselves. Having both long and short waves meant we were simultaneously dealing with two different kinds of movement—definitely more uncomfortable than what we'd experienced previously. However, because we were now in following seas instead of head seas, our tummies actually felt better than they did before, despite more motion.

The weather was nice today—warm, but not hot, with the cloud cover thinning to scattered clouds. There was a full moon tonight, its light reflecting off the water, creating a gentle, glistening, luminous light.

Each night it has gotten a little easier for Eric and Richard to stay awake during their watches. I have been sleeping less, but am still exhausted. I have found that with so much motion, even the most mundane of activities requires significantly more effort than it does on land, and since I haven't had energy, I haven't been doing anything. I keep thinking of all the things I should do, such as cooking, cleaning, and tackling the assorted projects I brought with me, but I just can't motivate myself. By nature, I am extremely driven and goal oriented, and for years was busy every waking minute of the day, so this lethargy is out of character for me. I'm overcome with guilt about wasting precious time.

I realize all my whining makes it sound like I despise life at sea, but actually, I enjoy being onboard and floating out in the middle of nowhere. I just wish the seas would calm down enough so that my lethargy goes away. I think Eric is suffering from a bit of lethargy, too, but not to the degree I am. Richard has as much energy as he did on land, of which I am envious.

Friday, May 4 – Day Seven

We are 818 miles from San Diego, putting us almost a third of the way there. At this pace, it looks like we'll be spending an extra day at sea. This is the longest Richard had ever been on a passage, so now all of us are in new territory. Our routine has become solidified. Eric and Richard have finally adjusted to their night shifts and we have all established a sleeping pattern that is in line with our respective watch schedules.

The weather has reverted back to gloomy, gray, and cool. We are in the tropics, but you would never know it. I pulled out my long-sleeved shirts again. The moon is full now, but due to the cloud cover, it is not visible at all. The wind picked up to twelve to eighteen knots from the port aft. Unfortunately, the seas followed suit and got significantly worse, with today the roughest yet. The swells were six to eight feet at ten to twelve seconds, along with three-to-four-foot wind waves on top of the swells. Or in more plain terms, the sea was lumpy and the lumps were dotted with white caps, with a few extra large waves here and there. Every minute or so, we were hit by a strong wave that rolled *Kosmos* over onto her side. Eric hid the anemometer from plain view, so we don't know exactly how many degrees we are rolling, but we know it is a lot. Enough to knock us over if we aren't holding onto the boat while standing up.

When the ocean gets that rough, it becomes difficult to function. *Everything*, including the most mundane things, requires tremendous effort and concentration. For example, we can't just open the refrigerator and rummage around. We have to know exactly what we want and exactly where it's located. When we're hungry, we stand in front of the fridge and wait for a wave to come. Then, just as the boat begins to right itself, we open the door, grab what we need as quickly as possible, then shut and lock the door before the next wave comes. If the door is open for one second too long, all the food starts to slide out. At this point, hand-eye coordination is imperative (and two hands really aren't enough) to shove all the food back in the fridge before it hits the floor. First, we stop the heavy things that would break our toes, like full jars and bottles. Our second priority is breakables, like eggs. Then, finally, we stop things that would cause the least damage, like the bread.

Inevitably, several more waves will come and go while we're trying to save the food. And since our hands are occupied, we aren't holding on to the boat—and not holding on to the boat at all times is a dire mistake. The waves slam us into the wall next to the fridge, and we lose our grip on the food, putting us back to square one with the food rescue mission. Meanwhile, the refrigerator door simultaneously tries to shut on our head

21

Getting food from the refrigerator isn't the only challenge. Another is retrieving the canned foods, located in an overhead cabinet. Invariably, a wave will come while the cabinet door is open and heavy tins come flying out, whacking us in the head.

Then there is the bathroom. When I wash my hands or my face, I can't hold on to anything—and thus I get slammed into the door, the counter, and then the door again, like a human ping-pong ball. The shower is no better. There's a bench inside so I can sit while the water is on, but when I stand up to towel off, I'm holding the towel, not the boat. So of course I get slammed back and forth between the shower door and the wall. Eric said he has mastered using his legs to brace himself, but I have not gotten that trick down. I did, however, figure out how to stay centered on the commode: holding myself upright by propping my elbow against the wall (on the right) and the counter (to the left), just like a statue.

This all contributes to me feeling like I'm living in a Marx Brothers movie. Anyone watching me has to be laughing their head off. I'm sure adjusting to the constant motion would be a challenge for most anyone, but I'm clumsy by nature, so it is probably especially difficult for me. As all my coworkers will attest, even on dry land I often walk into doorjambs and filing cabinets that are in plain sight. I'm literally bruised and battered now, physically punished for all my effort to move.

The most shocking part to me, though, is that Richard thinks the ride is still moderate. If this is moderate, I don't ever want to go to Oregon in the boat!

I am no longer tired, but more lethargic than ever. I'm also achy and stiff from sitting too much, and my body is desperately craving physical activity to make the sitting pains go away. I feel incredibly conflicted--half of me wants to move and the other half of me doesn't. (The half that doesn't, of course, is winning.) But the good news is I finally found something productive to do while I sit. We've been worried about not being able to communicate in French Polynesia, so I decided to study French. A friend had given us some French language lessons, so I started doing the lessons and watching at least one French movie with English subtitles each day. Having something to focus my energy on has made me happier.

We have solely been eating ready to eat foods or easy to prepare items. I expected to be doing a lot of cooking, but I am just too lethargic, and the waters are too rough; cooking could be dangerous. So we're eating a lot of fresh fruit, bread, eggs, yogurt, peanut butter, almond butter, and frozen foods.

Sunday May 6 – Day Nine

We are 1,084 miles from San Diego. Eric was excited when we crossed the 1,000-mile mark. Today, the sea conditions got even worse. The swells were up to six to ten feet, with wind waves of one to two feet. Those ten footers were brutal. Sometimes when they hit, we rolled a full thirty degrees. Then we rolled the other way almost thirty degrees before *Kosmos* started righting herself. Rocking a full sixty degrees is *not fun!* With each big wave, everything that was not securely locked down went flying across the room. The first time it happened, the dish drainer, toaster oven, and coffee maker went flying. Miraculously, nothing broke, and for now we're keeping the appliances on the floor so they don't fall over again.

To make matters worse, the seas also became "confused," with waves coming at us from multiple directions. Instead of merely rolling back and forth, we were shaken around like we were inside a washing machine. Eric and I didn't think the seas could get any worse than they were a couple days ago, but we were wrong.

Eric and Richard put out the paravanes yesterday in hopes it would make the ride better. We had the automatic stabilizers on already, but we were hoping that maybe dual stabilization would flatten out the ride. The ride was still absolutely miserable, but it was noticeably better with the dual systems. Unfortunately, the paravanes also slowed us down by almost a full knot, so they decided it was best to bring them back in today. They were concerned that slowing down so much while still burning the same amount of fuel could cause us to run out of fuel. Putting the paravanes out was easy, but bringing them in was hard. Getting the fish back into their holders was incredibly tricky. Those things are heavy!

It was still completely overcast today: no sun, no sunrises or sunsets, no moon, no stars. Just endless gray. Even the water looked gray. Of course, Richard, who is from the Pacific Northwest, is used to endless gray and he likes it. Not me. I like sunshine.

Between the bad seas, the gloom, and the aches from sitting all the time, I have become depressed. Richard has been trying to cheer me up. He told me some stories about his life and has tried to get me to appreciate the subtle nuances in the shades of gray so the world seemed less monochromatic to me. He has also been bringing me food. My lethargy has worsened to the point that I won't expend energy to get food. I prefer to sit on the couch ravenously hungry than walk three steps to the refrigerator to get something to eat. I have thrown myself into my French studies and spend almost every waking minute trying to learn French. It is a hard language. But at least I don't feel like I am wasting my time anymore, and it gives me a goal to achieve. I need goals. I don't function well without them.

Richard, however, is still functioning just as well as he did when we were on land. He still thinks we are experiencing a "nice, gentle, easy ride." I am amazed by—and envious of—him. I wish I could be a fraction as functional as he is. I'm thankful we chose him to be part of our crew. If we had someone who was also struggling with the bad seas, we would be in sorry shape. I think he helps me stay sane.

I have not seen much of Eric lately. The way our sleep schedules have worked out, usually one of us is sleeping while the other is awake. Now that he is fully adjusted, Eric is handling the seas okay. Better than me, but nowhere near as well as Richard.

Yesterday we saw two exciting things: a school of flying fish and a sailboat going the other direction. Eric and Richard were disproportionably excited about them both. God, our lives have really gotten pathetic.

Tuesday, May 8 – Day Eleven

Today at 2250 (10:50 p.m.), we made it to the halfway mark: 1,420 miles. Good news, indeed! Our current position must be the most remote place on earth. If it isn't the most remote, it is certainly in the top three.

The ocean was still miserable yesterday and today, but at least it was smoother. The dreaded giant waves that knocked us over before were, for the most part, gone. We should be to the ITCZ soon, where the seas are supposedly flatter. I am eagerly—desperately—looking forward to it flattening out.

The heat and humidity level has steadily increased. Yesterday the temperature was idyllic for Eric and me, though a touch too warm for Richard. Today, even Eric and I thought it was too hot. We're thankful for the cloud cover. If the sun were beating down on us, it would be sweltering.

Unfortunately, it is also much hotter in the engine room, and the equipment is running at significantly higher temperatures, particularly the propeller shaft. We're talking so hot that you can easily burn yourself if you touch any of the metal in there. This is probably due to a combination of factors: One, the air is hotter. Two, the water is significantly warmer, so the boat isn't getting cooled by the water as much. Three, the tanks have warmed up and are emanating heat as well. All the equipment is still within the normal temperature range, though, so we are not worried.

I'm feeling a little less lethargic and depressed, and I am guessing it is tied to the fact the seas are a bit calmer. I've been having vivid dreams about exercising, dreaming that I am going on a long, arduous hike or bike ride. As a result, I have started doing some yoga stretches, which has helped alleviate some of my stiffness and aches. One of the key components to yoga is balance, so given all the motion, the stretches are not easy. I'll bet if Eric video taped my yoga workouts, we could sell it as a comedy show.

Eric has been talking to Richard about various aspects of boating and has come to the realization that while Eric doesn't have Richard's hands on experience, Eric knows as much or maybe more than Richard. Eric now believes he has the books smarts to handle just about anything, that it is simply a matter of applying his theoretical knowledge to hands on situations. This is a huge relief to Eric, who wasn't ever one hundred percent sure that he was adequately prepared for our undertaking.

There is some rain in the forecast. It will be nice to wash the boat, since *Kosmos* is totally encrusted in a layer of salt and is kind of gross. But our biggest fear is getting hit by lightning, so we are a little anxious about the rain. Since boat masts are usually the tallest thing on the ocean, lightning strikes at sea are fairly common occurrences. We have a lightening rod and lightening ground, so we would likely survive a hit just fine, but it could wipe out our communications gear. That would mean trying to navigate using a sextant, which right now seems absolutely impossible since we can't see the sun or stars to get a fix.

Yesterday we saw another school of flying fish and a bird. Today we saw two more birds. What are birds doing all the way out here?

Thursday, May 10 – Day Thirteen

We are now 1,784 miles from San Diego. Almost the minute we finished typing up our report on Tuesday night, it tried to rain. By "tried to rain," I mean that it drizzled for a few minutes, stopped for a while, drizzled for a few minutes, and so on. The drizzle lasted for thirty-six hours before the storm finally hit us and the real rain came. It is still raining as of this writing.

Of course, as soon as the drizzle started, the wind and seas picked up. By 0400 (4:00 a.m.) on Wednesday, the seas were back to being as bad as they were on Sunday. Then when the rain hit, things got even worse. Today was definitely the roughest yet. The swells were six to ten feet at ten second intervals, and the ugly, breaking wind waves were four to six feet. Normally, if we're not holding onto the boat when a wave hits, we'll fall. Today, we literally flew across the room and slammed into the wall.

Even worse, the drizzle/rain forced us to keep the boat closed up. When we closed it early Wednesday morning, the inside quickly became hot, smelly, and uncomfortable without the ocean breeze. So all day yesterday and part of today we turned on the generator so we could run the air conditioner. The air conditioner is only working upstairs, though; the downstairs one keeps shutting off. The intake valve for the downstairs air conditioner is at the front of the boat. Eric said he thought the reason

the air is turning itself off is because the nose of the boat comes out of
the water with each wave, and once air gets sucked into the intake valve, it
shuts off.

Upstairs with the air on, it is actually comfortable. But downstairs, it
is unbearably hot and stinky. We all have found that the rougher it is, the
harder it is to sleep. Now that it is both super rough and super hot, none
of us are sleeping well in the bedrooms. Richard has taken to sleeping
upstairs on the living room couch. We're thankful we have air
conditioning, even if it is only working upstairs for now. Few boats have
air conditioning, and we honestly believe we all would go insane without
it.

When we turned the generator on, we decided to wash our sheets.
Ever since we got to the hot weather, we've been showering twice a day
to keep from smelling. Despite the showers, we sweat so much in our
sleep that the sheets were starting to stink. We're thankful to have a water
maker. Many boats do not have water makers, so water is seriously
rationed. That means only sponge baths and no laundry. I can't imagine
how heinous the stench must be in boats where the crew doesn't shower
or do laundry for weeks. *Eewww!*

Yesterday we entered the ITCZ ,where the waters were supposed to
calm down. The fact that it got rougher has been emotionally devastating
to me. I really can't take the rocking anymore and the heat is making me
even more lethargic. When I did my last engine room check, I bumped
into metal and burned my shoulder. I've become depressed than ever. A
couple days ago I started to pull my hair out again, which I will sometimes
do when I'm extremely anxious. Alarmingly, I've been pulling out huge
clumps, and I can't seem to stop myself. I'm not anxious about being on
the open ocean, so far from land, or about something bad happening to

us. I am simply anxious about the severe discomfort. At one point, I was cleaning up the hair on the carpet and wadded it up into a ball. Eric commented that it looked like a rodent.

I am praying hard that it calms down soon because I simply cannot do this for another week. I am sure Eric and Richard both wish this passage were already over, too. They were doing okay when it was cool, but adding the heat and humidity on top of the rough seas seems to be too much for them. They're starting to feel lethargic, as well. The forecast is for calmer seas near the equator, so hopefully the storm will pass quickly and we'll find that smoother water. If not, I'll probably be bald by the time we get to Nuka Hiva. We haven't seen any more ships or sailboats, and we are aware of how alone we are out here.

I make it sound like the trip is all bad. Really, it isn't. Some good things have happened. Oddly enough, after the drizzle started, the sun began to peek through the clouds here and there, so we were getting sun and drizzle simultaneously. There was a large, beautiful rainbow off the starboard bow yesterday and today. Thankfully, there was no lightening at all. We did, however, see some birds—more birds, in fact, since the drizzle began than we've seen in days. Last night, the stars came out for a few hours. There was no moon tonight, so the stars were amazingly bright. Seeing these things cheered me up, at least for a few minutes… until the next big wave came.

The best thing of all was that yesterday Richard caught a fish! He has been fishing this whole time, but hadn't caught anything. Eric and I went out to the cockpit to watch Richard pull it in. Eric bravely beat the seven-pound (two kilo) mahi mahi to death, an experience he did not enjoy. I couldn't bear to watch and shielded my eyes. When Richard pulled out the knife to fillet it, I had to go back inside. I can't take bloodshed. As soon as the fish was cut up, Richard immediately made us a family-style dinner. It was by far the best fish Eric and I have ever tasted. The fresher the fish, the better it tastes… and you don't get any fresher than that.

Sunday, May 13 – Day Sixteen

Yesterday, something happened that perfectly illustrates what life is like at sea. I decided to have a can of baked beans for lunch. I opened the can and filled a coffee mug about two thirds full of beans. I put the mug in the microwave. Then a big wave came. I heard the mug crash. I peered through the glass to see the mug leaning on its side with the beans all over the bottom. Sigh. I got some paper towels and opened the microwave door, grabbing at the mug before it came crashing down on the carpet. Beans immediately oozed down the wall the microwave is mounted on. While I was setting the mug on the counter, another wave came. The beans came flying at me like a swarm of bugs. There were beans all over my shirt and all over the counter below the microwave. As I started wiping up the beans, another wave came and the microwave door whacked me in the head. So, with one hand I held the microwave door and with the other hand I wiped up the mess. This was not a prudent decision. Remember, in rough seas, one must hold onto the boat at all times. Within seconds another wave came and knocked me into the wall. . Hmmm… I had a little dilemma here. I needed three hands to clean up the mess, and I only have two.

Fortunately, Eric was watching and came to my aid. He stood behind me, holding the boat with one hand and the microwave door with the other. I leaned against him for support and quickly wiped up the beans. I still can't believe I was attacked by a can of beans. Who would have thought heating food up in the microwave could be a dangerous activity?

This is an extreme example, but a good illustration of what life is like when the water is rough.

On to the less amusing details… We are now 2,048 nm from San Diego. Yesterday, we hit a horrendous current and have been moving dangerously slow since. We were averaging six knots overall, but in the last few days we have been down to only four-and-a-half knots. At first Eric thought something was caught on the propeller or something was wrong mechanically. But everything appeared fine. We turned around for a couple minutes to see how fast we would move in the other direction. We did indeed move faster the other way, despite the fact it was head seas, so we knew for sure it was a current. Those few minutes in the head seas were hellish. I have a new appreciation for why Richard keeps calling these waters "moderate."

This entire trip, Eric has been worried about something going wrong. Even when everything was great in terms of speed and mechanics, he never fully relaxed. Now that we've hit this current, Eric is freaking out that we will run out of fuel. He's constantly doing mathematical calculations about the probability of making it should the speed never improve. I keep trying to reassure him that we will eventually hit the current going the other way and the speed will even out, but he refuses to be consoled. He is making himself sick over this.

Eric is normally very logical and doesn't upset easily. I think his overreaction is a sign that he has had enough of being at sea. Eric hasn't complained much, but I believe he is having a harder time than he is letting on. I think he is trying to play the role of "brave captain", partly to be supportive of me as I fall apart, and partly to prove to himself that he can successfully accomplish this crazy adventure. I understand why he is stressed out. He's responsible for navigating us and maintaining the myriad of electrical and mechanical components—essentially keeping us safe. There is a lot of responsibility on his shoulders.

I also suspect that Richard is barely holding it together. Richard has never said or done anything to indicate he is unhappy, so I could be totally wrong. He is still chipper, has a good attitude overall and never complains, but his aura has changed. I sense that he is working hard at maintaining that cheerful façade, and that emotionally he has had enough of this passage, too. If what I am sensing is right, I have to give him tremendous amounts of kudos for working so hard at being a team player. It reinforces to me that we made a good choice when we picked him.

I may be overly emotional and overly sensitive, but I don't think Richard enjoys being locked in a small space with us. He lives alone and is used to both total privacy and doing everything his way. Now he is a guest in our house and has to do things our way. Richard is very clean and I think it bothers him that I have had no interest in cleaning.

More important, he has little privacy. Since it is so hot downstairs, we all spend most of our time upstairs, so he always has me or Eric up there with him. When he does go down to his bedroom, he likes to shut his door for the added privacy. But, when he shuts his door, we get mad at him. Our guest bedroom is located under the forward deck, and that room has dorade air vents in the ceiling that bring in fresh air. The master bedroom is under the pilot house, so there are no fresh air vents. To fix the ventilation issue in the master bedroom, Nordhavn installed a blower that forces in fresh air, but it simply doesn't bring in enough air to provide adequate ventilation. When Richard shuts his bedroom door, he cuts off the fresh airflow to our room, making our bedroom most unpleasant. Some people need their "alone time" with the door shut, and our insisting he leave it open must be hard on him.

As for me, my depression deepens daily and I've become a little teary eyed. I just want the rocking to stop, even for a bit. I need a reprieve from the constant motion. I'm also starting to feel incredibly lonely and isolated. I really need a friend to talk to, to console me and tell me everything is going to be okay. Eric and Richard do, of course, but it isn't enough. I suspect my depression is wearing on them, that it is hard to console me when they are miserable themselves. Meanwhile, my vivid dreams about exercise continue. So does the hair pulling. My French, however, is improving daily.

As far as weather and seas go, the waves were smaller today than last reported. But the countercurrent brought waves from another direction, putting us back in confused seas. It wasn't easy, but it was better, thankfully. The weather also turned truly tropical, with sunshine interspersed with black rain clouds. We got hit with several showers, but they passed quickly and we didn't have to keep the boat closed up for long. The seas definitely got rougher when the rain hit, but they calmed down as soon as it passed. (Of course, "calm" is a relative term.) The engine room is now so hot that it is somewhat dangerous. We've all gotten minor burns while doing engine room checks. Gloves are a must.

The bioluminescence in the water was insane the last few nights. The sea spray literally glowed as it came over the bow railing. The wake was so illuminated that it looked like there were lights under the water. We could actually see the white caps around us because they were emitting light, and the whole ocean was sparkly and pretty. Seeing it reminded us how awesome Mother Nature can be.

A few days ago, several flying fish and a couple baby squid began to land on the decks now and then. Today, one of the two GPS cut out. Eric went to investigate and found a dead baby squid on the antenna. He flicked the squid off and the GPS started working again. We couldn't believe the squid had made it up a good fifteen feet (5m) above the waterline. It is a little known fact that baby squid can fly. Once they get to be a certain size, they lose that aerial ability.

Tuesday, May 15 – Day Eighteen

We crossed the equator today! The event occurred at 0552 local time (one hour later than PST). It was still dark outside. It was a rare, clear night with the stars brilliantly shining. Our wake was sparkling and glowing with specks of bioluminescence, which was stunning. It was a spectacular setting for our huge milestone. We gathered in the pilothouse, watching the countdown on the GPS, then celebrated by drinking my favorite champagne (despite the hour). We went outside and stood on deck, enjoying the tranquil setting until the dawn broke. Eric wanted to do some silly hazing ritual, as is the custom for sailors crossing the equator, but Richard and I vetoed him.

But while crossing the equator is exciting, even more noteworthy is the fact that we spotted land on the long-range chart plotter screen. We have two chart plotters: One is set to short range (twelve miles), and the other to long range, which we have out as far as it will go. Until yesterday, the long-range view showed nothing but water. Seeing the shape of land was a huge relief—there is light at the end of the tunnel! Eric has been a little worried about somehow screwing up and missing the island, but seeing it on the chart means we will probably find it.

We are now 2,271 nm from San Diego. Unfortunately, while the waves were smaller today, they were "confused" again, so the ride was still miserable. The countercurrent eased, though, and we averaged five knots the last couple days, which made Eric less panicky. Then tonight our speed magically picked up by about 1.2 knots, which meant we had finally escaped the clutches of the evil equatorial countercurrent. Hallelujah! After four days of painfully slow speed, we were singing and dancing in the aisles.

This morning we turned on the generator so we could do some laundry. Eric tried turning on the air conditioning downstairs to help load up the generator, and much to our surprise, the air worked! It was a welcome reprieve from the heat and the stench. I took a nap while the air was on and slept soundly thanks to the cool, fresh air. Of course, as soon as the laundry was done, we turned the air back off because the generator uses precious fuel.

Yesterday, the inevitable finally happened. Richard had the refrigerator door open a moment too long and wasn't fast enough on the catch. Most of the contents of the fridge landed on the floor. Luckily, only a container of yogurt and a bottle of beer broke, so the food loss was minimal. Richard vacuumed up the mess (thank goodness for the wet/dry vacuum!), but it suddenly motivated me to vacuum the rest of the kitchen and living room. After meaning to vacuum for over a week, I felt good about myself for finally doing something. The only bummer is we need to wear shoes for a while because of potential slivers of glass that may be lurking in the carpet. Richard was really upset and kept berating himself about it. I kept trying to tell him I was glad it happened, but he wouldn't forgive himself.

Eric's blog post today helped me realize how conflicted I'm feeling. He wrote: "None of us feel any anxiety or nervousness (about being so far from land). We have a solid, well-equipped boat, and we are confident in our ability to run it. We all enjoy being on the water and the 'free' feeling that comes from having the whole ocean to yourself, with no one or nothing around."

All those things are true… yet I still feel miserable. His post continued: "Going from a frantic, fast-paced life to the slowest of slow speed life takes adjustment. Learning to function in the rocking seas is an adjustment. And, with the rocking of the seas, life becomes very sedentary, so that takes adjustment if you are not sedentary by nature. But you do adjust. Some days are better than others in terms of how well adjusted [you are] to sea life."

It's a succinct summary of my longwinded whining, but it doesn't convey how hard that adjustment really is. I'm more depressed than ever. Before I was a little teary eyed, but now I'm crying several times a day. I have also been having suicidal thoughts. I've never had thoughts like this in my life. But I just can't take the rocking anymore, and dying feels like the only way the rocking will end. I know my thoughts are irrational given that we will be on the island soon, but I can't seem to control them. I try to keep from crying in front of Richard, so Eric is bearing the brunt of my outbursts. Eric keeps assuring me that the rocking will stop when we get to the anchorage. He promises it will be calm and I'll be happy again. But right now it's hard for me to believe that it will ever be flat enough or calm enough on board, and I have made Eric promise at least a dozen times that we can stay in a hotel for a few nights. Knowing that I will have a few nights of absolute stillness gives me hope.

Of course, Eric is also having a hard time, and my depression just makes it that much harder for him. I think Eric is terrified that I want to sell the boat and cancel our trip. I don't—I just want the rocking to stop. But I do wonder what we have gotten ourselves into, and I think Eric is wondering the same thing, even if he hasn't voiced it.

Thursday, May 17 – Day Twenty

Yesterday, Richard and I had a huge fight. In retrospect, we were taking our misery out on one another. The fight was over something really insignificant. How a rote question could ever turn into a hysterical blowout that lasted for hours is beyond me. Now that it's over, we both feel incredibly bad. But it confirms my suspicions that Richard is miserable, too, and has been trying to hide it from us.

The seas were still rotten these last few days, but since they were no longer confused, they were somewhat more tolerable than before. The weather was better, too—not as cloudy or humid, with lots of stars at night. We even saw the sunset today! Normally, there are clouds on the horizon, so we can't see the sunset.

At the moment we are 2,574 nm from San Diego, so close to our landfall that we can almost smell it. Our speed has increased to 6.3 knots, and earlier today we were doing seven knots for a while. Every day, the images of land on the chart plotter screen get bigger and closer. We also saw a boat, the first one we've seen in ages. We should be seeing more birds and boats soon.

Needless to say, knowing we are so close gives us all hope that we will make it before we completely lose our marbles. But even so, none of us are any less miserable, emotionally speaking. We are so ready to get off this boat!

Saturday, May 19 – Day Twenty-Two

Yesterday we saw a variety of birds, a sign land was near. We saw several boats, which meant we were approaching civilization. Knowing that we were so close subdued us all. Our misery was replaced by hope and a strong sense that we were about to accomplish something big. Maybe the misery would be worth it, after all.

Last night, we had to slow down because we were on track to arrive to Taiohae Bay before sunrise. It was hard to slow down when we were so desperate to arrive. In the early hours of the morning, we could smell land. Before, I thought "smelling land" was a figurative saying, but it isn't. Earth and foliage have a distinct, rich odor, one that in our land life we had never noticed. Right now I think it is probably the most beautiful smell in the whole world.

We pulled into the bay at 0600 local time, just as the sun was starting to come up. Eric did an amazing job of timing our arrival so we didn't have to spend a single extra minute at sea. I cannot begin to tell you how we felt when we first saw the tropical paradise in front of us. After twenty-one days of staring at nothing but ocean, the lush, mountainous island seemed like a mirage. The mountains are so tall that the tops were enshrouded in mist, and so green they looked like they were out of a sixties movie, when color film first came out and all the colors were way too bright and unnatural. The whole vision was surreal.

The range of emotions we experienced was huge. Relief. Joy. Accomplishment. Pride. Humility. Thankfulness. Every doubt we had about being able to make it here melted away. We were—and are—all thrilled.

Much to my dismay, though, after we anchored the boat, it kept rolling. It was rolling far less than at sea, but Eric had promised me calm, and it wasn't calm—not even close.

I burst into tears.

The Statistics

We traveled 2,835 nautical miles (3,256 statute miles, 5,243 kilometers) on about 1,000 gallons (3,800 liters) in 500 hours. That means

5.67 knots average speed, 2.83 miles per gallon, and 2.00 gallons per hour burned. We had 200 gallons of fuel left.

In Retrospect

Since this was our first passage, we didn't know what to expect. We feel we made the best choices possible given what we knew at the time. But now that we have a lot of experience under our belts, we have some thoughts:

Bringing the paravanes back in was probably a huge mistake. We all began to melt down as a result of the harsh motion. If we had dampened the motion, we would have been more comfortable and thus more happy. Now that we have a better grasp on fuel burn ratios, we know we could have made it. Unfortunately, we didn't figure out the dual stabilization trick until we were two thirds of the way around the world.

I honestly don't know how people crossed oceans before without the modern amenities we had. I probably would have acted on those suicidal thoughts if it weren't for all the creature comforts. I wouldn't have eaten much without the deep freezer stocked full of heat and serve foods and the microwave. We all would have been more uncomfortable and cranky without the air conditioning when it rained outside. It would have been miserable without enough water to shower or do laundry—especially when we had to close the boat up. And time would have dragged even more slowly if it weren't for all the movies we watched and video games Eric played. So in retrospect, we outfitted our boat very well.

Chapter 2: Nuka Hiva, Marquesas Islands, French Polynesia

Saturday, May 19

Desperate to console me, Eric immediately deployed the paravanes. Richard and I helped. It took awhile and proved to be a pain, but once the paravanes were out, the roll eased enough to make the rocking tolerable. I immediately cheered up.

Getting the dinghy down proved to be as much of a headache as getting the paravanes out: Both tasks took us four hours. The waiting killed us! We just wanted to get to shore. Once the dinghy was down, we all quickly cleaned up and headed out. The "dinghy dock" turned out to be a small metal ladder mounted on the sea wall. We had to push our way through some other dinghies to get to the ladder, and we tied the dinghy up to the one of the rungs. The steps were so rusted out that it was a bit treacherous to climb. I needed a little assistance getting up.

For twenty-one days we had fantasized about this moment and now it was really here. I couldn't believe it. It was a beautiful feeling to have the nice, solid, motionless terra firma under my feet. For a few seconds I felt a bit dizzy, but it passed quickly. When the dizziness subsided, so did the depression. I couldn't believe how instantly I snapped out of it; it was as if someone had flipped a switch. Richard and Eric both said that they felt completely normal when stepping on land. We all half expected to experience land sickness, which is when you feel like you are still rocking, and were surprised that we didn't.

We went to the agent's office to check in, located literally a few steps from the sea wall. We decided before we left that since we didn't speak French and didn't know the ropes of checking into and out of countries, it would be better to hire someone to help us with the process. The agent was nice and the paperwork was simple. She helped us fill out some forms and told us she'd take care of the rest. The only disconcerting thing was that we had to leave our passports with her so she could clear us with immigration. Not having my passport in hand kind of scared me.

Then we got lunch at the first restaurant we saw, an outdoor cafe. It felt like a celebration of sorts—a victory party, even. It was so nice to be waited on, and the food was delicious. We were shocked to see several dogs and cats lounging in the restaurant, which is illegal in the U.S. We were also surprised that our waiter was a transsexual. We had read that throughout the South Pacific, at a young age effeminate boys are put in a dress and raised as girls by their parents. Culturally speaking, transsexuality is perfectly normal here. The combination of the animals and the waiter (waitress?) brought home the fact that we were in a completely different culture.

As we ate, we surveyed our surroundings. Taiohae is stunningly beautiful, with dramatic mountains and cliffs that drip with thick, lush foliage. It looks like Hawaii. The town itself is small without a lot of infrastructure. The buildings are mostly modest bungalows, and some even have bamboo walls and/or thatched roofs. It looks like a movie set. The people appear laid back, not hurried like people at home. Animals roam everywhere—cows, chickens, horses, dogs, and cats all just hang out. For the most part, the animals seem to know where they belong and stay put. It is totally different from home, which added to the euphoria we were already feeling.

After lunch, we walked up and down the main drag, which parallels the bay. I had literally been dreaming about a long, vigorous walk, and now my dream had come true. So I was shocked to find that I was feeling tired and weak. How could I be tired after three weeks of non-stop rest? The fact that it was oppressively hot and humid was also a deterrent. Richard and Eric weren't really up for it either, but we pushed ourselves, wanting to make the most of our first day on solid land.

We stopped by a park on the waterfront filled with traditional, indigenous hand carved statues. The statues were quite large, many of them eleven feet (four meters) tall. The South Pacific style of art was distinctive and beautiful; it gave us good insight into the culture.

After walking the main drag, we finally conceded exhaustion and decided to go back to the boat to rest. We picked up our passports and then went back to retrieve our dingy. I froze: It wasn't there! Nervously, we walked around the L-shaped sea wall and spotted the dinghy up against the perpendicular wall. It had apparently become untied and floated away. We were lucky it had floated into the wall. If it had floated out to sea, it would have been gone for good. The waterline was about nine feet below the top of the wall, so there was no way to reach it from above. I was taking off my shoes and socks, ready to go for a swim, when a local teenage boy came to our rescue. He lowered himself into the dinghy and brought it around for us. Another local helped us get the dinghy through the maze of boats and over to the ladder. The locals have all been very nice so far, but this was way beyond nice!

I expected my depression to return as soon as we got back on board, but it didn't. Actually, it was lovely onboard and I felt content. Without the engine running, it was quiet. It was peaceful to hear the gentle pounding of the surf on the sea wall instead of the smacking of huge waves on the hull. Although we were still rocking, it wasn't painfully harsh like it had been at sea. It was soothing to look at the stunningly beautiful island. Eric asked me about checking into a hotel, but I said I didn't think

I needed to now. I had gotten a few hours of total and complete flatness, and that was really all I needed. That was a relief for him. I think he was worried that I didn't like the boat anymore and would want to sell it. (Of course, he was probably wary knowing that we still had roughly twenty-six thousand miles of rocking to go!)

We went to bed early. I can't remember the last time I slept so well.

In Retrospect

We now realize that being tired and out of sorts upon completion of a passage is normal. Sea time is not rest time. Whether you realize it or not, your body works hard to keep its equilibrium with the motion. The rougher the motion, the less rested you feel when you come into port. Also, the odd sleep schedule that accompanies watches adds to the tiredness

Monday, May 21

You would think that yesterday we would have gotten up early, eager to get to shore, but we didn't. We slept late and lounged around the boat until lunchtime. We were all feeling lethargic and unmotivated. I was unbelievably sore from the first day's walk. I couldn't believe my muscles had atrophied that much from three weeks of sitting.

Then the three of us explored the town and met lots of other cruisers. We felt an instant bond with the other boaters. It's almost like getting accepted into an exclusive fraternity, because we've all accomplished something special in making it here. First, though, we had to convince them we are "real" cruisers. At first, no one believed we made the crossing in a powerboat and asked questions like "Did you have the boat shipped here?" Once convinced, they inundated us with questions about the nitty-gritty details of what made our boat capable of crossing oceans. Eric was happy to talk about *Kosmos* nonstop, but I was bored to tears with the repetitive conversations.

Interestingly enough, we only met one cruiser couple our own age. Most are retirees, with a handful in their early twenties. Between the odd age and the odd boat, we really stood out. The other couple in their thirties had a horrendous crossing. Their autopilot broke, so they had to hand-steer for seven days. Hand steering is tough, requiring tremendous concentration and some physical strength to stay on course when the waves keep pushing the boat in the wrong directions. Talking to them made us count our blessings about our own smooth crossing.

In a crazy small world coincidence, I met a sailor who teaches at a school I briefly attended. The school has less than a thousand students, so the chances of meeting her here are ridiculously low. She caught me up on what was happening with all the teachers I knew and told me one of my former classmates was now a teacher there, too. That was a fun conversation for me.

Eric and I had more energy today, though still not anywhere close to normal. He did some much needed maintenance on the boat, changing the oil on the main engine, cleaning the sea strainers, and changing the water maker filter. I cleaned and organized, rearranging a few cabinets so the contents would be easier to access at sea. In the afternoon, the three of us went to shore. Richard checked into a hotel, feeling like he needed a few days of personal space. Eric and I ran some errands, then had dinner with some new cruiser friends.

After dinner, we went on our first nighttime dinghy ride. It was pitch black outside. Going down the rickety ladder in the dark was scary, and it was downright spooky to be navigating through an obstacle course of boats, lines, and dinghies that were barely visible in the inky darkness. We

were worried we wouldn't be able to find *Kosmos*. But we found her just
fine didn't crash into anything and didn't fall in the water. Phew!

Tuesday, May 22

Today we awoke early, excited. We were going on an all-day
horseback ride through the beautiful mountains of Nuka Hiva. I had
managed to make reservations over the phone in French, which was quite
a feat. It was raining a little bit as we got ready and dinghied in, but the
rain didn't concern us. It has rained every day so far, and the rain has
never lasted very long.

Our tour guide, Patrice, met us at the dinghy landing. He spoke no
English and had traditional face and arm tattoos. In the indigenous
culture, men tattooed their entire faces with intricate designs so they
would look menacing to their enemies. In recent years, the tradition has
been revived and is becoming more commonplace. Despite the
intimidating tattoos, we intuitively knew the second we looked at Patrice
that he was a nice guy with a gentle soul.

He ushered us into the back of his pickup truck. Eric and I realized
that we hadn't been in a car for twenty-four days—a record for us both.
We drove up a steep road for what seemed like a long time. The
mountains were densely packed with a wide variety of plants. The view of
the bay below became more spectacular with each meter we climbed.

We arrived at our destination. Initially, it seemed as if we had just
pulled to the side of the road, but when we looked around, we saw a
bunch of horses in a field nearby. Patrice retrieved two horses from the
field and took them to a stable hidden behind some trees. The stable was
on a cliff about two thousand feet tall overlooking Taiohae Bay. The view
was stunning.

Near the stable were a couple of cows as well as another few dozen horses running freely. It was cool and drizzly, a welcome relief from the stifling heat and humidity of the last few days. Patrice put a traditional hand-carved wooden saddle on his own horse, but he gave us leather saddles (thank goodness!). While he prepped the horses, he pointed to the sky a few times and said things in French. The only word I understood was "big."

We traveled along the paved road before turning off onto a dirt road that led to our second viewpoint, the top of a 2,800-foot summit. The clouds slowly rolled in as we ascended. With the misty fog, lush greenery, tropical birds, and the *clop clop* sounds of hooves on the dirt, we felt like we had been transported to another time and place, an era akin to the movie *Lord of the Rings*. Neither of us would have been surprised if Patrice pulled out a huge sword and the *Lord* movie soundtrack started playing (except when we happened upon the construction crew building a road, but that is a side point).

At the top, the view was obstructed by the thick clouds. As we descended, the slight drizzle became stronger. We went back to the road and headed toward the third viewpoint, getting some close looks at the many cattle grazing nearby, including a baby calf nursing. The bulls were intimidating, seemingly ready to charge us if we got too close, but Patrice just shooed them away.

The third viewpoint was a cute little picnic area off the side of the road. Since it was a lower altitude, it didn't have the cloud cover and the view was spectacular. As we rode on, the sky opened up and it began to pour down rain. Hmmm… could this be what he was trying to tell us earlier? Too bad I hadn't gotten to the word for "rain" in the language lessons yet!

Patrice pulled out a rain slicker for each of us, but it was too late. We were already soaking wet. He apparently decided we needed to get back right away, and he abruptly turned us around and picked up the pace. It took some serious muscles for me to ride that trotting horse. I couldn't imagine riding at a full gallop! Our full day trip was over by noon, but that turned out to be a blessing in disguise since I was beginning to get saddle sore.

In the evening, we went out to dinner again and did another nighttime dinghy ride back to *Kosmos*. It was less scary the second time. Taiohae doesn't have streetlights, so the stars are amazingly vibrant. Once we were back on board, we sat outside and watched the stars. It felt good to be able to take the time to appreciate Mother Nature. In our old life, we rarely did.

Wednesday, May 23

I was in serious pain today. I was still sore from the walk on the first day, and I had large blisters from a new pair of shoes I'd worn on the second day. Yesterday's ride left me saddle sore beyond belief, with a big rash to boot. I had no idea that riding in wet clothes could give you such a severe rash. *Oww!* Now we know why Patrice took us back so abruptly.

Around 0930, *Special Blend*, another Nordhavn 43, pulled into the bay and anchored next to us. She came from Florida, through the Panama Canal, having stopped in the Galapagos Islands on the way. Last year we had met her owners, Jim and Martha, and had gone out to dinner with them. It was exciting to see familiar faces again, and just as exciting to have another powerboat around, especially *Kosmos*'s twin. (Well, fraternal twin. She has a fly bridge and a flopper stopper system that is different from our paravanes.) Jim and Martha are traveling with their adult children and one of their grandchildren.

In the afternoon, Eric and I went to the local museum. It was absolutely charming. The museum owner, Rose, is infamous and mentioned in all the cruising guides. An American, she moved to the Marquesas in 1972, when the chief still ran the show and there were no roads, electricity, or phones. She is passionate about the Marquesan culture and people. We found her fascinating to talk to and an absolutely lovely lady.

The museum has only one tiny room, but is crammed full of interesting historical information and exquisite artwork. Sadly, most of the Marquesan history has been lost. Prior to the arrival of white man, there was no written language. After the whites arrived, the local population was virtually wiped out. Some of the loss of life was from diseases the whites brought, but most of it was from the guns the newcomers gave to the locals. The various warring tribes used the guns on one another, each tribe trying to wipe out the other. The few that survived were forced to become Christian and to abandon their indigenous religion, culture, and lifestyle in favor of European ways. Few of the old traditions live on today. Even so, the Marquesas have a richer surviving culture than many of the other island groups since they were not as heavily colonized.

The Marquesan artwork is varied, but there are two general themes: local animals, like turtles and dolphins, and tikis. Prior to the arrival of the missionaries, the Polynesians were polytheistic. Tikis bear the images of their assorted gods, and they range in size from tiny to huge. We learned that all the statues in the park that we visited on the first day were tikis.

Thursday, May 24

Today, we went to the grocery store. In the Marquesas, the supply ship only comes once a month, and its arrival is a big deal. Everyone comes out to see the ship unload. We had stopped by the store before, and it was slim pickings. But the supply ship came in yesterday, and last night the boxes were unloaded. We were promised there would be a decent selection this morning.

As we walked down the aisle, a package caught my eye. At that moment, my life changed: Harp music started playing and angels started singing. I couldn't believe it. Was this a mirage? Joyfully, I picked up the package. I almost did a cartwheel in the aisle, but I decided to exercise some composure.

I pointed to the display. "We need eight boxes, two of each flavor," I informed Eric.

"They're just cookies," said Eric, looking at me blankly.

How wrong he was. They were Tim Tams, the best prepackaged cookies on earth! I had gotten addicted to them when I briefly lived in Australia and hadn't seen them since. I was eager to become re-addicted.

The real event of the day, however, was refueling. At about 1400 (2:00 p.m.), we lifted the paravanes and anchor, made a quick three mile jaunt out to sea to dump our septic holding tank then went to the fuel dock. We were nervous about getting fuel. At this station, you have to Mediterranean-moor against a concrete pier. We had never med moored before and were intimidated. Fortunately, there was no one next to us, so we didn't have to worry about crashing into neighbors, but it still wasn't easy. There was some wind and current, so getting the boat backed in perfectly straight was tricky. We did manage to get in and tied up okay, though.

The attendant handed us a hose, and we had to pump ourselves. We got 3,400 liters of diesel from the painfully slow pump, holding the nozzle the entire time since it didn't auto-lock. (Which is hard on the hands!) While we were fueling, though, we discovered we hadn't put out enough chain, so the anchor started dragging, slowly bringing us closer and closer to the pier. About halfway through the fueling, the waves had pushed us all the way into the pier. Not a good situation. In a contest between fiberglass (the boat) and concrete (the pier), concrete usually wins.

If we wanted to reset the anchor, we'd have to stop the fueling process and back the boat in again. That had been a nightmare, so we decided re-anchoring was out of the question. Eric ended up running the engine, trying to give it just enough thrust to keep us away from the wall, but not so much that we moved farther from the pier than the hose could reach. It was a delicate line. I was in the cockpit pumping, carefully watching our position. I would tell him when to move forward and by how much, and when to hold or back up. The problem was that we couldn't hear each other. We had to yell at the top of our lungs to communicate, and the yelling naturally inflamed the tension of the situation. We bumped into the pier a few more times until Eric figured out the right balance of throttle to maintain position, but once he got it, he was able to maintain pretty well. Fortunately, there was no damage to the hull. The situation was scary and stressful for us both. But our ability to work as team kept *Kosmos* safe.

It was 1720 (5:20 p.m.) by the time we were done fueling. When we asked the attendant where to pay, he said they had already closed and that we could pay tomorrow. Uh, Toto, I don't think we're in California anymore.

Richard also came back tonight. I guess he'd had enough space and was ready to be with us again.

Friday, May 25

Today's first order of business was to pay the fuel bill. Then Eric and I hired a local to give us a tour of the island. Richard opted not to join us.

50

A National Oceanic and Atmospheric Administration (NOAA) research vessel had pulled into port, and he went on a tour of their ship, instead. Our guide, Dean, was about the same age as us and spoke excellent English. We didn't go around the whole island, but we covered quite a bit and got a good feel for much of its scenery, culture, and lifestyle.

Rose had already told us that they only began putting roads on the Marquesan Islands in 1981. The road system doesn't go everywhere yet, and there are still parts of the island that are only accessible by boat. The roads that exist are mostly dirt. They are actively making new roads and paving the existing ones. We were glad we were being chauffeured; we wouldn't have been comfortable driving on the windy, steep, muddy mountain roads.

Taiohae is the administrative capital of the Marquesan Islands and by far the biggest city in the entire island group, boasting a whopping two thousand people. The other "towns" on Nuka Hiva are so tiny that you would miss them if you blinked. As we passed through the towns, Dean told us about each of them and how they generate income. Most make their money from coconut and noni farming.

The Marquesas are "young" volcanic islands, making them incredibly fertile. They have countless types of fruit trees and seem to grow just about every tropical plant imaginable. Dean picked us an assortment of fruit to eat, including star fruit and *pampelmousse. Pampelmousse* is French for "grapefruit," but the grapefruit here is so different from the grapefruit at home that we insisted on calling it *pampelmousse* to differentiate the two. It is almost as big as a basketball, and the meat is lime green. Incredibly sweet yet a touch tangy, *pampelmousse* is delicious—like a Midori sour.

Dean told us there are almost one hundred varieties of coconut in existence and most of them grow in the Marquesas. The majority of the exported coconut meat is dried before being shipped and eventually processed into coconut oil. He also pointed out noni fruit, though we didn't try it because apparently it tastes awful. Locals apply pieces of noni to wounds to help them heal faster. And they make a beverage out of it that is supposed to increase a man's sexual prowess and fertility. (Interestingly, the biggest customers of noni are the Mormons. Maybe that's why they have such big families!)

On the islands, no matter how poor people are, they never go hungry. Food is so abundant in the wild that people can always feed themselves. Similarly, most islanders can make houses from local natural materials, so no one has to be homeless. One can easily survive without an income here.

Until the early 1980s, everyone lived in tribes. There was no monetary currency, electricity, or roads. Dean lived in a tribe when he was young and told us how the chief assigned everyone job duties. Some people would build huts. Some would hunt, and some would cook. Others would fish or collect fruit. While each nuclear family had its own hut and family duties, the tribe worked as a team in order to survive. The concept of individual survival is a new one for the island people. Dean said there are some major pros and cons to both lifestyles. The modern lifestyle is certainly less physically laborious and more comfortable, but there is a mental stress that didn't exist before.

This modernization took place rapidly. In the West, modernization occurred over a couple hundred years. The Marquesans, however, skipped enormous steps in the technical evolution process. They went from horses to all-terrain trucks; from no electricity to lights, refrigeration, air conditioning, CDs, movies, and computers; from no modern communication to wireless phones—all in a few years.

Dean also took us to scenic viewpoints along the way, both coastal and mountain vistas. Because the mountains are so tall, Nuka Hiva gets a lot of rain, and consequently, there are numerous stunning waterfalls dotting the island. One especially scenic spot was where the set of *Survivor* was located and Dean proudly told us how he worked for the show during the production.

He also took us to several archeological sites, where he pointed out various ruins and told us more about the ancient culture. The layouts of the ancient villages reflected a class system. The foundations of the buildings were made of stone, but the structures themselves were fashioned from biodegradable materials like bamboo and palm fronds. The only things that have survived the test of time are the foundations, some stone statues, and some bone tools.

The focal point of these ancient villages was where humans were sacrificed. Throughout most of the South Pacific, cannibalism was commonplace until the European missionaries put a stop to it in the 17th century. The villagers would take prisoners from other villages and then kill the prisoners in a ceremony. Every bit of the dead person was utilized. They ate the meat and fat, shaped the bone into tools, and displayed the skulls as trophies. One of the sites we visited had an enormous banyan, one of the biggest trees we'd ever seen. When the Europeans first arrived at this village, the banyan had hundreds of skulls hanging from it, probably much like we hang ornaments on Christmas trees. Not surprisingly, the missionaries didn't like the choice of décor. It was probably like walking into a horror movie! The missionaries insisted that the villagers take the skulls down.

We also saw several old stone tikis, some dating back as far as two thousand years. The images on the ancient ones are weather-beaten and faint, so newer replicas have been carved so visitors can see what they used to look like.

We had a fabulous time touring the island. Nuka Hiva is truly beautiful--one of the few unspoiled places left in the world.

Saturday, May 26

This morning *Special Blend* pulled out around dawn, headed to Anaho Bay on the north side of Nuka Hiva. Later in the morning, five French *gendarme* personnel (rural military/police) pulled up alongside us in a dinghy. We almost had a heart attack when they told us they were boarding to question us and inspect the vessel.

One of our biggest fears was of being boarded and searched. Many people had told us about how corrupt officials often try to confiscate foreign boats and haul the crew off to jail unless the owner pays hefty bribes. We all panicked, thinking, *Oh my God! Oh my God! This is it. We're about to be shaken down for money.*

We tried to stay calm and play it cool. The officials spoke great English and they were nice, which helped us relax. They went through a series of questions: What is your citizenship? What is your home port? Where did you leave from? Did you stop anywhere in French Polynesia before coming to Taiohae?

When we said no, they looked suspicious and asked us a few more questions along the same lines, essentially rewording the same question over and over. We were wondering why they were harping on this point when it dawned on us: They thought we were *Special Blend!* By law, boats must go to Taiohae before they can visit any other place in the Marquesas. Since we came from the northwest, Nuka Hiva was the first island we came to, so there was no temptation to stop anywhere else. But *Special Blend* came from the southwest, and she had to pass several islands to get to Nuka Hiva. After crossing, they had needed a break, so they did stop briefly at the first island before coming to Nuka Hiva.

Holy crap! we thought, panicking. We're about to get busted for something we didn't do!

We asked the officials if they were aware an identical boat was en-route to Anaho. Given that our boat is so rare, especially in this part of the world, they didn't believe us. Fortunately, we had pictures of the two boats side by side, the background clearly Taiohae. Phew! Crisis averted.

From that point on, everything went smoothly. The military guys were joking and laughing with us. Even though they didn't demand to inspect us, Eric gave them a tour of the boat. We suspect that half the reason they boarded us was to get a look at our unique vessel.

In the evening, Eric and I went to a traditional Marquesan dinner hosted by Rose, the owner of the museum. Richard didn't join us, opting for alone time on board. We were surprised when we rode the dinghy in to see so many locals out and about. Usually, there were a handful of people around, but tonight—a Saturday—there were throngs.

Dinner was fun. In addition to cruisers, several people from the NOAA ship attended. I found them fascinating to talk to, and after hearing about the amazing technology they have on board, now understand why Richard was so eager to see their ship.

The buffet featured goat boiled in coconut milk (good, but it had a lot of small bones that had to be picked out); chicken with taro leaves (taro is a large leaf plant with edible tubular roots similar to yams. The leaves tasted like cooked spinach); three kinds of bananas prepared three different ways (one was really good, one good, one okay); breadfruit (a tasteless fruit with cheddar cheese-like texture); fermented breadfruit and coconut milk (an acquired taste, like beer, which I thought was gross); raw tuna in coconut milk with light veggies like tomato and cucumber (yummy); raw fish Chinese style (good); tropical fruit salad (good); and a banana-manioc cake (manioc is another root similar to a yam and the cake was yummy).

Musicians played traditional island music during dinner. We kind of expected the music to be slow and mellow, like Hawaiian music, but it was fast, pulsating, and sexy. After dinner, a group of women performed some traditional dances. The choreography was fabulous with some serious hip shaking action. Those women must have abs like rocks!

The dancers were wearing little black halter tops and long grass skirts. Some of the skirts were dyed red; some were natural colored. The waist of the skirts were adorned with what I thought was mother of pearl and fringe. They had on headdresses and were holding grass pompoms. Halfway through, they did a costume change, returning in brown halter tops and short, tight brown skirts. The backside of the skirt had a grass and feather overlay over the rump that made the girls look like they had big rear ends. They looked like peacocks with their feathery backsides. As they moved, the overlay flapped; it was erotic. The dancers also wore crowns decorated with seashells and matching belts.

It was a treat to be able to watch them. At the end, the girls gave everyone dance lessons. I tried to learn, but I don't think it's physically possible for me move my hips the way those women do! Too bad. I'd love to be as sexy as them.

On our way back to *Kosmos*, two very large, very drunk teenage boys approached us. They got closer than I would have preferred, which made me nervous, but I resisted the urge to step back. Eric was never worried, though. It turned out that one of the boys had heard us talking and simply wanted to practice his English. We talked to him for quite a while. His

English was pretty good, though it took awhile to get used to his drunken slur. He chatted animatedly and swayed a bit. I was sure he was going to fall over at any second, but he didn't. His friend didn't say much, but his gestures and body language were amusing.

And then we had another successful dingy ride in the dark. Yes!

Sunday, May 27

Today was quite an interesting cultural experience. In just a few hours, Eric and I received both our coldest and warmest reception from the locals. We had read in the guidebooks that Polynesians are deeply religious people and everyone goes to church. The singing was amazing, the books claimed, and it was worth a visit. Dean had told us that in his grandparents' day church was mandatory, but nowadays it was socially acceptable not to go. Based on the guidebook's emphasis, we figured most people still attend church and that it would be a great way to interact with the locals and get a glimpse of their culture. Richard had no interest in attending church.

The Catholic cathedral, located off the main drag, is imposing with two large stone turrets. You can't miss it. But finding the Protestant church was tricky; we had to ask for directions a couple of times to find it. The church turned out to be a plain bungalow with virtually no adornment, not even a cross. At first we thought we were in the wrong place. Dean had taken us to a few churches around the island, so we knew that most other churches had statues and art. We figured this must be an austere sect.

We arrived a bit early and sat down. Only one person welcomed us, and he asked a woman to sit with us. She did and said hello, but when she realized we didn't speak French, she ended all attempts at conversation. There were about forty people at the service, a lot of them kids, and no one else acknowledged us in any way, not even by nodding. It was really uncomfortable to be ignored. With 1,700 people in the town but only a handful of people at the church service, it was clear that religion is not the big deal that the guidebooks claim. We realized Dean had delicately tried to tell us that. The singing was good but not amazing. The sermon was in Marquesan, and while we had no idea what the minister was saying, we could guess based on the classic gestures and vocal tones. We left in the middle of his sermon at 10:30. We didn't walk out to be rude; we were planning to take *Kosmos* to Anaho Bay, and we needed to tell the officials we were moving. On Sundays the *gendarme* office is only open for a few hours, so we needed to get going before it closed.

We walked to the main drag and headed toward the office. One guy drove by, guzzling a beer with one hand and the other on the steering wheel. That gave a new meaning to "Sunday driver"! Then we passed a group of eight teenagers sitting under a tree along the shore. They called us over. As it turned out, the drunk guy from last night was there. Shockingly, he remembered our conversation. We were sure he would have blacked it out.

All the kids were drunk and wanted us to party with them, insisting that we take a drink from a communal tumbler filled with a mystery beverage. Talk about a 180-degree difference from the reception we got at the church! We thanked them for the invitation but explained that the officials we needed to see closed at 1100 and that we had to go. The last thing we needed was a mob of angry parents banging down our door for encouraging their children to drink.

Several hundred yards down the road a man who looked like he was homeless beckoned us. He offered us sandwiches and talked animatedly in French while pointing to the mountain. We had no idea what he was saying, but he was genuinely welcoming. Then a boy in a football (soccer) uniform ran up and walked with us for a bit. I chatted with him as best as I could in broken French.

Interestingly, almost everybody who saw us on the street today wanted to talk. Until now, not one person had spontaneously stopped to talk to us (except the boys last night); they needed a reason to engage us. We had thought the locals were kind and eager to help, but emotionally aloof. They seemed to want us to make the first move towards friendliness and would generally respond in kind. But after today our impression is changing.

Our visit with the *gendarme* was quick. They only wanted a list of places we planned to stop between here and Tahiti. We had expected more paperwork. Then we went to *Kosmos* and the three of us got her ready to go. We pulled up anchor at 1300 (1:00 p.m.). The ride to Anaho was rocky but tolerable. When we got there four hours later, we dropped anchor next to *Special Blend*. This anchorage was just as pretty as Taiohae, but the bay here was significantly calmer. Since sunset is at 1800 (6:00 p.m.), we didn't go to shore. Instead, we had a quiet night aboard.

Monday, May 28

Special Blend took off at sunrise. We were disappointed we didn't get a chance to hang out with our friends, but at least we were able to talk to them last night on the radio. Shortly after they left, the Gendarme Patrol ship pulled in—which wasn't surprising considering we'd alerted them *Special Blend* would be here. We couldn't believe that *Special Blend* escaped being busted by only a few hours yet again!

Anaho Bay is a special place. It is a glimpse of what all the Marquesas were probably like thirty years ago, and most likely what all the islands were like one hundred years ago. It may be one of the last genuinely unspoiled villages on earth. Like Taiohae Bay, Anaho Bay is surrounded by tall, vibrant green mountains. The bay itself looks like it is out of a picture book, with a horseshoe curve and sapphire blue water. Near the shoreline, the water color changes to a spectacular blue-green. The land along the water is odd – there are a few small isolated spots of white sandy beach where one could lay out, but the majority of the beach has only a tiny strip of sand that is enshrouded in thick, dense foliage. At the outskirts of the bay, the shoreline vanishes and instead sheer cliffs dramatically plunge into the water. There are only two ways to get to the town of Anaho: by boat or on foot. There are no roads that can accommodate a car. The "main road" is a small, one-person footpath that parallels the water. The footpath eventually takes you to the next bay over, where there is supposedly a real road.

We landed the dinghy at the edge of town. The town consists of a small *pension* (motel), a church, a town square, several small homes, and a couple of sheds for animals. (Like in Taiohae, animals roam everywhere.) The town square has a covered patio and a grassy area with a volleyball net. The land is cleared around the buildings and square, but the buildings are spread out, with lots of jungle in between. Standing in the lush jungle and looking out at the scenic bay, we felt like we were on the set of the TV show *Lost*.

We walked along the path for a while, enjoying the pretty scenery. After the walk, we went snorkeling in the warm water. Anaho Bay has the only coral reef in all the Marquesan Islands. Since the Marquesas are "young" islands, the reefs haven't formed yet. This reef is quite small and the water isn't very clear. But while the coral was disappointing, the swim was wonderful and refreshing.

After the sunset, we sat outside for a while, enjoying the warm night. The moon was only three quarters full but still bright enough to cast shadows. We could clearly see each of the boats in the bay and the land around us. Gosh, on a night like tonight, doing the dinghy ride in the dark wouldn't be scary. As always, there were scattered clouds, and when the clouds moved in front of the moon, they would glow in the moonlight. The stars near the moon were invisible in the bright light, but the stars farther away twinkled brilliantly in the sky. It was the perfect end to a perfect day in paradise. We are so glad we came here. It probably won't be much longer before this little village is introduced to "civilization."

Tuesday, May 29

We were up at 0630, preparing the boat for sea. Our next destination was Fatu Hiva, an island about twenty-four hours away. We were planning to make a stop to make along the way, and we needed to make it as early as possible.

There is a particular spot on the southeast side of Nuka Hiva where dolphins congregate by the hundreds in the mornings. You can actually jump in and swim with them. It is the only place where this happens; no one knows why. They aren't always there, but we had our fingers crossed.

Eric told us he didn't think we should swim with the dolphins since the seas were rough. Richard and I were bummed, but we agreed. Swimming in rough seas is dangerous in and of itself, and the danger is compounded by the fact that it can be difficult to get back aboard when the boat is swaying too much. One reason we never swam on our twenty-one-day crossing was because we never had a calm enough day.

We cruised over to the spot and sure enough, six dolphins came to play in the wake of our bow. Soon more joined them. As we motored around, there were always between a half dozen and two dozen dolphins at the bow. We could see tons more—the water was literally teeming with them. We cruised up and down for a while, delighting in watching the dolphins play. They followed the boat whichever way we turned, and when we stopped, they waited below the surface for us to get going again. Sometimes they poked their heads out and floated vertically for a while. It was incredible.

These dolphins were different from what we're used to seeing. At home, they are grey with a sleek head and long nose. In Nuka Hiva, the dolphins are light brown, with a rounder head and shorter nose. They are also smaller.

Richard and I both thought we could handle the rough waters. It didn't take much cajoling to get Eric to throw caution to the wind and let us swim. As soon as he said yes, we changed into swimwear; grabbed our masks, snorkels, and fins; and hopped in. Eric manned the boat.

The swim was nothing short of amazing. We watched the dolphins play under the water and chased them around a bit. Most of the dolphins kept their distance, but some got within a few feet of us. Swimming with so many dolphins in the wild was truly a once in a lifetime experience. The fact that it was warm, tropical water made it even better. Oddly enough, neither of us saw other fish in the water. Maybe the dolphins scare everything else away.

After twenty minutes of swimming, Eric told us to come in. He had been keeping the boat stationary, so the automatic stabilizers weren't working and he was getting sick. We had no problems getting back on board. We turned the boat around and headed out to sea. At first, a swarm of dolphins followed us, but one by one they dropped away until eventually they were all gone.

The scenery on this passage was incredible. During the entire ride, we were able to see an island or two or three in the distance. At sunset, we were near the island Ua Poa. The sun dipped behind the island, surrounding it with a red glow that almost looked like a halo. It was truly glorious. As the night progressed, the moon—almost full now—became so bright that it lit up the whole ocean. Even in the dark, we could clearly see the islands we passed. It was the brightest, clearest night we have ever had on the water.

The comfortableness of the ride was another story altogether. The seas today were some of the roughest we've experienced yet, and we took water over the bow a few times. Unfortunately, we were going into head seas, hence the ugly ride. Thank goodness this is a short trip. However, we have to admit that even though head seas are an unpleasant motion, we prefer them to the multiple motions that come with confused seas.

Chapter 3: Fatu Hiva, Marquesas Islands, French Polynesia

Wednesday, May 30

We pulled into the Bay of Virgins on Fatu Hiva at 0830. We were dismayed to see that the anchorage was crowded, and we had a hard time finding a spot far enough from the other boats that felt safe. The anchorage here is unusually deep at one hundred feet. The deeper the anchorage, the more chain you have to let out—and therefore the more space you need to leave between boats to prevent crashing. It took a couple of tries, but we finally anchored near the outer edge. We were a little nervous about our spot, but it looked like the best one available. Unfortunately, this anchorage is rolly and uncomfortable, but we knew that putting out the paravanes wasn't an option given how close the neighboring boats are.

As promised, the Bay of Virgins is spectacular. Fatu Hiva has the most rainfall of all the islands and is the most lush. Like in Nuka Hiva, steep mountains dramatically shoot out of the water; there is very little shoreline. Interesting rock formations dot the landscape around the bay. Its indigenous name was Bay of the Phalli, because several of the rock formations strongly resemble penises of various shapes and sizes. Not surprisingly, the French missionaries were unhappy with that name (*Baie des Verges* in French) and changed it to the Bay of Virgins (*Baie des Vierges*) by adding an "i" to the name.

We hadn't originally planned to visit Fatu Hiva since it was a little bit off our route, but so many cruisers had told us we had to come here that we changed our itinerary. Fatu Hiva has two towns that are connected by a mostly dirt road, and just over five hundred people. It is extremely

64

difficult for tourists to get to without a private boat since there is no airport and no regular ferry. The ability to go to isolated islands like this is a reason why people choose to travel by private boat.

After anchoring, we waited a few hours, carefully watching to make sure *Kosmos* didn't drift into any other boats. When we were sure that the spot was safe, we dinghied into shore. The town is called Hanavave, and it is not much bigger than Anaho, consisting of a church, a market, a tiny clinic, and a handful of homes. We saw the whole town in five minutes, then set off on a what was supposed to be a short hike to see the island's biggest tourist attraction: a waterfall. We didn't have a map, but according to the guidebooks, the trail was marked.

We made the first turn off the main road, which took us up a hill to a spot with a pretty view of the bay and rock formations. The small road ended at a house. Oops. Wrong turn! We backtracked to the main road. Fortunately, at the second turn we met a couple on their way back from the waterfall who affirmed that was the right trail. They warned us it was difficult to see the trail, but to look for the rock markers, and said the waterfall was worth the hike.

We turned onto the small road, which soon narrowed to a footpath. The footpath led to rocks that we had to climb over, and the defined trail vanished, replaced by an occasional small marker that vaguely pointed the direction to take. Richard was leading the way, and Eric and I are ashamed to admit that we had a hard time keeping up. (Richard is at least decades older than we are!). I was thankful Richard kept blazing ahead, because if Eric and I had been alone, we probably would have given up. We generally like to stick to well-marked trails and don't do a lot of wandering where it is easy to get lost. While the hike was absolutely beautiful, it was longer and more vigorous than we had originally anticipated, and I had started to worry that we were lost. I was relieved when we arrived.

The waterfall was stunning, with a majestic two hundred foot drop into an inviting pond. We sat there for a long time, enjoying the cool mist from the fall. Richard told us that the mist is charged with negative ions which are scientifically proven to improve lung function, lower heart rate, and improve moods.

As we passed through town on our way back from the hike, a woman named Theresa invited us to come into her home and look at her artwork. Traditional Polynesian cloth, called tapa, used to be made from tree bark. Fatu Hiva is the only island in French Polynesia where the custom is still practiced. Several locals sell indigenous style paintings on this cloth to tourists.

Theresa showed us a few pieces of tapa art and some other things for sale, but nothing interested us. As we were leaving, she asked if we had sunglasses to trade. We did have a pair of cheapies on board in case of emergency that we offered up. She gave us four *pampelmousse* (grapefruit) in exchange right then, trusting us to come back with the glasses. She also asked if I had any perfume. I told her I would check. On the small islands, the locals prefer to barter. Few retail goods ever make it to such remote places, so cash means little to them because they have nothing to spend it on.

Back at the boat we made lunch and took a nap, still tired from the passage. When we got up, I dug out a sixteen-ounce (480 ml) bottle of knockoff perfume, grabbed the cheap sunglasses, and Eric and I headed back to the village. Theresa's eyes practically popped out of her head when she saw how big the bottle was. She gave us two baguettes, two onions, and another *pampelmousse* in exchange. After we left, though, I realized we are terrible barterers. We traded thirty dollars worth of stuff for ten dollars worth of food. We need to work on our negotiating skills!

We went back to the boat and sat outside to watch the sunset. The sunset was gorgeous, but after the sun dipped below the horizon, the sky became almost magical. For a few minutes, the whole sky turned periwinkle (a shade of purple). We've never seen anything quite like it.

After dinner, we went back outside. Even though it was dark, it was still enchanting. The almost full moon was so bright that we joked about needing sunscreen, and the water sparkled as it reflected the light, giving the whole scene a soft, mystical feel. As we appreciated the beauty surrounding us, we decided it was definitely worth all the hellish days at sea to get here.

Chapter 4: Manihi, Tuomotus Islands, French Polynesia

We just pulled into Manihi after the worst three days at sea of all time. We knew it was going to be rough when we left, but we figured it couldn't be any more awful than it had been on our twenty-one day passage.

How wrong we were.

We left on Friday morning at the first light of dawn. Even in our protected anchorage, the wind was blowing at thirty-two knots and there were whitecaps in the bay. It only got worse out on the open ocean. The waves were twelve to fourteen feet, coming at rapid intervals, and hitting from the port aft. When waves come from the back corners, they often make the boat roll in a strange corkscrew pattern. Corkscrewing is heinous. We were rolling like crazy, often as much as thirty-five degrees (essentially seventy degrees as you go back and forth). If we weren't holding on to the boat when a wave came, we would literally get thrown across the room--and that is not an exaggeration. We felt like human pinballs.

With all the rolling, water regularly came up over the sides and sometimes splashed all the way up to the roof, so we had to keep everything closed up, including the pilothouse hatch. Because of the corkscrew motion, all three air conditioning intake valves were periodically exposed to air, so all three air conditioners (one downstairs and two upstairs) frequently turned themselves off. The heat and stuffiness were stifling. None of us slept well. We were all grouchy and irritable.

Emotionally speaking, Eric and I both endured the ride okay. Once again I was severely lethargic, but this time I didn't get depressed. I think Richard had a hard time, though. He never complained, but I sense that he's had enough of being locked up with us and needs his own space. It's not personal; I think Richard enjoys our company as much as we do his. It has simply been too long of a visit, in a much too confined space, and in mostly unpleasant circumstances (due to perpetually rough seas). Richard's misery was compounded last night when he bashed his finger. It swelled all the way to his second knuckle and turned black.

This morning, the seas calmed down right before dawn and the ride actually became pleasant. Too bad it didn't flatten out sooner. We spotted land midmorning. From a distance, it looked exactly like what we had always imagined a deserted tropical island to look like—so low it was barely above sea level, with lots of palm trees swaying in the wind.

There's a geological explanation for this: When volcanic islands first form, they are mountainous. Over time, the mountains slowly sink under their own weight and a reef forms around the edges. Eventually, the reef grows into its own landmass. The Marquesas are young islands, with huge mountains and reef that are just beginning to develop. But the Tuomotus islands are very old. Most of them, in fact, are atolls. An atoll is a volcanic island that has already completely sunk, leaving only a narrow ring of coral landmass with a lagoon in the middle (where the volcanic island once was). To enter the lagoon of an atoll, you must go through a pass—a spot in the reef where coral doesn't grow. These passes were once river mouths where coral never formed because it was unable to survive in the brackish water.

We approached Manihi's pass around 1100. We were all nervous. The atoll lagoons in the Tuomotus have a reputation for being tricky:

There are lots of stories about various boats that have hit the coral and sunk. Mahini is one of the easier passes to navigate, which is why we chose to visit this atoll, but doing so still requires skill and caution.

The pass is only eleven feet deep and one hundred feet wide—not much latitude for maneuvering. The currents are notoriously strong, too, making it difficult to steer. We were advised to go in and out against the current for better steering control. Before we left Fatu Hiva, we had calculated how long it would take to get to Manihi and consulted tide charts to see when the current would be outgoing. We specifically left Fatu Hiva at dawn to make sure we got here when the current was suitable for us to enter.

We all took deep breaths as Eric gunned the engine and entered the narrow channel. So many things can go wrong when navigating a pass. There might be an uncharted coral head or rock. The bottom of the pass could become built up with silt. A sudden, large gust of wind could push us off course. Or, with it being a full moon, the current could be so strong that we might not be able to get in. We hoped the pass would be clear so we could have full latitude in case any evasive maneuvering was necessary, but much to our dismay, a small dingy of fishermen was anchored there. Fortunately, they were off to the side and didn't get in our way. The current was indeed strong. At full throttle we were only doing three and a half knots, so it was probably a five knot current! Eric navigated us in with no problem. I was so proud of him

Once inside the pass, we still had to avoid dozens of coral heads as we motored us over to the anchorage on the southeast side of the lagoon, not too far from the pass. Richard and I stood outside and intently watched the water for any uncharted underwater hazards, and Eric drove slowly, carefully weaving around the heads noted on the charts.

Manihi looks like a postcard. The whole island appeared to be a giant white sand beach filled with coconut trees and evergreens. The evergreens are bent over from the wind, but the palm trees naturally grow against the wind, which blows them upright. The water is a majestic quilt of blues and greens with some patches of very light aquamarine, deep cobalt, and every shade of blue-green in between. The turquoise patches are so bright they practically glow. It looks like a scene out of the movies *South Pacific*. The most incredible things about Manihi, though, are the floating houses. Here, people have actually built houses on stilts atop some of the coral heads, giving the illusion that the houses are floating on the water. It doesn't look real.

The lagoon is so big that you can't see the other side, but the strip of land between the lagoon and ocean is so narrow that you can see the ocean through the trees. That thin strip is magical: On the lagoon side it is flat calm, while only a few hundred feet away are tumultuous big waves.

We pulled up to the anchorage and saw three sailboats. One of the cruisers hailed us on the radio, warning us to be careful about anchoring. His boat and another boat's anchor chains were both stuck on coral. They were waiting for a local diver to go down and unwind the chain from the coral. Getting stuck on coral is a common problem out here and is one of the risks of visiting paradise.

We had just started to relax, but that news made us nervous again. Richard, Eric, and I studied the water, looking carefully for a light area without any dark spots—that is, a section that was probably all sand with no coral heads. We dropped anchor, hoping we made a good choice. Unfortunately, we won't know if we are stuck until it is time to leave.

We got the dinghy down and headed to the island's only hotel and restaurant, located on the southwest side of the island. It was a long ride, taking us more than a half hour. The hotel is rustic and charming, a series of bungalows made of bamboo rods with palm frond ceilings. Many of the rooms are built on stilts over shallow water. The beach has alluring white sand. Richard made reservations to check in tomorrow. Apparently, the rooms are not cheap. Guess you have to pay for paradise, huh?

We had lunch, feeling celebratory for enduring another rough time at sea and successfully navigating the pass. The ride back was really wet. Whenever we go against the wind waves and current in the dinghy, we generally get splashed. But today we got drenched. Once I got wet, I became really cold, despite the fact that it was quite warm out.

We watched a spectacular sunset and then crashed early, tired from the previous three days. We all slept great in the calm lagoon.

In Retrospect:

We eventually found out that lethargy is a common form of seasickness, one that I would suffer with for the entire world journey. In hindsight, I should have known it would be a problem for me. All my adult life, I became lethargic every time I went out on a boat, but I always wrote it off to working too much. I assumed once I wasn't working, the lethargy would vanish. Wrong!

Tuesday, June 5

First thing this morning, some divers came and freed the two sailboats. The divers are based out of the hotel, so they gave Richard a ride. Richard was thrilled that he and his luggage were in a faster, drier boat. Around the same time, the third boat also pulled up anchor and left. Eric and I were suddenly alone. There was no one inside with us, and no one outside around us. The exotic setting couldn't have been any more romantic. It was serious paradise!

This afternoon we went into town to explore. The town of Paeua is on the south side of the island between the anchorage and the hotel. It is three quarters of a mile long and about a fifth of mile wide. Manihi's total population is five hundred people, and most of them live in Paeua. There is one main road with several side streets. The side streets are lined with densely packed, small houses on tiny lots. All were fenced, single story, metal-roofed bungalows. We found the fences a bit surprising. There are two markets that are stocked almost as well as the stores in Taiohae. (One even has five flavors of Tim Tams!) Paeua also has a church, a soccer field, and a cemetery.

The thing we found most curious were the roads themselves, unpaved white dirt embedded with chunks of shells and coral. We've never seen white dirt before. There were just a handful of vehicles on the road, but a large collection of hard bottomed dinghies parked along the lagoon; we realized here a boat is necessary to get around the island, not a car. Oddly enough, there is no sandy beach. What looks like sand from afar is actually a collection of dead coral. It feels almost irreverent to step on the coral, even if it is dead. After all, each chunk was made by millions of living polyps over hundreds of years.

Eric spent the rest of the day doing boat maintenance, including changing the fuel filters, and I did some cleaning and organizing. I have come to the realization I will need to clean and organize after every single passage. Despite a good night of sleep, Eric and I were out of it and moving slow; we still hadn't fully recuperated from that last rough passage.

We enjoyed a spectacular sunset and sat outside for a while after dark, admiring the bright stars.

Wednesday, June 6

Richard is flying home tomorrow. He wanted to see us again before he took off, so he offered to buy us lunch at the hotel. Eric and I arrived early to explore the general area. We walked out to the main road and followed it half a mile north to the airport, passing a handful of houses along the way. Unlike the houses in Paeua, these are on fairly large lots and have no fences. We decided this area must be Manihi's equivalent of the suburbs. Just outside the airport were three small souvenir shops that sold jewelry made with locally raised black pearls. On most of the Tuomotu Islands there are only two real sources of income: coconut and black pearl farming.

The airport has a single landing strip with one small terminal and a passenger loading/unloading boat dock. There's also a sign that warns people not to walk across the strip when a plane is approaching. Eric and I carefully scanned the sky for oncoming planes and then walked to the breakwater wall along the ocean. The waves were tumultuous. There was no beach—just dead coral that had piled up along the shore. We realized that Manihi doesn't have the fabled white sand that one expects from a tropical island, and the beach at the hotel must be man made. Unfortunately, there was also a lot of trash strewn among the coral. In addition to the usual bottles and cans, there were broken buoys and sandals, and an odd assortment of things like diapers, toys, and curlers.

We left the breakwater wall and headed back to the hotel, walking along the shore of the lagoon instead of on the road. In retrospect, it probably wasn't the greatest idea because we traipsed through some private yards and were chased by a couple of dogs. But the views were pretty.

At lunch, Richard was in genuinely good spirits. I was kind of sad to see him go. We owe him many thanks for helping us get across a big chunk of the Pacific Ocean!

After we said good-bye to Richard, we continued our walk, this time going south toward Paeua along the lagoon shore. We passed through what looked like a coconut grove. And again, there were copious amounts of trash strewn about. We were beginning to think the locals are pigs. Beyond the western edge of the coconut grove the land seemed barren. We ventured over to have a closer look and realized that the ground was mushy and sandy. Was this really quicksand? I was skeptical. In all honesty, I thought quicksand was something the writers made up on the TV show *Gilligan's Island*. Of course, I had to step in it to see if you really sink. You do. Eric had to pull me out!

The southern edge of the coconut grove ended where the land had sunk under the water.

The word *Tuomotu* means "many islands." Visually speaking, these atolls look like a string of small, separate islands. The reality is that it is the ring is one continuous land mass (except for the passes), but some spots are barely above the water line and some are just below the water line. We walked across the water, which was only ankle deep, towards the next *motu*, happily splashing and playing like kids. But before we reached the shore, we decided we'd had enough exercise, and headed back to *Kosmos*.

The sunset was memorable tonight. The entire western sky was socked in by clouds, so we didn't actually see the sun go down, but the eastern side was painted in vivid red, pink, gold, and blue-gray. In our old life, we took the wonders of nature for granted. Now we appreciate her majesty so much more.

In Retrospect:

Over the next few months, we went to several more island paradises that were also riddled with trash. We just couldn't believe the locals would pollute their fragile environment like that. It wasn't until we went to an uninhabited nature preserve hundreds of miles from any kind of civilization that we figured out the pollution wasn't from the locals. The trash was being dumped in civilization – in places like Asia and North America, and the tide and currents were bringing the trash all the way out here. It is heartbreaking that something I dropped in the water back in San Diego probably washed up in the South Pacific, especially because in the islanders have no way of properly disposing of trash.

Thursday, June 7

One thing that must be regularly scrubbed on boats is the bottom—the part that sits in the water. Since Eric doesn't like deep water, it is my job, which is fine with me. I love to be in the water.

This morning, I got in to do some scrubbing, and I almost had a heart attack when I saw grass growing all over the bottom. It was lush—so full and thick that you could mow it with a lawnmower. I thought, *We used to have to work really hard at home to get the yard to look half as healthy as the bottom does right now! Why didn't anyone tell us we needed to bring a weed whacker?* Needless to say, it took quite a bit of scrubbing to get all the grass off.

Tonight, we had another unusual sunset. The whole sky was socked in with clouds, a mix of white and gray. There was a small sliver of sky visible on the horizon. Where the sun was visible, it was bright red. All the clouds in the sky turned various shades of purple, depending on the color of the cloud. The wispy white clouds were violet, the dark, ominous clouds turned a blue-gray-purple, and the others were every shade in between. No stars tonight due to the cloud cover.

Friday, June 8

Today we went SCUBA diving. Before we left San Diego, Eric decided we needed to become SCUBA divers as part of our adventure. I thought Eric had lost his mind; SCUBA didn't seem to be the right kind of sport for either of us. My lungs are weak; I have trouble adjusting to the change in atmospheric pressure; and I hate cold water. I absolutely love to swim in the ocean—but only if the water is warm. Eric doesn't like to swim in the ocean at all and gets panicky if the visibility isn't phenomenal. He's afraid something will sneak up and eat him. The week before we left for our trip, Eric bravely faced his fears and got SCUBA certified in the murky waters of San Diego. I was still working full time plus, so I couldn't take the class with him, but the truth is that I wouldn't have gotten in the cold water anyway.

So now we are in the tropics, where the water is warm and the visibility is wonderful. Being that we are out of excuses not to dive, we finally took the plunge—literally. It was Eric's first non-training dive as an entry level certified diver, and my third dive ever.

The dive shop is at the hotel, so we took the dinghy there and joined a group that was scheduled to go out. The whole group piled into a fast boat, and the guides navigated us out of the pass and into the ocean. They dropped anchor close to the pass, about one hundred feet from shore. We were divided into two groups: certified and non-certified.

Each dive master briefed his group. When Eric heard his group was going to feed the sharks, he practically began to hyperventilate. But he got in anyway. It turned out that the dive master had put chopped up fish in a box to attract sharks to the general area—the group wasn't feeding them by hand as Eric had first thought. The sharks were little, only three to four feet, and much to Eric's relief, they didn't seem to be interested in eating any of the divers.

After the initial shark feeding, Eric's group swam along a coral wall sixty feet below. Along the wall, the visibility was excellent and the scenery was pretty, but just a few feet away, the wall plunged into a dark, scary abyss which made him nervous. The longer he was under without being mauled by a sea monster, the more he relaxed. Unfortunately, he sucked his air so fast that he had to come up after forty-five minutes, whereas the rest of the group was under for a full hour.

My dive was good, too. We were under just forty minutes and we only went down twenty feet, so we missed the shark feeding below us. I had a hard time equalizing, which is standard for me. But after my initial discomfort during the descent, I became totally absorbed in my surroundings. The coral was colorful with shades of purples and browns, as well as some reds and blues. We saw all kinds of interesting sea life, but sadly, I had no clue what most of them were. I was able to identify one strange thing, though: neon-lipped clams. Yes, there were clams with neon-blue and neon-purple lips!

Overall, it was a good experience for both of us. We'll try SCUBA diving again soon.

Saturday, June 9

We swore we weren't going to do it. But we just couldn't resist. They were just too cool....

This morning, a flat-bottomed boat with a large outboard motor pulled up with some locals inside. There were two men, a woman, and a three-year-old with dark skin and blonde hair. Given all the groceries they had in the boat, we figured they had to be on their way back from the market.

One of the guys asked if we wanted to see a pearl farm. We said sure. We had read in a guidebook that the hotel offered tours of pearl farms. While we had wondered what happened on a pearl farm, we weren't curious enough to spend the money to see one. So, we were excited about getting a free (at least we hoped) tour.

The guy told us to follow them in our dinghy, but our little six horsepower motor wasn't keeping up with their forty horsepower motor very well. After a few minutes, they stopped and insisted Eric and I get into their boat. Then they actually picked up our dinghy with their hands and put it inside their boat. It was hilarious! Our dinghy looked like a toy inside this bigger boat. Then we went roaring off. The motor didn't seem to be at all bothered by the extra 375 lbs. of weight.

We rode up along the west shore of the lagoon for about six or seven miles. The man who had asked us to visit, Jean Paul, was outgoing and gregarious, chatting animatedly the entire boat ride in broken English. The shoreline looked much the same as it did at the south end. Here and there we saw a few small bungalows clustered around a dock. Each of the docks had a small building on the water end. These little pockets of bungalows were few and far between, with no other development at all. We were surprised to hear that these were pearl farms.

The farm we stopped at looked almost the same as the others we'd seen from the water. When the engine turned off, we heard reggae music blaring. The little compound was deserted. Jean-Paul explained that since it was Saturday, the farm was closed. At first we were confused, then disappointed as realization dawned on us: This guy had brought us here to buy pearls, not to see how the farm operates. And we had no interest in buying pearls since I don't wear jewelry.

Jean-Paul ushered us into his workshop. As it turned out, Jean-Paul hand engraves beautiful, intricate designs into the low quality pearls. Almost all of his designs are different. He incorporates the pearl's flaws into the patterns so the imperfections are hard to see, and he does an incredible job. Some of the pearls he sells loose, and some he weaves into necklaces made of coconut fibers. He soaks the fibers in the ocean for a couple of weeks to make them strong, weaving together about a dozen fibers per necklace. Most of the necklaces we looked at had just one large pearl, but there were a few that had two or three, and some that also had mother of pearl (the inside of an oyster shell). The necklaces were simple, yet intricate and classy. They were way too unique to pass up, so I got one.

We hung out and talked to Jean Paul for an hour or so. He was fun to talk to even though we didn't understand much of what he said. He told us all about his family; the pearl farm; his bitterness about having to pay such high taxes to the French government; his recent trip to America to visit his brother; his upcoming trip to Hong Kong; and on and on. We were almost sad when it was time to go because we were enjoying his company so much.

After we got back to the boat, I cut Eric's hair for the first time, and I have to say, it didn't come out too badly!

Chapter 5: Apataki, Tuomotus Islands, French Polynesia

Sunday, June 10

This morning we were up before dawn. Our goal was to arrive at the next atoll destination, Apataki, before the sun went down. We held our breath as we pulled up anchor. At first it seemed to come up okay… then *bam*—it stopped. We were stuck. Our hearts sank. Eric drove the boat around in a circular pattern to help jar the chain loose, and it worked. When we tried again, the chain came right up, at least for a couple minutes. Then it got stuck again. Eric tried to jar the chain loose a second time by moving the boat. Fortunately, the chain began to come up and a couple minutes later, the anchor came out of the water. We were free!

When we went through Manihi's pass, we were going with the current, which made steering trickier than normal, but it wasn't bad. No one else was in the pass and no evasive actions were necessary. The current was so strong that we flew through the pass, enjoying a few minutes of fast speed.

Believe it or not, the passage from Manihi to Apataki was pleasant. The seas were calm, which was a huge relief. Although I'd been fine emotionally on the last passage, physically I had been very uncomfortable. Since then, I'd been having doubts about traveling by boat. We planned to be at sea twenty five to thirty percent of the time, and I wasn't sure that I could handle so many days of misery. Now that I am reminded there can be nice days at sea, too, the doubts are gone.

We spotted Apataki at about 1400 (2:00 pm). It looked much like Manihi from the distance, but bigger, with more obvious stretches of sand (or maybe coral). We approached the northwest tip of the atoll at about

1500. The entrance is four hundred feet wide, so it looked easy to navigate at first. But, once we entered the pass, we realized it wasn't going to be simple. The current was three and a half to four knots against us. Close to the land were huge eddies of water that looked like glass, and all around the eddies the water was moving so violently that it looked like it was boiling. The bizarreness of the water flow was intimidating. Thankfully, we entered with no problem, but it was stressful.

Once we were inside the lagoon, we relaxed a little. We made our way toward the recommended anchorage on the north side. Fortunately, there weren't many charted coral patches to maneuver around. I still stood lookout outside for any underwater hazards, but the water was deep all the way.

We were in a great mood as we pulled into the anchorage. There were many things that could have gone wrong today, but everything had gone smoothly. It had been a really good day, the kind of day that makes you glad to be on your own boat. We picked a spot that looked to be one hundred percent sand, all light with no dark spots at all, and dropped anchor around 1530. Ahh… anchored in paradise.

When you anchor, the boat rotates around the anchor as it gets pushed by the wind and current. According to our chart, there was a shallow reef nearby. We dropped anchor in a place that looked like it was far enough away, but slowly we watched ourselves get closer and closer to the reef. When we finally settled in a spot, we were ominously close; the coral was just fifty feet away. It might be possible to drift another fifty feet and hit the reef if the wind or currents changed.

Needless to say, we decided to move. This wasn't a big deal. We still had a bit of daylight left, but night was coming quickly. I walked to the front of the boat and pushed the button for the windlass. A good amount of chain came up, but the windlass was struggling. I had never seen it groan and complain like this before. Then the chain stopped coming up completely. Oh shoot, we must be stuck on coral.

No worries, I thought. *We'll do the same dance we did this morning and move the boat around in circles.* We tried that strategy several times, but to no avail: The chain wasn't moving. Talk about irony! This morning we were so worried about being stuck and everything was fine. Now we were super stuck when we'd been so sure everything would be okay.

Meanwhile, we noticed a few things that didn't add up. First, for almost a minute I saw a consistent trail of air bubbles coming to the surface, but could see no creature in the water making the bubbles. Then Eric noticed that we had only twenty-five feet of chain out, but the depth sounder said we were in forty feet of water. Granted, the coral could rise up sharply out of nowhere, causing a difference between the depth sounder location and the anchor location, but you would think we could see the coral if it was only twenty-five feet below. Then Eric noticed oil coming up out of the water. *Oh, good God,* I worried. *What if we're stuck on some kind of pipeline?*

This was much worse than we'd thought.

I put on the mask and snorkel and got in the water to have a look. Because the sun was low in the sky, visibility wasn't too good, but I could see there was definitely something strange stuck to the anchor. It could be a pipeline, but it looked more like a long, skinny tree trunk, and I assumed it was a palm tree. Then I noticed several ropes floating around the tree. It looked like a typical boating rope, and I figured some discarded rope must have gotten itself wrapped around the tree. One of these ropes appeared to be stuck to our anchor, indirectly attaching us to the tree. I thought it should be easy to cut.

The more I studied the area, the more I realized that the ground didn't look quite right. While the ground was sand colored, it didn't look sandy. Oddly, there were also two boxes on the bottom. I could see the tops of the boxes, but not the sides; as if they had sunk into the ground. Hmmm…

I went back on board and grabbed a knife, a weight belt, and my air hose, then hopped back in, intending to try to cut the line. When I had been looking before, I had stayed close to the surface. But once I had gone deeper, I realized that we were above a sunken boat! The "tree" was actually the mast, but it was covered in marine growth, which made it look textured like tree bark. The rope that had hooked onto our anchor was part of the rigging. The "boxes" were the boat's hatches, and the "ground" was its hull.

I panicked as I realized that this sunken ship had probably hit the very coral we were trying to avoid—she had died and was buried in our exact spot. It felt like she was looking for an eternal companion and was trying to pull *Kosmos* into her watery grave with her.

The anchor was only down twenty-five feet, but I couldn't get my ears equalized beyond twenty feet. It was really frustrating. I was so close to the rope! I tried to reach it several times, and considered diving deeper anyway, but Eric and I agreed it wasn't worth the risk for me to go down the extra five feet without equalizing. Jean Paul, the local we had just met yesterday, had told us he'd gotten permanent hearing damage from diving too deep and having his ears pop. I gave up and came in. By then it was almost dark, and there was nothing more we could do until dawn. We dropped the anchor again, hoping it would land on the ground instead of getting further tangled in the wreckage.

And now, all Eric and I can do is just sit tight and hope that the anchor/sailboat will hold us in place so we don't drift into the coral behind us. If the rope suddenly breaks, it could literally be disastrous for us. We're also worried about cutting the rope tomorrow. So many things could go wrong. What if we can't cut the rope? What if we do cut the rope and the sudden release of pressure sends *Kosmos* shooting into the coral? Or what if one of us gets hit by the mast and rigging due to the sudden release of pressure?

We tried to call the only village on the island, but we didn't get any response. It is on the south side, out of radio range. We doubt we'll get much sleep tonight. We have an "anchor alarm" on the GPS, which goes off if *Kosmos* moves more than a predetermined distance. Eric set it as close as he could, sixty feet, and is going to sleep on the couch in the pilothouse tonight. We decided not to set a stern anchor since it could potentially make the situation worse. If the primary anchor does fail, we'll need to start the engine and drive *Kosmos* to safety as fast as possible. A stern anchor wouldn't stop us from drifting into the reef, but would inhibit our ability to move as quickly.

We are astounded by the odds of this happening. It is unbelievable that in this enormous lagoon, we would randomly try to anchor in the one spot where there is a sunken ship below!

Monday, June 11

We awoke at first light, 0600, after a restless night. The closely set anchor alarm had gone off a few times, but overall we hadn't moved much. Still, when we looked outside, we saw that instead of being fifty feet from the shallow reef, we were only twenty feet away. Oy vey. Thank God the anchor had held and we hadn't drifted any more than that!

We decided to go SCUBA diving together to cut the rope that was holding us to the wreck. Thank goodness we did that dive last week! While we were both still terrified about diving by ourselves, we couldn't imagine how much more intimidating it would be if we hadn't just gone SCUBA diving. (Of course, when we said a few days ago that we'd like to go diving again, we didn't mean in circumstances like this!)

Eric wanted to wait until the sun was higher in the sky and the visibility was good, so we sat nervously for three hours, too on edge to do anything. At 0900, we put on our SCUBA gear and jumped in. I had a hard time on two fronts. One, we couldn't get the amount of weight set properly to get me down safely (when you SCUBA dive, you wear extra weight to help you sink). I either wasn't sinking at all or was sinking faster than I could equalize. And the crazy ups and downs I experienced as we adjusted my weight were wreaking havoc with my ears. I wasn't equalizing, so Eric wound up going down alone, which made him even more nervous. I stayed in the water and monitored him from the surface. I'm not sure that I could have done anything to help Eric if he had a problem below, but having me close by comforted him.

The visibility was much better today. We could see that the anchor was set in sand, which was a huge relief. Had it been on the boat or on coral, our problems would have been compounded. Also, the wrecked boat was now on its side. Yesterday it had been upright. We realized that we must have pulled the boat up by the mast when we raised the anchor, which would explain why the windlass struggled so much to get the chain up. When we let the anchor down, we must have laid the boat back down on its side.

The wreck was about thirty feet long and made of fiberglass. Seeing the boat upset Eric as much as it did me. We agree it looks haunted. We figured that since it only had a little marine growth, it must have sunk relatively recently. The fact that it was a newer wreck made it even scarier. What if there were bodies inside that hadn't decomposed yet? I half expected a dead body to float out of the hatch or for a shark to swim past us carrying a limb in its jaws. Eric was sure that the creature from the Black Lagoon would come out of the hatch, riding on the back of a great white shark and holding the severed heads of the crew.

Nervously, Eric focused on getting to the bottom and cutting the rope, trying not to look at the wreck. He was breathing hard and fast; his air bubbles were the size of baseballs. Once he was down, he saw that the problem was significantly worse than we thought. Yes, the rope was stuck and he was able to quickly cut it with his dive knife. But there was also a 3/8-inch steel cable that was wrapped several times around our anchor. Oh no! When we had done all those circles, thinking we were stuck on coral, we had inadvertently wound the cable around the anchor!

Eric obviously couldn't cut the cable. Instead, he had to untangle it from the anchor, which meant lifting the eighty-eight pound (forty kilos) anchor several times to get the cable out from underneath. He was standing on the ground, using his full force to manhandle the anchor. With all the physical exertion, he was sucking air faster than ever. A tank of air generally lasts about an hour when someone breathes normally. He was at the bottom for twelve minutes at fifty-one feet and came dangerously close to using up all his air.

As a safety precaution, divers are supposed to ascend slowly, taking at least five minutes to go from the bottom to the surface. But, that was a luxury Eric didn't have because we weren't out of danger yet. With the anchor untangled, we knew we could drift that last twenty feet into the reef. Eric quickly swam to the surface and we hustled back on board, then pulled up anchor as quickly as possible. We picked a new location in deeper water, far from that reef. By 1030, we were safely anchored in a new spot.

I'm so proud of Eric—not just for freeing the anchor, not just for going SCUBA diving without a professional there to monitor him, but also for facing his worst fear by diving alone. After all, no one was there to help him fend off an attacking monster!

Tuesday, June 12

When we woke up this morning, there was no wind and the water was so smooth that it was literally a mirror, reflecting the clouds in the sky above. You couldn't see where the water ended and the sky began. Up until the last couple of days, the trade winds had been very strong. We thought the wind never died around here, so the calm was a surprise.

Yesterday, after we took some time to calm down on board, we went for a three mile walk in the afternoon. We realized the reason this side of the island is deserted is because it is sinking. The land is dotted with big pools of water. The pools smell like sulfur and are mosquito infested. The foliage is mostly thick shrubs with a few palm trees. There were no signs of human life anywhere, and the only animals were crabs. Like in Manihi, the alluring "beach" is actually a collection of dead coral. Last night some mosquitoes managed to get inside our boat and ate us alive as we slept.

Today we went on a four mile dinghy ride along another section of shore. During that stretch we only saw one house and four metal shacks. One of the shacks was on a *motu*, an itty-bitty island in the middle of the lagoon. We also spotted a speedboat in the distance—the only local boat we've seen since arriving. We are definitely in a remote place! We saw a lot of cool fish in the water. We found a large, shallow reef teeming with fish that looked like an ideal snorkeling spot, so we'll go back tomorrow for a swim.

After dark, we sat outside to watch the stars. It was a new moon, so the sky was pitch black and the stars were amazingly bright. There were millions of stars twinkling at us, reflecting on the mirror-like water. We felt as if we were floating in outer space, with nothing but endless stars above and below us. It was another unique, incredibly special moment. Unfortunately, we weren't outside long. We were chased off by the mosquitoes and the sulfur smell.

Wednesday, June 13

We spent the day snorkeling. The coral wasn't as colorful as in Manihi, mostly shades of beige with some spots of dark yellow and purple. There were neon-lipped clams here, too. On the coral, we noticed little orange creatures that look like bottle brushes. When we got too close to them, they would vanish into a hole.

The fish were better here, though. There were thousands of unique, colorful fish flitting about. We wish we could name them all, but we can only identify two: angel fish and parrotfish, and there were several varieties of each. An odd fish that stood out to us looked like a tube with a long snout. There were two versions of this one: one was small and translucent and the other large and putty color. There were several schools of fish that moved in unison, which we found fascinating. They reminded us of a marching band, especially when they all turned at once. We saw three sharks, too, but they were babies—only about a foot long.

Chapter 6: Fakarava, Tuomotus Islands, French Polynesia

Thursday, June 14

We were planning to leave Apataki in the early morning to go to the island of Fakarava, but. when we tried to pull up the anchor, the chain didn't come up. We weren't surprised. The water had been choppy when we last anchored the boat, so it had been tough to tell whether we were in sand or coral. When the wind died down a few days ago, we were able to see the bottom clearly: We were anchored in coral.

Worse, there hadn't been wind to push us in any one particular direction, so the boat had been slowly circling the anchor, wrapping our chain more and more tightly around the coral head. We had to do a lot of the circular maneuvering to get the chain unwound, but fortunately it did the trick. Eventually we got the anchor up without having to dive in and manually unwind it, which was a relief. Neither of us wanted to do another scary dive.

On the ride out, we were moving with the current. We hit a new record of twelve knots—double our normal speed! We joked about painting flames on the sides of Kosmos.

The passage to Fakarava was fairly calm and pleasant overall. We could see it was raining hard on three sides of us. Large storm clouds tend to show up on our radar, and all three squalls were on the screen. They were moving towards one another, and it looked like they would converge on us, but they didn't. We made it the whole way without getting hit with any wind or rain. We're beginning to think Kosmos has developed some kind of special force field. All week the rain has missed us. On Monday, we could see it raining just to the north. On Tuesday and Wednesday, we could see it raining to the south. The only problem with this new anti-rain force-field shield is that the boat is now getting dirty and I will have to wash it soon!

We were headed to the island's northern pass, near the main village of Rotoava. As we approached, Fakarava looked like two islands set close together, but the charts show it is one island with a giant lagoon pass. The landscape is much the same as in Manihi and Apatiki.

It was close to sunset when we entered. Going through the pass was easy. It is a full mile wide, didn't seem to have much coral, and we only had two knots of current going against us. We could see buildings and other signs of civilization as soon as we were inside. A few minutes later, we arrived at the anchorage, in the heart of town.

We were delighted to see that *Special Blend* was there, tied up to the sea wall med-moor style. Jim came out to greet us and encouraged us to tie up to the sea wall, too. The med-moor parking was easy because we had lots of room to maneuver on both sides.

Just after we pulled in, the storms converged in the distance. There was tons of lightening. I was fascinated by the storm. I don't know why I was so drawn to it, other than maybe I've developed a fascination with the power of Mother Nature. The *Special Blend* crew is from Florida and they said they see heat- lightening storms all the time, but to me it was exotic. Thankfully, the storm by-passed us. We want rain without lightening.

Jim invited us over for dinner, and had the crew from the sailboat *Priscilla* over as well. We had a great time with them.

We went to bed happy. Once again, many things could have gone wrong today, and none did. We didn't get stuck on the coral and we didn't get hit by lightening. We had a nice passage and got to spend time with friends. It was a good day.

Friday, June 15

We may have spoken too soon with that last comment. At midnight, we awoke to odd noises. The wind had picked up and shifted, and Eric was worried that *Kosmos* was shifting out of position and was going to bang into the sea wall. We had to bring up the anchor, untie ourselves from the dock (leaving our lines behind), and re-anchor out in the bay. Anchoring in the dark—and in strong winds— is scary. You're never quite sure what potential hazards are around or below you. We re-anchored with no problems and went back to bed, but Eric didn't sleep well, worrying about dragging.

This morning, I grudgingly performed a rain dance. Out came the brush, soap, and hose. I figured since it always worked with the car, maybe it would work with the boat, too. I only washed the areas most in need of a scrubbing, hoping that Mother Nature would take care of the rest. Brad from Special Blend retrieved our lines and delivered them to us, which was a relief.

In the afternoon, we went for a bike ride, using the handy dandy folding bikes that we had brought along. The island has just seven hundred people, and most of them live in Rotoava. The town is tiny, with a few blocks of houses, scattered administrative buildings, a clinic, a post office, a gas station, an airport, and not much more. In terms of places to eat, there is one restaurant, a pizza stand, and a snack bar that serves hot food on Friday and Saturday nights. The town is adorable and well kept. People make an effort to landscape their yards and sweep dirt walkways to keep them clear of debris.

I am also pleased to report that the rain dance worked. In the afternoon it poured!

Tuesday, June 19

The last few days have been mellow. We've done a lot of exploring on shore. Outside of town there are several farms, mostly coconut and pearl, and a few hotels. The people are nice, but few of them speak English, so we haven't had much interaction with the locals.

One day, we saw a group practicing for the upcoming Heiva competition, so we sat down and watched them. A Heiva is a traditional Polynesian war dance, and each year from late June through early July the islanders have a celebration by the same name. As part of the festivities, there is a big competition to determine the best dancers. This group had male musicians and female dancers. Most of the music was fast, with only one slow song. The dances were well choreographed and similar to what we saw in Nuka Hiva.

After a while, a woman who was also watching walked up made a request. The dancers and musicians nodded. Then three very skinny, very beautiful teenage girls in bikini tops and sarong skirts joined the dancers and tried to follow along. The girls had a video camera man, a sound person, and a photographer recording them, plus an entourage of people standing on the sidelines, so we assumed they were celebrities. We asked one of the entourage, who explained that every few years there is a *Miss Tahiti* model search. The three contest winners get five- year modeling contracts with a New York agency, and these were the winners. They did three or four dances, and then the big group took off. Rehearsal ended shortly thereafter. It was fun to be able to see the traditional singing and dancing, and intriguing to see the models.

Meanwhile, we've also done some diving with a local dive company. We did one dive inside the lagoon, which was good, and a second dive on the ocean side that was spectacular. The coral was beautiful and there were tons of fascinating sea creatures. The dive master taught us the names of some of the fish. We were most interested in the Napoleon Wrasse. It's huge—as big as a shark! The water has been crystal clear, and Eric is getting more comfortable in the water. I'm also having an easier time equalizing. We've both become more confident about our SCUBA skills and have decided that we like diving and will do more of it.

Although we haven't conversed with many of the locals, we've been socializing a lot with the cruisers. Now even Eric is starting to get tired of the questions about our boat. Everyone always asks the same questions in the same order and makes more or less the same comments, so we feel like we are living in the movie *Groundhog Day*. While we haven't said anything snide as of yet, we've come up with some joke answers that we are tempted to start using to break the monotony. For instance, when they say, "How much fuel do you carry?" We say, "One tablespoon of plutonium." And, when they ask, "Did you have enough fuel to get here?" We reply, "No, dolphins towed us here."

We've had lunch at the restaurant twice, once a few days ago and again today. It's on the water and it has a chic, unique atmosphere. Last time I ordered raw fish with onion in a vinaigrette sauce. The preparation was simple but unique (and good!). Eric had mahi mahi with a vanilla sauce. The fish was perfectly cooked and the sauce almost tasted like crème brûlée. He had to restrain himself from licking the bowl.

Today, I ordered coconut-crusted fish, which was great. Eric ordered Tahitian style raw fish, which was similar to what we were served in the Marquesas, tuna with coconut milk and light veggies. While we were waiting to order, a small speedboat took off from the dock at a neighboring house. Three dogs ran into the water, chasing after the boat, just like dogs follow cars down the street at home. The dogs swam to a coral reef before giving up the chase. They stood on the reef howling at the boat long after it was gone. It was hilarious!

At the table next to us, two guys asked us if we had sailed here. We replied we had come on a powerboat, waiting for the usual questions. One of the guys lit up and said, "I want to buy a Nordhavn!" We spent the whole meal talking about the pros and cons of each model Nordhavn makes. It turned out that he is seriously considering buying a sixty-two foot model. We invited them back to see our boat and Eric tried to convince him that the 43 was a better choice than the 62.

Tomorrow we're heading to the south end of the island, where people can apparently drift-snorkel through the pass. The reef down there is a protected UNESCO site and is supposed to be incredible.

In Retrospect:

Our new friend did actually buy a Nordhavn 43, which probably costs less than half of a 62. The salesman probably has voodoo dolls of us hanging in his office.

Friday, June 22

On Wednesday morning, we pulled up anchor and headed to the south side of the island. We were relived that the anchor came up with no problems. The ride in the lagoon was calm. We hugged the east shore most of the way and enjoyed the views. We arrived at the town of Tetamanu in the southwest corner of the island in the late afternoon and dropped anchor.

By the time we got *Kosmos* situated, we decided we'd better not go to shore. We had just a couple hours of sunlight left, and when the sun is low it is tough to spot coral. Plus, the wind was screaming at twenty knots, which would have made the dinghy ride to shore slow, bouncy and wet.

Yesterday, we took the dinghy out to explore. On this end of the island, there are lots of *motus*, which makes it especially scenic. It looks like a string of itty bitty islands with white sand beaches and a few palm trees on each island. Since the "water" is actually low-lying land, it is a stunning light blue-green. The whole scene is postcard perfect—totally surreal.

We landed on a couple of *motu* mini-islands and walked around. Much to our surprise, there really was sand, and it was pinkish in color. However, there were still small, sharp coral rocks everywhere, so we wore shoes. We did find one small stretch of beach where the rocks were minimal and the shoes could come off.

We also explored the town. Tetamanu consists of two small hotels, a church, a couple of homes, and a couple of non-residential buildings. We suspect the only residents of this town are the hotel staff. Like in Anaho, there are no roads here, just a footpath going from one end of town to the other. What distinguishes the footpath from the rest of the grass is that the path is mowed. There is something so charming about towns that have no need for cars. It's like going back in time. (That is, as long as you can turn a blind eye to the satellites, radio tower and solar cell panels at the side of the grass "road."). We met a staff person at each of the hotels. Both of them talked to us for a long time.

One of the guys, Raymond, invited us to have lunch today at the hotel's restaurant. We expected to eat with the other hotel guests and to pay for our meal. As it turned out, the hotel was empty; Raymond was simply looking for company. The restaurant is on stilts above shallow water on the edge of the renowned reef, with a small wooden walkway connecting it to the shore. Lunch was nice. The appetizer was marinated olives, bell peppers (capsicum), and pearl onions. Raymond made us yellow fin tuna (thoroughly cooked) in a sauce that was almost like gravy. It was served with pasta salad made with beets and small pieces of fish, as well as rice and bread. He also served us watered down juice. He had asked us to bring wine or beer, so we brought a bottle of wine. Conversation was not easy with his broken English and my terrible French. He is a nice guy who loves the solitude of this tiny town.

After lunch, Raymond gave us some whole fish to make for dinner. We dropped off the fish at the boat then went snorkeling in the famous pass. We followed the instructions the other cruisers gave us: Wait until the incoming tide is at its strongest, take your dinghy out to the edge of the ocean, then jump in the water and let the current push you through the pass and into the lagoon. And hold on tight to the dingy rope to keep it moving with you. We hadn't been sure what to expect and were surprised it felt like being on a roller coaster! The current was strong, so we flew down the pass. Like in the Apataki pass, the water was moving so fast that it looked like it was boiling, so we bounced a lot as we floated along.

The ride was lots of fun, but it was hard to see much. We were moving too fast. Still, we saw beautiful shades of coral, such as hot pink, and large schools of fish. We spotted a good variety of fish, too, including several new species. My favorite fish were the black ones that each had one yellow stripe. The fish seemed to swim in duos and they almost looked like they were dancing with one another. We also saw several fish with horns like a unicorn—and a good number of sharks.

Afterward, we snorkeled in other areas around the reef. Some of the fish here are huge, much bigger than the same species we've seen in the other areas. Fishing is illegal in the protected area, and that seems to make a big difference in their size.

Then we went back to the boat to make our fish dinner. But Eric and I both looked at the little red squirrel fish with their big, sad eyes and said to each other, "I'm not cleaning it. You clean it." Since neither of us wanted to do the deed of cutting the heads off, we settled for frozen pizza and cookies instead.

Saturday, June 23

I awoke feeling brave. *I can do it. I can clean the fish!* I chanted to myself. I pulled the fish out of the refrigerator and found an instruction book. But I wasn't sure whether to follow the small fish directions or the flat fish directions—the book used technical language I didn't understand, and it wasn't clear whether this fish would be classified as "small." I grabbed a different instruction book, but that one was no help either. This was a desperate situation. Time was ticking on the freshness factor.

Fortunately, the family on the boat next to us are professional fishermen, and we knew they could help us in our time of need. We made a mayday call. They laughed and two of them came right over. The guys patiently showed me how to clean the fish. I'm proud to report that I did the last two (almost) all by myself. And I didn't faint, not even when I accidentally poked the fish's eyes with my bare fingers!

We threw the scales, guts and heads overboard as we worked. Within seconds, the back of the boat was surrounded by dozens of fish and some circling sharks. The fish fought viciously over each scrap while the sharks lurked behind them. It was amazing to watch. I was a little nervous about falling in, knowing that the sharks had smelled blood.

Afterward, we spent part of the day practicing our SCUBA skills in shallow water. Eric is trying to teach me everything he learned in his certification course. It has been as much of a refresher for him as it has been a learning experience for me. Later in the day, on the incoming tide, we snorkeled the pass a few more times. It gets more fun each time you do it!

The fishermen family had invited us to SCUBA dive the pass with them, but we decided against it. Given how strong the currents were, we felt like it was too advanced of a dive for beginners, especially without a professional. Also, the pass is a special shark breeding ground, which is why it has been protected by UNESCO, and hundreds of sharks live at the bottom of the pass. While Eric was now okay with seeing a shark or two, he was pretty sure he'd freak out if he saw swarms of them. The family reported to us that the dive was nothing short of amazing.

Chapter 7: Tahiti, Society Islands, French Polynesia

Tuesday, June 26

On Sunday afternoon, we pulled up anchor and headed to Tahiti. We went out the narrow and shallow southern pass. We knew this would be trickier than the northern pass, but navigating it turned out fine.

When we left, we knew the winds were strong and that it would be a rough ride. Unfortunately, we had to go anyway. I need to fly home. I closed my mortgage business literally a few days before we left the country, and I still have many loose ends that need to be wrapped up. I have a few people helping me at home, but most of the work I need to do myself. I've been trying to do it from here, but I don't have consistent Internet access or reliable mail service, and both satellite and cell phone calls are ungodly expensive. I've realized it's actually going to be cheaper and easier for me to fly home for a few days. My flight leaves on Thursday.

The ride was as unpleasant as anticipated. The waves were six to eight feet, with a few ten footers. Occasionally we were hit with a beam wave that gave us an extra big roll. The air conditioner downstairs turned itself off again, so we had to sleep on the couches upstairs. But the passage only lasted for a day and a half, and we knew we could handle anything for that length of time. It was the longest passage Eric and I have ever done alone.

At sunrise this morning, we pulled into Tahiti's lagoon using the main pass in downtown Papeete (the main city). From the lagoon entrance, Tahiti looked like a large cone-shaped mountain. It is less imposing than the Marquesas, which are taller, steeper, and more

100

mountainous. The Society Islands are older than the Marquesas, so the mountains have started eroding and reefs have already formed. The entire shoreline and most of the mountain was covered in buildings, including many that were four to five stories tall. It's a "real" city, all right.

Since *Kosmos* is just over thirty feet tall, we needed to get permission from the port captain to pass the airport, which is near the entrance to the lagoon. Just beyond the airport is where the anchorage begins.

Driving through the anchorage, we recognized several boats, including *Special Blend*. The anchorage was crowded and we had trouble finding a spot. We almost re-anchored because we felt a little too close to the boat next to us, but there was no better place to go. The guy next to us agreed we were too close, but said he would be leaving soon anyway.

Once we got *Kosmos* situated, we took the dingy down so we could go to shore.

As we climbed into the dinghy, we heard a siren wailing in the distance—something we hadn't heard in a long time. We parked the dinghy in the marina and walked to the street. It is an extremely busy four-lane highway. Seeing the traffic just reinforced what we were already feeling: We weren't ready to be back in a big city again.

We did some exploring. We noticed a couple of gas (petrol) stations, a McDonald's, and a small mall that sells Starbucks iced coffees. The mall has a big grocery store with a selection comparable to back home, so we stocked up. After having such a limited selection for so long, we were excited.

Neither of us had gotten much sleep on the passage, so we laid low the rest of the day. During the late afternoon and early evening, dozens and dozens of outrigger canoes went by. Outrigger canoeing is the favorite sport of French Polynesia and is a major part of the Heiva festival that just officially began.

The sunset was spectacular, possibly the best we've ever seen. The island of Moorea is only ten miles from Tahiti, and we have an excellent view of it from where we're anchored. The sun sank behind Moorea, making the entire island glow. The sky turned gold with streaks of blue, almost like a spotlight in reverse. Little canoes dotted the waterline. It was magical.

Wednesday, June 27

Yesterday, we booked a guided tour of Tahiti's undeveloped interior. Our tour guide, Aaron, picked us up around 0900 at the marina. It turned out to be just the three of us. We climbed into a four-wheel drive Land Rover that looked like it was ready for combat. It actually had a snorkel so the car could be almost fully immersed under water and still keep going!

We drove through downtown Papeete. Eric thinks it looks like Miami with its crowded streets, palm trees, and the views of the ocean. Something we found interesting is you can see where the ocean ends and the lagoon begins, even though you can't see the actual reef. It looks like smooth water ringed by tumultuous water.

As we left downtown, the road went from four lanes to two and became increasingly residential as we continued along. At a couple points in time, we saw beaches with waves hitting the sand—there must have been breaks in the reef—and large numbers of people surfing. Tahiti is supposedly where surfing was invented. I was surprised to see that the beaches have black sand. For some reason, I had always associated Tahiti with white sand beaches.

After what seemed like a long drive, we turned onto a dirt road that took us to a river valley called Papenoo Valley, which was surrounded by mountains. There are no houses here and the land is thick with vegetation. We made our first stop at a pretty waterfall. Aaron said it is believed that in the pre-European days, the natives threw criminals down this waterfall. The pool at the bottom is so shallow that no one could survive.

Aaron was full of information about the history, culture, and politics of the region. It was nice having him to ourselves, and we bombarded him with questions. One of the things he told us about was the non-native vegetation and animals. Tahiti and the rest of the islands were completely different one hundred years ago. When Europeans discovered the islands, they introduced new plants, animals, bugs, and (unwittingly) parasites. Over the years many other people brought additional foreign species to the islands. Now the non-native species are dominant, and have completely changed the ecosystem of the islands. For example, native birds are rarely seen, their numbers drastically reduced by a mean bird species from Indonesia and from new predators such as rats. Another example is a fast growing vine that was brought over during World War II by the U.S. to use as camouflage for its equipment. That vine has taken over the island, killing the plants it climbs over.

Our next stop was a hydroelectric plant. The river that runs through this valley is utilized for making electricity, producing ten to fifty percent of the necessary power for the island, depending on the rainfall. Aaron said that that in French Polynesia, they are concerned about utilizing environmentally friendly and renewable power.

We then visited a beautiful waterfall with a swimming hole nearby. We had to turn off the main road and travel on a badly rutted out dirt road to get to there. Aaron explained that the main road is relatively new. Until a couple of years ago, this rough, pothole-ridden road was the only one in the area. It parallels the river, is usually muddy, and is often completely covered with water when the river is full, which is why the tour company uses four-wheel drive vehicles with snorkels. Aaron said that they still do the tour even when the water level is up to the passengers' feet and legs. They stow all the gear on the roof of the vehicle to keep it dry. Everyone holds on to the roll bars for dear life and Aaron reassures them all is fine while his heart is pounding.

We drove on, steadily climbing in altitude, stopping by a lake that feeds a second hydroelectric plant. We were surprised to see eels. We thought they were saltwater creatures, but apparently they are brackish and can live in both oceans and lakes.

Aaron told us that in the old days there were several tribes that lived in this valley. The natives preferred the valley to the beach, since it provided more protection from the other tribes. Once modern conveniences like electricity were introduced to the island, everyone moved to the beach to enjoy those comforts. We found it ironic that there is no electricity in the valley that they make electricity in.

Our last stop was a viewpoint where we could see the top of the mountain. Aaron said that the mountain shrinks by about three centimeters every year. Someday, Tahiti will become an atoll like the Tuomotus.

On the way back, we talked about the local culture. Aaron affirmed what Rose and Dean had already told us: that for about one hundred years, thanks to missionary pressure, the islanders had abandoned their own ways to follow European culture and traditions. It was only twenty-five years ago that a cultural revival movement began to resurrect the native traditions. While some customs have been preserved, many have been lost forever.

We had another unique sunset, completely different from the night before. We just cannot get over the spectacular sunsets out here.

Sunday, July 1

I flew home on Thursday. Only my dad, Eric's parents, my sister, and the people who were helping me with assorted business matters knew I was back. I needed to get as much work done as possible and didn't have time for socializing.

One of the things I intended to do was file a lawsuit against two mortgage banks that had stiffed me out of a significant amount of money. In February 2007, Wall Street had announced that effective immediately, it was no longer buying mortgage-backed securities, and the entire mortgage banking industry collapsed within days. Banks ran out of money and couldn't honor their lending commitments, leaving all my clients who were in escrow high and dry. They also could not pay the commissions on recently booked loans.

The night I arrived home, I went to the grocery store. I was standing in front of the milk when I realized that the guy standing next to me was the representative for one of the banks I was suing—the actual person scheduled to be served. My heart stopped. He hadn't seen me, so I quickly turned and walked off. I slunk around the market carefully, pretending to look for foods behind aisle displays and on low shelves where I was hidden by the shopping cart. At one point, I was so busy looking to my left and right that I didn't see him coming straight toward me. Again, my heart stopped, and I quickly turned down an aisle. After what seemed like an eternity, I saw him go towards the registers. *Phew,* I thought. *He's leaving.* I waited a full ten minutes before I went to the check out line, wanting to be certain I didn't run into him in the parking lot. I got in line. And then he got into line behind me.

It turned out to be a providential meeting. I found out that he too had been stiffed several weeks' worth of pay and bonuses, and that the company was expected to go bankrupt and close its doors that week. He filled me in on the numerous other mortgage banks that had gone under since I had left. The other bank I was planning to sue was rumored to be going under soon, too, so it looked like neither lawsuit would happen. For four years, I'd planned to leave the business in March 2007. I almost could not have planned the departure date better if I'd had a crystal ball.

The rest of my time at home has been busy, but uneventful. I picked a good time to be away from *Kosmos*. Every time I talked to Eric, he has said the weather in Tahiti was awful. There is a big storm to the south, and they have been getting some of the rain, wind and waves from it. On Friday afternoon it began to pour, and the heavy rains lasted all night. It rained so hard that Eric had to go outside twice to bail out the dinghy. It rained yesterday and today, too, but not as much as it did on Friday.

The wind speed in the protected anchorage has been averaging twenty four knots and shifting often, sometimes coming from directions that are abnormal for the area's weather patterns. Every time the wind shifts, so do the positions of the boats in the anchorage. All the boaters have been perpetually worried about whether their boat will hit anything with each re-settling. One boat dragged its anchor and crashed into another boat. Fortunately, there was no damage. They were lucky!

The waves have been twelve feet high outside the reef, and inside the normally calm lagoon it's so rocky that people are getting seasick at anchor. Eric put out one of the paravanes to help stop the rolling. Unfortunately, the boat on the other side was too close for him to put both of them out.

Needless to say, going out wasn't much fun, so Eric mostly stayed on board. On Saturday, he went out to dinner with the crew of *Special Blend*. He said the ride to and from the dinghy dock was the scariest he has ever been on. It was dark and the waves were huge, so it was difficult to see potential hazards, while also being rough and wet.

Eric tried to get some projects done around the boat that we hadn't gotten to before leaving, but with the heavy rocking, it was difficult to do anything. So he basically spent the last four days sitting all alone, waiting for the weather to improve. He really misses me.

Thursday, July 5

The weather in Tahiti was miserable up until yesterday. And since I just happened to come back yesterday, I lucked out in missing it completely! Jim from *Special Blend* had also gone back to Florida for a few days to deal with his own affairs, and we happened to be on the same flight from Los Angeles to Tahiti. We managed to sit next to one another. Having him to talk to made the flight go by more quickly.

When we woke up, the sky above us was sunny and beautiful, so we decided to go sightseeing. There was more rain in the forecast, and we could see dark clouds on the horizon. But Eric needed to get off the boat, so we took our chances.

We caught a bus that took us into the heart of downtown Papeete and strolled along the waterfront, enjoying the views. We wandered into a handicraft market that sells goods made on all the islands in French Polynesia. There are 120 islands in total and most have less than one thousand residents. Sixty-five percent of French Polynesia's entire population lives on Tahiti, so it's naturally a center of commerce. A musician was playing, and we enjoyed listening to the music as we looked around.

Next to the market was a fairground with carnival rides, games, and food venders. Beyond the carnival area was a grassy park with a sea wall where people could dock their boats. We were surprised to see there were no boats parked at the quay. Our guidebook said it is always packed because everyone wants to be in the heart of downtown.

From the park, we turned and headed inland, checking out the assorted shops. While Papeete is small by city standards, it is a typical city with the usual array of restaurants, coffee houses, nightclubs, government offices, hair salons, and so on. Papeete is a dramatic contrast from all the other islands we have visited that are so rural.

We went to the pearl museum. The tiny museum gives a history of pearl cultivation and use throughout the world. Most of the displays include wax figures. For example, in talking about diving for pearls, there is a figure dressed in a diving suit. In talking about using peals for jewelry, there is a figure of a woman wearing outlandish pearl jewelry. We found the museum informative and cute.

I was jetlagged, so we headed back to the boat after the museum. It was great timing—it started pouring almost as soon as we got back on board.

Saturday, July 7

This weekend, the Tahiti Tourism Board is putting on a series of special events for cruisers. Last night the weekend kicked off with a great Polynesian dance show and dinner. In addition to the female dancers, there were also male dancers, which we haven't seen yet. While the female dances involve excessive hip gyration and flowing arm movements, the male dances involve lots of squatting, hitting one's own legs and chest, and arm movements mimicking the rowing of canoes and thrusting of spears. They are quite masculine. Eric and I were recruited to go on stage

108

to learn one of the male dances. It was easy to pick up, much easier than the female dance moves. All those squats gave our legs and buttocks a major workout!

This morning, there was a rally where dozens of boats crossed from Tahiti to Moorea in a big convoy. We weren't taking *Kosmos*, but we had been invited to join our friends Tom and Suzie on the sailboat *Priscilla*. Tom and Suzie know we aren't sailors, so we weren't sure if we were getting sailing lessons or just keeping them company. It turned out to be the latter. The ride over was slow since there wasn't much wind, but the day was sunny and beautiful, and we had a great time socializing.

Since the wind was so light, most of the boats put out their spinnaker sail. Usually, all the sails on a boat are white except for the spinnaker, which is brightly colored. It was pretty to watch the boats go by us with their colorful sails. Yes, go by. Sadly, we started in the lead but fell to the back by the end.

In Moorea, we attended a cruiser's luau which featured a traditional Tahitian food buffet. The food was similar to the Marquesan buffet. There was breadfruit and taro (a root similar to potato), which were both completely tasteless; yummy raw fish in coconut milk with veggies; pig roasted in the ground, which was disappointingly fatty and flavorless; and cooked spinach and chicken in coconut milk, which was similar to the taro leaf dish in the Marquesas, but tastier. We also tried pork and cabbage, which tasted like chow mein; excellent cooked bananas; bland sweet potatoes; and another raw fish dish with shredded coconut that was good, but not as good as the fish in coconut milk.

The most noteworthy items were Tahitian cakes. At the time we had no idea what they were. One cake looked like raw tuna in coconut milk and the other like raw salmon in coconut milk. They were fruity tasting and incredibly sweet, obviously a dessert item, with a texture similar to raw tuna. Our entire table had a heated discussion about whether they were fish in a sweet sauce or some sort of strange fruit. A lady at our table asked a local, who explained to us that Tahitian cakes are made of mashed fruit with cornstarch. The red one was banana and the orange one was pumpkin.

After lunch, we met some people from the San Diego area named Eric and Gisela. In a crazy coincidence, it turned out we have mutual friends from back home. Shortly after, the outrigger canoe race began. Each boat in the rally sent three people to row, and Eric was recruited. Christy from *Special Blend* had also volunteered. At first they told her no, then yes, then no, then yes, then no. By the last no, she was super annoyed and ranted to us, "I'm in. I'm out. I'm in. I'm out."

Suzie replied, "Is it fish or fruit? Am I in or out? Are we at a luau or making a porno?"

Those canoes take more power to row than one would think, and Eric has a new respect for the sport. He and his crewmates came in second in their heat, but we didn't stick around long enough to find out how they ranked overall. We were taking the ferry back to Papeete, and we had to get to the terminal before the last one left for the day.

When the ferry pulled up, hundreds of passengers, all wearing clothing of the same material disembarked. There were also people with them wearing regular clothing. Eric and I tried to figure out who they were. There were old people and young people, men and women of all sizes and fitness levels. One of the women in the group handed me the hat she was wearing and told me I could have it. The hat was woven from the leaves of some sort of plant and was so fresh that the leaves were still green. I proudly wore it the rest of the day.

After we landed in Tahiti, we decided to watch a round of the Heiva competition. We walked a few blocks to the theater and bought tickets. The emcee began the show by explaining that every night, two groups compete in each category. We were impressed by the first group of dancers. There were fifteen musicians in the back, forty female dancers and twenty-five male dancers. Their performance was almost like an opera in Tahitian, with the musicians singing the narration as the dancers acted out the story. One person was clearly the chief. Another person died, causing a war with another tribe. The music and dancing were incredible. The dances were mostly fast, but there were a few slow ones, too.

The dancers went through a number of costume changes. For each costume, the women had on a bikini top and a skirt of some sort. At the end they wore grass skirts and elaborate headdresses. The men were bare-chested and wore little skirt-like cloths around their waists. Their performance lasted an hour and a half. We couldn't believe the endurance of those dancers!

Then a three-hundred-person choir came out in matching outfits. We realized the group we had seen getting off the ferry was a competing choir. They sang for a half hour, and all but one song was a capella. A ukulele was the only instrument used in the one song with music. When the first choir was done, a second choir, also three hundred people, came out and did the same routine, but singing different songs.

Then the second dance group came out. This group had the same number of musicians and male/female dancers as the first group. This act seemed like it was more of a compilation of dances than an actual story, but since it was in Tahitian, we weren't sure. The routine lasted about an hour and fifteen minutes. Once again, there were amazing dancing and costumes. The costumes were colorful and flashier than the first group's.

The men wore little breastplates that looked like they were made of the same plant as my new hat. Their skirts were risqué, with a flap of material covering the loin and another covering the buttocks, leaving the hips exposed. As the men danced, the flaps would fly up. Some of the men had on banana hammocks underneath, but not all of them. No wonder there weren't many children in the audience!

Monday, July 9

Today we rented a car and took a tour of the island. The road around Tahiti parallels the ocean. Eric did all the driving—the first time he has been behind the wheel in two and a half months! A friend of ours put us in touch with Peter, a local on the island he knows, and Peter and his wife were kind enough to play tour guide for us.

Our first stop was Maraa Grotto, a series of caverns that have pools of water at the bottom. The caverns are right off the main highway in a small, pretty park dripping with a variety of foliage, including some gigantic, odd looking birds of paradise.

Next, we had lunch at the Gauguin Museum and Botanical Gardens, named after the French artist Paul Gauguin, who moved to Tahiti in the latter part of his life. He was broke and wanted to be someplace he could live off the land without money, which back then was possible in Tahiti. Peter didn't recommend going to the museum or gardens, so we just went to the restaurant. Lunch was nice. The roof is metal, and there is colorful cloth tacked to the ceiling, which gives it a festive feel. The supporting pillars are covered with palm fronds and flowers, and the floor is dirt. Since the edge of the restaurant is right on the water, sea spray comes up right though the open windows.

After lunch we drove around Tahiti Iti. Tahiti is shaped like a figure eight. The small part of the eight is called Tahiti Iti ("small Tahiti") and the big part is called Tahiti Nui ("big Tahiti"). Tahiti Iti used to be home to the French submarine fleet. The bay is four hundred feet deep— enough space to accommodate submarines. Near the shore, there are enormous concrete and metal cleats that are as big as a car. Cleats for forty-five foot boats are generally smaller than a foot (1/3 meter); the subs must have been gigantic to need cleats so big.

Tahiti Iti is also home to one of the most famous surf spots in the world, Teahupo, called the "jaws of water" for its enormous waves. Eighteen foot waves are common, though today the waves weren't nearly that big. The surf championships had just taken place here a few weeks ago.

Next, we stopped at the Arahoho Blowhole. We pulled into in a little parking lot off the side of the road and looked over at the rocky shoreline, and waiting for something to happen. Nothing did. Peter explained to us that since the seas were calm today, the blowhole wasn't spurting. He was disappointed because he'd been trying to play a gag on us. The blowhole is actually on the other side of the road—the water travels into an underground cavern and if the swell is right, will shoot through a crack between the rocks like a geyser. He was hoping that while watching the wrong spot, we'd unwittingly get drenched from behind. The blowhole sprays the cars on other side of the highway. We couldn't imagine driving on this scary, narrow ledge overlooking the ocean and suddenly being hit by a huge spray of water. We're surprised our guidebook didn't warn about it.

Our last stop was Point Venus, named because of Captain James Cook, who established an observatory there. As a nautical astronomer for the British navy, Cook had been sent to Tahiti to observe the movement of Venus against the sun during a specific period of time. Scientists compared Cook's observations with data collected from England on the same days, which helped them determine the distance between Earth and the sun. After he was done with his celestial assignment, Cook explored the South Pacific, becoming the first European to discover numerous Pacific islands (and on a later voyage, Australia). Peter told us that Point Venus is also where the missionaries first started converting people. Today, the only lighthouse on the island stands here. The area contains a nice public park and beach, which is crowded with locals swimming and rowing outrigger canoes.

We had a great time on our tour, but Tahiti was definitely different than what we had expected. We had envisioned endless, deserted beaches without much development (at least outside Papeete). In reality, the entire shoreline is built up and there aren't many beaches.

Tuesday, July 10

Tomorrow, we're taking *Kosmos* to Moorea. Since we were leaving the only real city we would be in for a long time, we needed to do some things before we left.

Eric changed the oil on the main engine and generator since there was an oil disposal site nearby. We also loaded up with fuel. We were by no means low, and we knew we could get fuel at other places, but we wanted to get it in Papeete since the dock is modern and the fuel is clean.

After we re-anchored, we went to the grocery store and stocked up on "passage food": easy-to-prepare and premade foods like soup, crackers, yogurt, lunch meats, cereal, canned pasta, and bread products. In the rough seas it is too easy to get burned by the stove or oven, and it is better to eat cold food or food heated in the microwave. We had intended to buy lots of microwave dinners, and were dismayed to find that they don't carry such things in Tahiti.

114

Then we had to finish our formalities with the government. Even though we officially checked into the country at Nuka Hiva and would check out from Bora Bora, we still had to complete the bulk of our paperwork in Papeete. Papeete is the administrative center of the islands; all boats are required to go here. We went to the agent's office (who works with the agent in Nuka Hiva), and he helped us fill out a few more forms. He told us he'd take care of the rest. All we needed to do was tell the Gendarme when we left the country.

Our last issue was emailing our blog posts to Mike S., our friend who has been administering our site for us. Finding decent Internet connections has been a tremendous logistical headache, and getting the large files successfully sent off was the most difficult task on the list.

Then we completed the usual preparations that need to be done before getting underway, such as hoisting and securing the dinghy. The paravanes and the dinghy share a rigging, and in order to lift the dinghy on and off, you have to configure the setup one way, and then switch it around to bring in or put out the paravanes. It takes a while to do the re-configuring. We always leave the rigging in paravane mode when we go to sea in case we need to deploy them for some reason, so even if we hadn't had the paravane out, we would have still had to reconfigure nonetheless. We brought the paravane in and secured it. Doing tasks like these was awkward and difficult for us back in Nuka Hiva, but we are slowly but getting better at them.

We also packed all storage areas, including the refrigerators, so that nothing would shift (and thus break or leak), and locked all the cabinets so the doors wouldn't fly open at sea. Everything out in the open needed to be secured or put away. Then we then took off the window covers (used to reduce glare and keep the furniture from fading) and stowed the fenders in the anchor locker. After that, we were finally ready to go.

First thing tomorrow, we will roll out of bed, notify our "guardian angels" Mike and Kim F. that we're moving, and pull up the anchor. Mike and Kim are our emergency contacts. Should we have an emergency at sea and set off our emergency beacon, the authorities would contact Mike and Kim to verify our location and get any other pertinent information about us. As such, we always keep them aware of our current location.

Chapter 8: Moorea, Society Islands, French Polynesia

Thursday, July 12

Yesterday morning we went to an anchorage at the edge of Opunohu Bay on the north side of Moorea. We had an easy ride over, but anchoring was a challenge. The wind and current were strong. We would pick a spot and start lowering the anchor, but by the time the anchor hit the sand, we had drifted and were either too close to another boat or right above a coral head. It took several tries, but eventually we wound up in a suitable spot.

Part of the movie *South Pacific* was filmed in Opunohu. The anchorage here is absolutely beautiful, with clear, light blue water and a white, sandy beach. (Finally, a white sand beach! We were beginning to doubt they existed.) Moorea, like Tahiti, doesn't have many beaches, so we feel lucky to be here.

This morning, we planned to rent scooters and take a tour of the island. We took the dinghy to the town of Paopao, located in the next bay over. The dinghy ride was interesting. There is coral everywhere, so you have to be careful. The small boat channel is clearly marked, and in theory you should be fine as long as you stay in the channel. Since the water is so clear, the coral looks closer to the surface than it really is and we passed over many coral heads that we were sure would scrape the bottom of our dingy. Fortunately, the channel was deep enough and the dingy was just fine, although we were a little shaken up about what we perceived to be several "close calls."

We got to the rental place in Paopao forty-five minutes after it opened. Much to our disappointment, the guy in line ahead of us got the last scooter. We wound up with a tiny, no frills car. Just a few minutes later, though, it started pouring. Suddenly, we weren't so sad about not getting the scooters. The most vivid double rainbow we've ever seen stretched across the sky. It was incredible.

We drove toward the interior of the island on a steep, curvy, and unpaved road. As we inched up the dirt road in the pouring rain, we were even more thankful we hadn't gotten scooters! Our first stop was the local agricultural school, which grows several kinds of crops, including banana, pineapple, and vanilla. Eric loves vanilla, so he was excited to see how vanilla plants are raised and harvested.

We got out of the car and walked to a food stand in front of the school. The stand sells ice cream, sorbet, pineapples, pineapple chips, jams, honey, vanilla beans, and other things made at the school. We went up to the counter and asked about a tour of the plantation, and were disappointed to find out the tours had been cancelled due to the rain. We got to try some food samples, so it was still worth the stop.

After we left the agricultural school, we stopped at a scenic viewpoint at the top of the road. Despite the thick clouds, we could see the ocean. There are a couple of trail heads located here that take you through the forest down to the bays, but they are one-way hikes; someone would have to pick us up at the other end. We contemplated walking for a little bit and then turning back, but it was still drizzling. It looked as if more serious rain was yet to come, so we headed back to the car.

Next, we turned off at an archeological site that holds the remains of one of the villages. Like in Tahiti, most of the natives lived in the lush interior of the island before the Europeans came. The ruins themselves look similar to what we saw on Nuka Hiva: essentially, piles of stones that used to be foundations for bamboo/palm buildings. In Nuka Hiva, the ruins were in close proximity to one another and the ground between them was mowed grass. But here, the ruins are spread out pretty far, with a walkway that takes you from one ruin to the next. The scenery in between is gorgeous—green, damp, and lush.

After Eric and I spent a good fifteen minutes walking around the circular site, it started pouring rain again. Unfortunately, we had no idea how much farther we had to go to complete the circle. We debated about whether to continue forward or turn back and opted to turn back. At the entrance, we looked at a map and saw that we had been three quarters of the way. Darn!

We headed back down the mountain and turned onto the main road. There, we saw a handwritten sign on a chalkboard that read, "Crepes and Juice." Yum. Crepes! Much to our surprise, the only place we've seen crepes before today was in downtown Papeete. We'd expected crepes to be a staple in French Polynesia. It was almost lunchtime, so we stopped. It turned out that the shop was actually a catamaran (boat) with a big wooden deck built over the two hulls and a palm frond roof thrown on top. No one was there, so we left.

Much to our delight, there was a place that serves both pizza and crepes a few miles down the road. In French Polynesia, pizza is a little different than in the States. Most pizzas here are thin crust and served with a thin layer of cream sauce on top of the tomato sauce. The sauce, cheese, and toppings are a little sparse, which is just the way Eric likes pizza. In addition to the usual toppings you see in the States, most pizza parlors also have several seafood toppings available. Fresh tuna and mahi mahi are common, as are "fruits of the sea"—a random assortment of whatever seafood is on hand. Another common topping is egg, where they crack a raw egg on top before they bake it. We ordered tuna pizza and got rum crepes for dessert. Eric's was sugar and rum, and mine was banana, chocolate, and rum. Both could have used more sugar.

Our crepes craving satiated, we headed out. Like in Tahiti, Moorea's entire shoreline is developed. It is comprised of mostly residences, with commercial buildings scattered here and there and lots of restaurants. Unfortunately, there weren't many places for us to stop. Most of the activities listed in the guidebook were beaches or shopping, but it wasn't beach weather and we don't enjoy shopping. Nevertheless, it was a pleasant drive with pretty ocean views.

Our last stop—the Rotui juice factory—brought us almost all the way back to the car rental return. Rotui is the most common brand of juice in French Polynesia and we thought it would be fun to tour the factory. We parked and entered what looked like the visitor's center. Inside, was a store that sold juice, soaps, perfumes, lotions, clothing, bric a brac with Hinano beer logos, and a variety of liqueurs.

We walked to the counter at the back of the store and asked if they gave tours. The employee stated that they didn't offer tours, but he would be happy to give us some samples. As it turned out, they only offered samples of the booze, not the juice. There were white and brown rums (which we passed on), and chocolate, mocha, and vanilla crème liqueurs, which were yummy and similar to Bailey's Irish Cream. There was also an assortment of tropical flavored liqueurs, including pineapple, banana, *pampelmousse*, coconut, and orange. Those were pretty good, although some flavors were better than others.

After all that booze, we hopped back in the car and went back to the rental place. (Don't worry, we only took small sips!) We got back to the boat shortly before sunset and enjoyed one of the most beautiful sunsets to date. The entire sky and ocean turned red.

Saturday, July 14

Yesterday was our chore day. Eric changed the fuel filters, which is easy to do with full tanks in a flat anchorage. He also took advantage of the fact that we are in shallow water and changed some sacrificial zincs. (When the water is shallow, it's easy to retrieve any tools/parts that may get dropped.) Meanwhile, I cleaned the bottom of the boat. The grass was back with a vengeance, and the whole time I scrubbed, I thought of that Chinese proverb that says to be careful what you wish for. I had always wished for a thick lawn at our house. Now my wish had come true, but it happened at the wrong house!

Today is Bastille Day, one of the biggest French holidays of the year. We started the day by going snorkeling in the coral reef next to our boat. As we swam toward the reef, Eric and Gisela approached us in their dinghy. They were also going snorkeling, so they joined us.

The coral here isn't particularly colorful, but it has some interesting shapes. There weren't many fish either, but we did see two new species, as well as a black-tipped reef shark that was about five feet long. The most noteworthy plant looked like a single dark pink rose stuck on the side of a coral head. It almost looked like someone had glued a plastic flower to the coral. We only saw one and I found it odd.

After snorkeling, Eric and I had planed to go to the Bastille Day celebration in Cook's Bay, and we convinced Eric and Gisela to join us. The problem was, we weren't sure how to get there. We knew it would be too much work to move *Kosmos* to Cook's Bay. And we were afraid to take our dinghy since the channel markers aren't lit. Going through the coral-filled water in the dark would be a disaster waiting to happen.

Eventually, we decided the best option was to take the dinghy to the beach and walk over to the Sheraton, pose as guests, and get a ride from the hotel. If the hotel staff wouldn't take us, we could hitchhike or walk, although it would be a long walk. I didn't like the idea of hitchhiking, though. My parents had ingrained in me that only axe murderers pick up hitchhikers, but Eric and Gisela assured us that it was safe.

We left our boats at 1500 (3:00 p.m.), figuring that would give us plenty of time to walk to the bay if necessary, buy tickets to the show, and eat dinner before the celebration started at 1930 (7:30 p.m.). We went to the Sheraton, who told us they didn't have a shuttle. So we started walking and stuck out our thumbs. It didn't take long before a pickup truck stopped. Two older Polynesian women sat in the bed, carrying Bibles. Seeing them made me a little less fearful. The four of us hopped into the truck bed next to them, and a few minutes later we were at our destination. By 1615, we had our tickets in hand.

We wandered around town looking for something to do. In French Polynesia, restaurants close between lunch and dinner, and almost everything else was shut down for the holiday. We wound up hanging out a time-share resort, sitting on the deck overlooking the bay until dinnertime.

After dinner we went to the soccer field where the show would take place. It seemed every person on the island was there. The bleachers were already full, but we grabbed some folding chairs and found a place to sit on the field. For a few minutes we were in the front row, but people put chairs in front of us. Even so, our seats were excellent.

The show was three hours long. The first half was comprised of a variety of individual dances put on by different groups: young boys, men, teenage girls, and finally, a professional dance troupe. During the second half of the show, the troupe performed an "operetta." The narrator gave the introduction in both French and English, explaining that it told the

122

story of someone or something coming out of a long, deep sleep and deciding to procreate. The men were warriors from heaven and the women were earth maidens, and they were joining together to copulate in hopes of fertility. No, we are not making this up. That really is what he said. We were expecting an especially erotic show, but it wasn't much different than any of the other dances we have seen. Although, the dancing style in and of itself is sexy, so who knows, maybe every dance is about copulation.

For most of the performance, the men and women danced separately, but toward the end they danced as one big group before pairing off as couples. Now and then four women dressed in white also came out and danced, separate from everyone else. But we couldn't figure out who they were and what their role was in the copulation process. As for costumes, the men all wore the little skirts that are just a flap over each side (didn't notice any flashing, though). Usually they were bare-chested, but for a few dances they wore grass breastplates and grass arm and leg bandanas. We're noticing a pattern with the female costumes. It seems that at every show, the women are always dressed in costumes with tight, short skirts and either no or small headdresses. With each costume change, their skirts get longer and/or puffier and their headdresses get progressively bigger.

After the show was over, we hitchhiked back to the dingy. We were picked up by a sweet-looking lady who had been sitting near us.

Sunday, July 15

Our longtime friends Pete and Shelley are flying into Tahiti tonight. We are so excited about seeing them. We've met a lot of new people and have started to form some great friendships, but we are a bit homesick for our old friends. There's something so easy—almost comforting—about being with people that you've known for years.

Today we took *Kosmos* back to Papeete, opting to tie up at the quay downtown instead of using the anchorage. It felt strange to pull in, tie up, and just hop off the boat onto dry land. It was too easy. No re-anchoring multiple times, no stressing about where we would settle, and no getting the dinghy down.

Near the quay there are a dozen or more "roulette trucks." We'd heard that they were great, but had no idea what they were. They turned out to be mobile food trucks, which in the U.S. we affectionately call "roach coaches." Over a dozen trucks were congregated in an open area, neatly parked in rows, with a few plastic chairs and tables in front of each truck. There is a festive feel to the area. Most of them offer Chinese, crepes, pizza, or hamburgers.

We found a truck that served crepes and went to the counter to order. Much to our surprise, a woman told us to sit down and served us like it was a regular restaurant. I had a crepe stuffed with smoked salmon in cream sauce, and a pear and dark chocolate crepe for dessert. Eric had a crepe stuffed with ham and onion in a bouillabaisse sauce, and a crepe with banana and ice cream on top for dessert. The food was excellent.

It was really convenient to have a variety of wonderful restaurants just steps away. If we'd docked at the anchorage, it would have taken us at least an hour each way to get to dinner. But we also discovered there are drawbacks to being on the wall. There was a lot of traffic noise, pedestrians kept peeping into our windows, and there was a nasty surge from the ferry ship's wake. Each time the ferry went by, *Kosmos* would rock like we were at sea, swishing violently against the fenders that protected it from the concrete wall. Now we understand why everyone keeps their boat in the anchorage.

Pete and Shelley arrived around 2000. It was almost surreal to see our friends from home here in Tahiti. We took them over to the roulette trucks for dinner, then for a stroll along the waterfront.

Chapter 9: Tahaa, Society Islands, French Polynesia

Tuesday, July 17

Yesterday we pulled out of Tahiti in the early morning for our twenty-four hour trip to Tahaa. We've noticed a pattern for our passages: Any time we do a short day run, the seas are nice and calm, but the overnight trips always seem to be miserable. This run was no exception. We had strong winds on our port aft quarter producing six to eight foot following seas and periodic ten-foot beam waves that knocked us all over the place. It drizzled all day, and as soon as it got dark, it rained hard all night. Poor Shelley was sick for the entire passage. Pete and I both had moments of sickness, too. Oddly, Eric was the only one who didn't get sick. Usually, he is the one who struggles with sea sickness.

We approached the south entrance to the reef at 0400 this morning. With the rain clouds blocking the stars and moon, we couldn't see anything outside. Not too long ago we would have waited outside the reef until dawn so we could see exactly where we were going, but Eric has gotten comfortable navigating by the charts, as long as they are high resolution. He confirms their accuracy by using radar, depth sounder, and navigation aids such as channel markers and buoys. The entrance and channel markers were lit, and everything lined up perfectly with the charts, so Eric decided to go for it. This was our first night entry through a pass, and it went smoothly.

Then we headed to the north end of the lagoon, threading through a narrow channel with coral on both sides. It was "fly by instruments" the whole way, and Eric was intently focused on making sure everything continued to line up with the charts. Had anything not matched, we

126

would have stopped, but the charts were accurate. We anchored shortly after sunrise and were welcomed by a beautiful rainbow over the reef. We were all so proud of Eric.

Tahaa is another island that is accessible only by boat, so it is not a big tourist destination. It must be an older island than Tahiti and Moorea. The mountain peaks are much lower—about half as tall. The reef surrounding Tahaa also has a few *motus*, which neither Tahiti or Moorea have yet. This is the first time we have been able to see land on both sides of the lagoon. We could also see the island of Bora Bora in the distance.

We were eager to go exploring. We secured *Kosmos*, blew up the inflatable dinghy (which handles four people better than our hard dinghy), and headed into Tapuamu, the closest town on Tahaa. It was a cold, wet ride in the rain. Since Tapuamu is a small town, we were done exploring in only a few minutes. We were planning to go out to breakfast and then rent a car to tour the island, but we found out there were no restaurants within walking distance and no car rentals anywhere on the island. We did arrange to take a half-day tour of the island tomorrow, though.

We had seen a hotel on one of the *motus*, so we piled into the dinghy and went over there for breakfast, figuring they had to have a restaurant on site. As soon as we pulled up to the dock, we were shooed off, told that we needed to make restaurant reservations at least a month in advance. Defeated, we went back to *Kosmos* and cooked for ourselves. We looked up the hotel in the tourist guide and found out that rooms start at one thousand dollars (US) per night.

The rain had stopped, so after we finished eating, we decided to go snorkeling. While we were changing into our bathing suits, a boat pulled up. On the boat was a local guy wearing a *pureu* (the local word for sarong) wrapped around him like a diaper and no shirt. We had been told by other cruisers to expect him. His name is Norman and he grows fruit at his home, and then sells it to cruisers. Unfortunately, he doesn't speak a word of English, so we couldn't talk to him. I bought some *pamplemousse*, papaya, and bananas. Pete really wanted a coconut despite hearing how hard they are to open and eat, so we got one. Norman then serenaded us with a song, playing his ukulele and singing. It was great. Norman gave us four extra red bananas and took off. He was the highlight of our day.

We went snorkeling at the reef closest to the boat. It was disappointing: There wasn't much to see other than urchins. After snorkeling, Pete went to work on the coconut. He tried a variety of knives and techniques to get it open and get the meat out of the shell. He was working so hard that he was sweating. A half hour later, he proudly displayed the "fruit of his labor." It was good!

Wednesday, July 18

This morning we met our tour guide, Vincent, at 0830. We climbed into his truck and drove for a while. The road parallels the water, with scenic views of the lagoon. Most of the area around the bay had development of some sort on it, mostly houses. We pulled into a church parking lot where another six people were waiting. Once everyone was seated, Vincent played a couple songs for us on his ukulele, which set the tone for a fun adventure.

After a short drive, we turned off onto a dirt road that took us into the interior of the island. The road was steep, full of potholes, and scary. There's no way anyone could navigate that road without four-wheel drive!

Vincent stopped frequently to tell us about the local flora and fauna. Like in the Marquesas, a lot of fruit is grown here. We saw breadfruit, star fruit, *pampelmousse*, noni, and coconut. Vincent hopped out of the car and picked a few pieces of each ripe fruit for us. He even cut open a *noni* and passed it around for us to smell. It has a foul odor that could be easily mistaken for Camembert, the smelly French cheese. He also explained to us that there are both male and female papaya trees. The male trees never bear fruit, and the female trees only bear fruit if there is a male tree close by.

While driving along the main road, we noticed several low, wide structures that looked like a roof covering a large, single shelf. Vincent told us that the shelves are sliding trays and the structures are for air drying coconut pieces prior to processing. In Nuka Hiva, they dry coconut using fire, and we found it interesting that different islands have different drying methods.

Then we passed a pineapple plantation. The pineapple in this part of the world is phenomenally good: smaller, sweeter, more flavorful, and much better than what we get at home. It was harvest time, so Vincent grabbed a couple of pineapples for us, too.

Next, much to Eric's delight, we passed a vanilla plantation and got a full explanation of how vanilla is made. Vanilla plants are vines with white orchid flowers. The flowers are bisexual, meaning they have both male and female reproductive parts. Most flowers are pollinated by insects, but vanilla is not. Each vanilla flower must be pollinated by hand. The plantation workers break the stamen and put the pollen on a small stick, then smear the pollen along the female part of the flower. Vincent said the plantation workers come every day during the four-month fertility season to look for new flowers to pollinate. After nine months, the beans are picked and then left to dry in the sun for another nine months. No wonder vanilla is so darned expensive!

As we climbed the mountain, the views became prettier and prettier. The scenery was spectacular at the peak, probably the most beautiful we've seen yet. We could see two bays, the lagoon, the ocean, and an island named Raiatea in the distance.

There, Vincent gave us a brief lesson in the art of tying a *pareus*, the traditional clothing worn by the natives. It is basically a big piece of rectangular cloth that can be tied dozens of fashionable ways. Vincent showed us the most basic ties for men and women, including the diaper style worn by Norman.

Then we learned how to open and carve a coconut. Pete volunteered to be Vincent's guinea pig for the demonstration. What took Pete a half hour of hard labor took Vincent about ten seconds. Vincent said the secret was to use the dull side of a machete, not the blade. He showed us where the weakest point of the shell is, tapped the spot twice with the knife, then gave it a single hard whack--V*oila*, the coconut was split in half. Vincent told us that the clear liquid inside is called coconut water. Coconut water is refreshing and a favorite beverage on the islands. Vincent also showed us how to make coconut milk He shredded the coconut using a special tool then squeezed the shredded pulp, and out came the milk. The milk is used for cooking.

Afterward, Vincent brought out a fruit tray and played songs for us on his ukulele while we ate. When we finished, we piled back into the car and went drove the mountain to the other side of the island and around several bays. The drive was lovely.

Our last stop was a pearl farm. This one was similar to the farms we saw on Manihi, with several bungalows on the shore and a dock with a small building on the water end. We all walked down the dock to the building, and there a young French man explained how pearls are created.

The process starts when the oysters are young. First, the worker opens the oyster just a small crack—anything bigger will kill it—and

130

inserts a small mirror. If the oyster has an especially colorful shell, it becomes a seed oyster. If not, the grafter implants a seed inside by taking a small piece from the seed oyster and a round piece of mother of pearl, called a nucleus, and surgically implanting them in the female reproductive area. Interestingly enough, most farms buy pre-made nucleuses from Mississippi, USA.

Oysters naturally secrete a fluid that coats the inside of their shell, creating the mother of pearl interior. The seed enhances the color of the secretion. This fluid also coats the nucleus, which makes the pearl. Polynesian pearls are colored instead of white because the indigenous warm water oysters produce colorful secretions. The pearls are called black pearls, but they're actually various shades of gray. Some are lighter, some are darker, and many have tints of blue, green, purple, pink, and yellow.

Once the surgery is done, the pearl farmer puts several oysters in a bag and places the bag in seven meters (twenty-one feet) of water for a year and a half. After this time, there should be one to two millimeters of coating on the pearls. Oysters that have produced nicely shaped pearls are implanted with another seed, while oysters with deformed pearls are discarded.

We were taken to a showroom, where we learned about how pearls are graded. Depending on the grade and size, they cost anywhere from forty dollars to thousands of dollars each.

When we first arrived at the pearl farm, we asked Vincent if he knew where we could get lunch at the end of the tour. As the group loaded into the truck to leave the pearl farm, he told us he had made arrangements for us at Chez Louise. He would drop us off there and they would take us back to our dinghy. He had also taken all the fruit that had been rolling around in the back of the truck and piled it into the backpack we had left there. Apparently, Vincent had taken a liking to us and wanted us to have all the fruit he had picked for the group. Nice!

After a few minutes of scenic driving, we got to Chez Louise, a small, outdoor restaurant overlooking the water with a spectacular view, with a serene, tranquil feel to it. We were the only people there. An older Polynesian woman welcomed us and told us to sit down.

"What do you want to eat?" she asked us.

We looked at her blankly.

"You like fish?" she said.

We all replied, "Yes!"

A few minutes later, she brought out salads, followed by a main course of tuna and rice. The food was excellent and the portions were enormous—literally four times as much tuna as we'd normally get in a restaurant.

After the food came out, two older teenage boys hopped into a boat tied at a nearby dock and took off. The woman explained that her older son was the chef, and now that lunch was over, he and her younger son were going surfing. What a life!

When we were done eating, she brought us some *pampelmousse* for dessert. Then an older man drove us to the dinghy dock and we went back to *Kosmos* for the night.

Chapter 10: Bora Bora, Society Islands, French Polynesia

Thursday, July 19

Yesterday, we noticed some people snorkeling near the hotel and decided to give that spot a try this morning. The snorkeling was nice, with pretty coral formations that had some nice colors. There were a lot of sea anemones, as well as a decent amount of fish, though not many of them were colorful. The fish were obviously used to being fed. They had no fear of people. While they wouldn't let us touch them, we got within inches—the closest we've ever gotten to a fish in the wild.

After snorkeling, we got *Kosmos* prepared for sea and made the short trip over to Bora Bora. With Shelley and Pete helping, we were ready in record time. Of course, since it was a day trip, the seas were calm and no one got sick.

Like Tahaa, Bora Bora has a main island in the middle of the lagoon and *motus* along the reef surrounding the main island. Bora Bora looks tall from the distance, but in reality there is only one tall peak and the rest of the land is quite low, much lower than Tahaa. There are a few small islands in the lagoon between the reef and main island. The majority of the lagoon is light blue-green, with patches of sapphire blue. It is gorgeous.

We arrived in Bora Bora at 1530 and anchored in Povai Bay, which has a wireless Internet connection. We got *Kosmos* situated and the dinghies down in record time. Shelley and Pete are such good worker bees that we may never let them leave!

On Povai Bay there is a famous restaurant called Bloody Mary's. We'd been told that Bloody Mary's is an "experience" and that we needed to eat there at least once, so we headed there for dinner. It has a new-looking dinghy dock. The restaurant is a palm frond structure with a neatly landscaped entranceway. When we walked in, we noticed the ground is covered in white sand, and there is a shoe check. Funny, in America you won't get served without shoes on and here you have to take them off.

The guys went to the bathroom and came out laughing. To flush the urinal, you have to pull a penis-shaped handle. They said there's also a waterfall sink where water comes out of the top of the waterfall, down the rocks, and into the bowl at the bottom. Of course, Shelley and I had to check out the women's bathroom. The sink is the same, but obviously there's no urinal!

They called our name and ushered us to a display table featuring lots of raw seafood and meat on ice. The owner pointed out each item and described it, then took our order right there. All the cooking was done on open grills near the display table. The food arrived shortly after we were escorted to our table. We each got a different main fish course to share. Everything was good, but we all agreed the pink opah (moonfish) was the best. There was seasoned wahoo (ono), peppered ahi, and broadbill (swordfish). We had crème brûlée and warm coconut tart for dessert.

Overall, we had a great time. The environment is laid back and fun, the food is good, and the portions are big. No wonder Bloody Mary's is so popular!

Friday, July 20

This morning, we took the dinghy into the main town of Vaitape, which by boat is about a mile north from where we're anchored. (By land it is farther since the road follows the curvy lagoon.) We walked around town a bit, but we didn't find it very interesting. We passed an outdoor theater where they were setting up for tonight's show, the final round of the Heiva competition. We also saw a grocery store, post office, police station, bank, a Catholic church, and an evangelical Protestant temple. There are not many real restaurants—mostly "snack" places that serve sandwiches. There is a big handicraft market that sells goods similar to what we saw in Tahiti. We were taken aback by the large numbers of tourist souvenir shops—many of them high end—lining the road.

We headed back to *Kosmos* and changed into swimsuits to go snorkeling at a recommended spot a mile south of where we'd docked. The coral covers a large area and has a variety of depths, so it is a good place to go diving, too. Most of the coral formations are quite large, with a variety of shapes. The reef isn't very colorful, but there are some spots of color. There were a lot of fish and a lot of variety to the fish, including a napoleon fish. We also spotted the biggest moray eel we've ever seen and lots of neon-lipped clams.

After snorkeling, we headed back to the boat, made dinner, and then went into town for the Heiva show. We were excited to hear that the president of French Polynesia was in attendance.

This was the third major Heiva dance production we've seen—and it was probably the best. Once again, we scored great seats. The show opened with a speech in English, French, and Tahitian about the importance of cultural identity. In the first act, a couple of singers performed a modern tune accompanied by a group of children. Then the dancing began. It was fabulous, and it seemed more overtly erotic than any of the other dancing we've seen. The audience was really into it, cheering for the dancers and going wild when the music sped up and the dancing became really fast. At the end, a group of singers came out and repeated the same song that started the show.

Saturday, July 21

This morning we went for a hike near the anchorage, where there is a TV tower. We followed the service road up. It was a relatively short hike, but very steep: In a car, we would have needed four-wheel drive. The hike was worth it. The view was spectacular. We could see the whole southern half of the island, including all the *motus* in the bay and around the reef. We could also see Tahaa and Raiatea in the distance.

At the top, we met a local who had a traditional Polynesian tattoo. Pete has been contemplating getting a tattoo here, so he asked the man where he'd had his done. The man replied that his brother had done it and gave Pete his brother's name and the location of the parlor.

After the hike, we went to a nearby restaurant for lunch. I ordered breadfruit gnocchi. It tasted like regular gnocchi, which is not surprising since neither potatoes nor breadfruit have any real flavor. For dessert, Eric got pineapple wrapped in a thin phyllo pastry. The food was excellent.

While we were eating, Pete asked the waitress where she'd gotten her tattoo. She told us she'd had hers done by the same man we had heard about earlier.

Shelley nodded excitedly and said, "Oh, yeah, we met his brother today!"

The waitress gave her an odd look. Shelley assumed the lady, who isn't a native English speaker, didn't understand and repeated "brother" a couple of times.

After a minute, the waitress explained her confusion. "He's my brother. Who did you meet?"

We couldn't believe that the only two locals we've met are siblings! What are the odds of that?

After lunch we went back to *Kosmos* to change. Then we headed out to a site on the southeast side of the lagoon that two guidebooks said had the best snorkeling on the entire island. The ride in the dinghy took over an hour, but it was gorgeous. Along the way, we saw a spotted eagle ray and followed it, trying to get a decent photo.

We were totally baffled, however, when we arrived at the snorkeling spot only to find sea urchins and small patches of dead coral. We scoured the entire area looking for the supposedly amazing stretch of reef, but never saw anything of interest except for an enormous puffer fish and a large porcelain tiger shell. Feeling defeated, we went back to *Kosmos* for the night. Later, we found out that the spot had been destroyed by El Niño a few years ago.

Sunday, July 22

Our plan for the day was to rent a car and tour the island. By the time we got the car, it was noon and the rental agency would only let us have it until 1600 (4:00 pm). That seemed like plenty of time, since the island is so small. We felt confident that we would find everything worth seeing. The rental agent had given us a brochure entitled "Ten Things You Must See," which had at least thirty things listed. We were also armed with a travel guide.

According to the guidebook, most of the locals live in or near Vaitape, but most of the development is at the southern end of the island, where the majority of the hotels are congregated.

Our first stop was an art gallery near Vaitape, but it turned out to be closed on Sundays. Next, we decided to get lunch at a restaurant recommended in our guidebook. After we parked, though, Eric noticed the restaurant across the street served Tex-Mex. He was sold! Being as we live about ten miles from Mexico, Mexican food was a staple of our diet.

We both miss it, but Eric was literally suffering from Mexican food withdrawal. He insisted we go there.

We all ordered, with Eric getting shrimp fajitas. A half hour later, the owner came out and told Eric he was out of shrimp. Was fish okay? Eric didn't mind. Fifteen minutes later, Pete, Shelley and I were served. Another twenty-five minutes later, after the three of us were totally done eating, Eric's food finally came out. Eric inhaled his food and we paid. We were antsy to go since the clock was ticking on the car.

Slow service in restaurants is actually the norm here on the islands, but we still haven't gotten used to it. Another norm is restaurants being out of many of the menu items, so we have gotten in the habit of having second and third choices ready in case the first choice is unavailable. The food tasted fine, but it only vaguely resembled real Mexican food. Pete, Shelley, and I were disappointed. But, Eric was happy to have had something to help satiate his craving.

After lunch, we set out in search of the next site: a World War II cannon at the top of a nearby hill. We couldn't find the trail, so we asked about it at the reception desk of a hotel. Apparently, there's no trail. You just push through the brush on your way up and you'll find the cannon. The hill looked steep with dense foliage, like something you'd need a machete and rock climbing gear to do. We decided to skip it.

Next was Belvedere Point. According to the brochure from the car rental place, it is a pleasant twenty-minute walk to the viewpoint, with the trail starting at a staircase across from Club Med. We found the staircase and headed up, expecting it to lead to a walking trail. It turns out that the mountain is so steep that the staircase goes all the way to the top. Fortunately, the surrounding forest was pretty, and the view at the top was phenomenal with fabulous vistas to the east and southwest. Going back down was a wee bit treacherous, since the leaves on the staircase were slippery, but we all made it just fine.

Our next destination was a three-in-one combo with a viewpoint, ancient Polynesian temple, and two World War II cannons. When we found the dirt road that led to the top, though, we realized our little vehicle couldn't tackle it, so we parked and made the short trek up the hill. Once again, the view was breathtaking. There was a concrete slab at the peak, and we could see where the cannons were once embedded into the slab, but we didn't see any indicators of an ancient temple. (Unless the especially big rock that happens to be there is part of the temple.) Chances are the ruins were covered by the concrete slab. We did notice a hiking trail that looked like it headed down to the water, but we were too short on time to go exploring. As we were about to leave, a beautiful White-Tailed Tropicbird swooped by us.

From there we struck out on everything. We couldn't find Marlon Brando's condos or the marine museum, and the yacht club was closed. Nonetheless, the drive was still pretty. We made it back to Vaitape promptly at 1600, then headed back to *Kosmos* for dinner and a movie.

We had been told that Bora Bora is the most beautiful of all the islands but that it is by far the most touristy. We agree that Bora Bora is the most touristy, and it is definitely the most expensive. Now that we've seen the whole thing, we can say that Bora Bora is beautiful, but it isn't necessarily the most beautiful. All the islands are gorgeous.

Monday, July 23

This morning, Pete finally decided to get the tattoo he's been debating about. In the pre-European days, tattoos were an important part of the Polynesian culture, especially for the warriors. When the first Europeans sailors arrived in Polynesia, they were fascinated by the locals' tattoos—a foreign concept to Europeans at the time. Many European sailors got tattooed while in Polynesia; in fact, the tradition of sailors getting tattoos originated here.

The Polynesians, especially the Marquesans, are some of the most noted and respected tattoo artists in the world. The tattoos offered in French Polynesia utilize traditional artistry, with incredibly intricate and beautiful designs. The tattoos here are only black ink, and they usually depict sea creatures and tikis. A couple tattoo parlors here are so traditional that they still use the old style bamboo rods that needles have since replaced. Eric and I are not tattoo fans, but we think the traditional artwork is beautiful and that the tattoos are impressive.

Pete started calling around and found a Marquesan guy named Fati that could take him at noon. At 1500 (3:00 p.m.), Pete was back, sporting a giant manta ray on his calf. Inside the manta ray is a turtle and inside the turtle is a tiki. The tattoo is extremely well done. Pete is thrilled with his "Fati Tatty." Shelley is less than thrilled with the size, but even she has to admit that the tat is cool.

Later, we went out to dinner. The restaurant gave us a complimentary appetizer—a puff pastry stuffed with a fish pate. It was good, but a bit fishy. Eric ordered a yummy gazpacho with salmon mousse as an appetizer. Pete ordered mahi pate, which was okay.

Tuesday, July 24

We started our day snorkeling again at the reef south of our boat. It's one of the best snorkeling spots we have been to, mostly because of the sheer number of fish. Today, we finally remembered to bring bread to feed the fish. There were lots of fish around when we jumped in, but once Eric pulled out the bread, he was surrounded by hundreds of them—mostly sergeant and butterfly fish—all fighting for food. The fish came up and ate right out of his hands. He could feel them nibbling on his skin as they attacked the bread.

After a minute, some larger fish joined the swarm. A big parrotfish came toward Eric, clearly after the bread. Eric freaked out and dropped it. We've seen parrotfish bite off good-sized pieces of coral and crush them into fine sand, so Eric wasn't about to let this one anywhere close to his hands! As a side note, parrotfish play a key role in the creation of sand.

I spent a lot of time watching a school of small yellow fish with thin black stripes. They moved as a wall from one coral head to the next. It's incredible that they can swim in unison, seeming to know instinctively which coral head they will feed at next. This behavior is a natural defense mechanism. To predators, they look like one big fish.

When we were done, we went back to *Kosmos*, and Shelley and Pete got ready to fly out. Once they were packed up, we dinghied into town and got lunch at a small restaurant in the center of town. The mood at lunch was melancholy. None of us was ready for them to leave.

And now I'm trying to use up all the fruit we acquired in Tahaa before it goes bad. This afternoon I made papaya salsa and papaya-banana muffins. Both turned out tasty. The papayas out here are huge, yielding three times a typical papaya, so I wound up making triple batches of each. We can freeze the excess muffins, but it looks like we'll be eating salsa for the next few days. For dinner, I served the salsa on crackers with cream cheese and we had the muffins for dessert. Yum!

Thursday, July 26

Our plan for yesterday was to go diving in the morning, head into town to check out of the country in the afternoon, and spend the evening getting the boat ready for departure. Unfortunately, Eric awoke with a bad cold, so diving was out. Leaving was out, too. The wind in our protected anchorage was howling at twenty knots, and the weather forecast for today was twelve-foot seas at eight-second intervals (for non-boaters, this is nasty!).

Since he hasn't been feeling good, Eric laid low yesterday and today. About the only activity he did was to equalize the batteries, maintenance that needs to be done once a year on our Lifeline AGM batteries. Once Eric charged the batteries as usual, he put a high voltage (15.5 volts) on them for a solid eight hours to refresh them. This meant we had to stay on board all day and monitor them in case there was a problem. Since we weren't going out anyway, it was a good day to do it.

Meanwhile, I continued to use up all our fruit. Yesterday, I made smoothies with papaya, banana, and vanilla yogurt for breakfast. For lunch, I made quesadillas with brie topped with papaya salsa. In the afternoon, I made blended drinks with papaya, pineapple, and ice. I finished the day with a triple batch of papaya-pineapple muffins. They were even better than the papaya-banana muffins. Today, I made a double batch of coconut brownies. The brownies are incredibly decadent.

We also tried a new juice. In French, the juice is called *corossol*, and our translation book says in English it is called *soursop*. We've never heard of *soursop* before. The juice is white—definitely a citrus fruit. It is sweet and tastes good. It doesn't taste like pineapple juice, but that is the closest we can come to describing the flavor.

Tonight we went out to dinner and tried marlin. We didn't like it that much. Marlin is similar to swordfish in texture, and we prefer light, flaky fish.

Friday, July 27

When Eric woke up, he was feeling a bit better, but now I'm sick. The weather forecast for this weekend says the seas will be okay. Not good, but tolerable. Unfortunately, we need to get moving and can't wait for better seas. We have to maintain a fairly fast pace if we're going to get to Indonesia before hurricane season starts in the Pacific.

We went into town to check out with the officials. Since all our paperwork was done in Papeete, checkout was quick and easy. Basically, we said we were going to leave tomorrow and the officials stamped our passports out.

For dinner, we went to the famous Hotel Bora Bora, the first hotel on the island. It is one of the most expensive places we've ever eaten! The restaurant was very French, with small portions of high quality foods. But the portions were extra tiny, which we weren't too happy about given the super expensive cost. For example, we got a cup of asparagus coconut soup that was literally a single measuring cup of soup (240 ml). It cost twenty-five dollars (US)! All the food tasted great, especially the soup, but it wasn't good enough to justify the price and portion size.

During dinner we sat on a balcony overlooking the ocean. Below us, a couple was having a romantic dinner at a table on the sand. As we were getting up to leave, we saw that a private performance was beginning for them, so went down to the beach to watch. A Polynesian man dressed in a *pareu* wrapped like boxer-briefs was doing tricks with two flaming batons. What's ironic is that Eric had just mentioned yesterday that he was surprised we hadn't seen any flaming baton performances in French Polynesia. You see them a lot in Hawaii. The man dropped the batons in the sand a few times, but even so, his performance was impressive.

Saturday, July 28

We awoke to gray skies, rain, white caps in the lagoon, and seventeen- to twenty-knot winds with gusts of up to twenty-eight knots. The wind kept changing direction, too, so we were being blown all over the place. Supposedly, it was going to clear up this afternoon, and we were planning to leave as soon as it did.

I still wasn't feeling good, but I forced myself to finish cooking all the fruit that would likely go bad before we made it to Suwarrow, our next destination. I made banana-coconut waffles from scratch for breakfast, which were good, but not as flavorful as I had anticipated. Then I used the last of the ripe bananas making puff pastries stuffed with a banana-coconut filling. I didn't actually bake the puffs—we'll cook them in the toaster oven while we're at sea when we want a hot dessert. Then I grated and toasted the last of the coconut so it would be ready for us to use in Suwarrow.

Meanwhile, Eric started getting *Kosmos* ready for sea. First, he pulled the inflatable dinghy out of the water, which was tricky to do in the strong winds. We have to lift the dinghies from the side of the boat, where the wind was blowing head-on. Keeping the dinghy from flipping over as it was being lifted was not easy. Once he got the dinghy to the top deck, he left it out to dry for a few minutes. When he returned to deflate and stow it, he saw the dinghy had been blown onto the railings and was dangerously close to flying away. Losing the dinghy would have been really bad. He quickly stowed it.

By 1600 (4:00 p.m.), the wind was getting stronger and it was clear that we weren't going anywhere. We had *Kosmos* mostly ready to leave, but we hadn't brought in our hard dinghy yet. We decided it was better to wait until the last minute to bring in the dinghy in case we needed to get to shore for some reason.

Around 2200 (10:00 p.m.), we were ready to go to bed. As usual, Eric poked his head out the back door to make sure all looked okay and saw that the hard dinghy had flipped over. This was really bad. He pulled the

144

rope in until he could reach the dinghy and flipped it upright. We normally keep the dinghy loaded with miscellaneous useful items, like life jackets, a jerry can of gas, etc. Fortunately, most of what was in the dinghy floated and had gotten trapped under the hull when it initially flipped over, but when Eric turned it right side up, it all started to float away. Eric jumped into the dinghy, despite it being almost full of water, and started gathering things, but sadly, didn't get them all. He was able to retrieve the gas can and oars, which was a relief.

I handed Eric a large bucket and he bailed like crazy. I then pulled the dinghy over to the side of the boat with Eric in it, which was not easy to do against the wind. Eric clipped the rigging to the dinghy and got out. As usual, Eric went up top and I stayed below. I normally hold the dinghy to keep it from swinging as the crane pulls it from the water to the top deck, and then when the dinghy is beyond my reach, Eric grabs it and holds it from swinging. Tonight, I had to use a lot of force to keep it from completely flipping over, and no matter how hard I tried, I couldn't stop the swaying. A couple times, the dinghy blew into the cockpit. Once the dinghy was out of my reach, I ran to the top to help Eric. Even with two of us, it was a struggle to get it situated properly in the twenty-five to thirty knot gusts of wind.

Then we went through the rest of the routine of getting ready to go: stowing the stuff that was loose on the deck inside the dinghy, putting the dinghy cover on, switching the rigging from dinghy mode to paravane mode, and so on. The whole routine was challenging with the wind, but everything went fine.

We are counting our blessings. We could have lost both dinghies today in the wind. Then we'd be in a world of hurt. We could have lost the oars, which would be a problem. The dagger board that helps steady the dinghy was our biggest loss—it was unsecured and is now resting in peace at the bottom of the lagoon. But we can live without it. Our real concern now is the outboard motor. In the morning, we will follow the "what to do in case of submersion directions" and hopefully the motor will still work.

So, when all was said and done, tonight's little ordeal was not that bad, after all. We did have a bright full moon to help us see, which helped a lot.

Thursday, August 2

On Sunday morning, Eric checked the outboard engine motor as soon as we got up. He washed off the outside of the engine and then opened it. The cylinder was dry, which was a good sign, so he drained the fuel from the carburetor and tried starting it. Nothing happened, so he drained all the fuel in the tank and put in fresh fuel, thinking maybe water had gotten in the tank. It still wouldn't start. He repeated the first steps— draining the carburetor again and checking the cylinder. Still nothing happened. About to give up, he tried cranking it one more time. And this time it started! Yippee!

Had it not started, it wouldn't have been the end of the world. The reason we have two complete dinghies is because dinghies are a critical piece of equipment, one that we cannot live without. Should something happen to one of them, we have a back up. However, the thought of losing an engine, and thus no longer having a backup, so early on in the trip was disconcerting.

We left for our four and a half day passage late Sunday afternoon. At first, it was our usual fare, with six- to nine-foot waves coming from starboard aft, making for uncomfortable rolling. On Monday, though, the seas flattened to four to six feet. While it wasn't a smooth ride, it was better than any other long passage so far. Much to or delight, on Wednesday morning, the seas flattened out some more, down to three to five feet, making the ride more pleasant. Of course, it didn't last long. On Wednesday night the seas became mildly confused, so the ride became rockier, but it wasn't bad.

Even so, I've been miserable. I'm still sick, and being sick when you're at sea compounds the misery. I'm also struggling with loneliness again. I miss my friends. I have many lifelong friends who go back all the way to junior high school. They've watched me grow and change, and they know the major events of my life. They understand me. Yes, we have made some fun new friends on our travels, but it isn't the same. For example, I was with a new friend in Bora Bora when I mentioned that something we saw reminded me of my mother. My new friend said, "Oh, that's nice." But an old friend would have understood that my comment was bittersweet—and most likely would have made a sarcastic joke. I miss that deep camaraderie. I have it with Eric, but I need that kind of connection with more than one person.

The days drag slowly and blur together. We read, play video games, watch movies, and spend a lot of time staring at the horizon. We are doing four-hour watches, and we both sleep a lot when we're not on watch. The sunrises and sunsets have been unspectacular, but nice to watch nonetheless. The moon has been full to mostly full and incredibly bright. We can clearly see unlit islands in the distance in the moonlight, but it is hard to see the stars in the bright light. Every other day we check email and blog comments via the satellite phone, which is the highlight of our day. We should be there tomorrow morning, and we can't wait!

Chapter 11: Suwarrow, Northern Group Islands, Cook Islands

Friday, August 3

Suwarrow is an isolated atoll within the Cook Island chain, a good 230 nm away from its nearest neighbor and 440 nm from the closest town (and it's a very small town). A nature preserve, Suwarrow can only be accessed by private boat. No ferries or planes go there. The only inhabitants of the island are the park ranger and his family. It is probably the most remote place we will visit on our journey.

We were within view of Suwarrow at first light. From the distance, we could see the long reef line dotted with small, green *motus* in the deep blue water; behind the *motus* was a layer of gray clouds low on the horizon. Above the line of clouds, the sky was pink with the early morning light. All the colors together were a majestic sight. After the sun rose, we saw three dolphins.

We radioed the park ranger and got permission to enter the lagoon. As we neared the pass, the water quickly became shallow. It was so clear we could see the bottom! The pass into Suwarrow is potentially tricky. Since there are two reefs in the pass, we had to enter it from one angle and change course to another angle once we were inside. There are lots of coral heads around, so Eric had to carefully follow the charts while I kept a close eye on the water. Eric masterfully navigated the pass and we headed over to the nearby anchorage. This is the longest passage the two of us have completed by ourselves and we are delighted to report it was a success.

The only place you are allowed to anchor in the atoll is near the shore where the ranger lives, specifically so he can keep an eye on you.

148

The water around the anchorage is colorful: light blue-green near the shore, gradually turning to turquoise, and then changing to sapphire toward the center of the lagoon. It is also crystal clear, which allowed us to see the large number of coral heads. We crossed our fingers as we picked a spot and dropped anchor.

After situating *Kosmos* and getting the hard dinghy down, we headed to shore to check in. There is a small concrete and rock pier jutting out from a small white sandy beach. The sand is laden with small pieces of coral and shell, so shoes are a must. Suwarrow looks exactly like the Tuomotus. The low lying land is dense with foliage, especially coconut trees. We were greeted at the shore by the ranger's four adorable children. The boys escorted us down a narrow footpath through the coconut trees to their home, the only structure on the island.

Technically, we are not supposed to be here since we did not check into the Cook Islands at an official entry port. But we had been told the ranger and his wife turn a blind eye to those who have not checked in. The ranger's wife, Veronica, gave us a three-page list of rules and regulations and reviewed them with us, telling us emphatically that the rules were as much for our own good as for the good of the island.

Wanting to enjoy more time on land, we walked around the *motu*. Like the Tuomotus, some of the shoreline was dark, jagged rock, and some was comprised of big chunks of broken coral and shells. There were a few small stretches of rocky white sand. We spent most of our time walking in the water since the shoreline was so rough. We saw a half dozen baby sharks, two of which were chasing a potential meal that was almost as large as they were, and a school of fish jumping out of the water in unison. There were lots of little lizards around. The view of the ocean, lagoon, and surrounding *motus* was spectacular. Even though this *motu* is one of the largest in Suwarrow, it is tiny; we were done with our walk in an hour.

As we were walking back to our dinghy, Veronica asked us if we would like to go to Bird Island. We said yes! The *motu* we were on is the only one we would be allowed to wander freely—the rest would require us to be escorted by the ranger. We joined four other cruisers, along with the ranger, John, and his family.

As we approached the small *motu*, we saw dozens of birds flying around. We anchored the boat and trudged to shore, and suddenly the sky was filled with literally thousands of birds. Our presence must have scared them. Some of the birds were soaring high, but most were close to the ground. It looked like that famous scene from Alfred Hitchcock's *The Birds*.

Even with thousands of birds in the sky, there were still several hundred birds sitting contentedly on the ground. We were allowed to walk the perimeter of the island, but warned not to go into the bushes, since the sterns lay their eggs directly on the dirt underneath them. Bird Island is all lava rock with a number of bushes and no trees.

We were able to identify several kinds of birds. The most obvious were the frigates. Male frigates have a red pouch on the front of their necks called a gula pouch. Most of the time, it is shriveled up and barely noticeable. During mating season, though, the males puff up their gula pouch, making it disproportionately large—like a big red balloon tied around their little necks. The red pouches look so odd that when we first arrived at the *motu* and saw the males perched in the bushes, I mistook their red orbs for fruit.

The male frigates sit in the bushes, trying to look sexy, and wait while the females circle above them and check out the candidates. Then the female chooses a partner and they mate. After mating, the male gathers twigs and builds a small nest. The female only lays one egg, and she and her mate take turns sitting on the egg while the other hunts for food. Once the chick has hatched, both parents hunt for food to bring back to the chick. After three months, the male flies off to another breeding ground to repeat the process, while the mother and her chick stay behind. The female continues to feed the chick for another eight months before it goes off on its own. Frigates have a longer period of parental care than any other bird.

In addition to frigates, we also identified brown noddy, sotty sterns, and petrels, and saw a number of different species of adorable baby chicks. We saw many nests in the bushes, as well as stern eggs lying on the ground without a nest. It was amazing. Of course, with so many birds flying overhead, we were a bit paranoid about being hit by "bombs." Eric miraculously escaped without a single turd. I was hit with a small one to the left shoulder. We think that we were pretty darn lucky, given the odds.

Saturday, August 4

This morning, we woke up to eighteen-knot winds, swells in the normally flat lagoon, and overcast skies. We were going diving with another cruising couple, and we were nervous. Except for the anchor rescue, we've only dived with a professional. John, the ranger, had warned us that the sharks here are especially aggressive. He said that as long as there's no blood in the water, they will ignore us, so diving should be safe—but knowing there are so many sharks here added another layer of fear and doubt. The bad weather seemed an ominous sign.

The other couple chose a site near the pass. It was a rocky and wet ride, and the closer we got, the more nervous we became. Was it too rough to be in the water? As we were putting on our tanks, though, they told us they have been on eight hundred dives. This was a tremendous relief. *We'll be okay with them,* I thought, relaxing. *They're practically professionals!*

Under the water, it was perfect. We had timed the dive for slack tide, so there was little current. It was just as clear below the water as above. Both Eric and I had some difficulty equalizing, but within a few minutes we were down. The coral here isn't particularly colorful, but the formations are beautiful. We didn't see nearly as many fish as we'd hoped, but there were still plenty to keep us enthralled. The fish here are generally larger than anywhere else we've been. We saw a giant angelfish, a couple of sharks (that fortunately didn't seem interested in us!), an enormous tuna, and a couple surgeonfish doing a mating dance. One particular species of starfish were the highlight for me. Shaped like a five-pointed star, they are a pinky-beige color with a light brown design. They are more than two feet in circumference and puffy. They look like a decorative pillow on a little girl's bed, not a sea animal.

After the dive and back aboard *Kosmos*, we finally saw our first sea turtle swimming nonchalantly through the anchorage. We decided to go snorkeling around the boat. We couldn't believe how great this spot is! There are a few large coral formations under *Kosmos* and a lot of reef fish living there. Unfortunately, we also saw that our anchor chain had gotten wrapped around a coral head And we do mean wrapped around good. Getting out of here is going to be a challenge!

In the evening, we sat outside and watched the stars. It was totally dark outside except for the feeble anchor lights from a handful of boats. The sky had only a few small clouds. The moon didn't rise until midnight. It was ideal for star gazing. There were several millions of brilliant stars in the sky, and we spotted several shooting stars. The Milky Way looked like a long, skinny illuminated cloud. It is hard to believe those millions of stars are always here.

Sunday, August 5

John and Veronica only get supplies dropped off to them once every six months. They have limited refrigeration and their freezer is broken. We were told before we came here that they appreciate perishable foods. Today we traded the last of our fresh produce—a *pampelmousse*, some bananas, an apple, and a bell pepper (capsicum)—for fresh fish fillets. We also gave them some chicken, muffins, bread, and lollipops. Veronica's eyes lit up when she saw the *pampelmousse*, and the kids were excited about the bananas. We couldn't believe that the kids were happier about fresh bananas than lollipops, and it made Eric and I realize that we take produce for granted.

Today, Eric decided to look at our dinghy motor, which hasn't been working right since the dunking. It's not engaging the transmission properly, so he decided to change the transmission gear oil and the regular oil to see if that would help. But it was windy and drops of oil sprayed everywhere, including all over Eric. It was not fun to clean up. After changing the oils, we gave the dinghy a long test ride and realized that the more we ran it, the better it worked. The two horsepower Honda has an automatic clutch that engages at higher RPM. Eric thinks that part of the clutch system was probably wet, and is now drying out.

While we were out, we visited with some other cruisers in the anchorage. One guy, Ian, told us about a friend of his who died a few weeks ago in Bora Bora while spear fishing. It is believed the guy dove too deep and blacked out. Then Ian went on to tell us that he has been spear fishing here in Suwarrow. We were shocked: Spear fishing is strictly prohibited here. John told us that in most places the sharks don't get too riled up over small amounts of blood, but that the sharks here will attack when they smell even a trace of it. Ian said the other day that he had caught a beautiful fish and as he was pulling it in, he saw a shark swimming toward him. He managed to get into his dinghy with the fish before the shark got to them. Yesterday, he went again, but this time the shark got the speared fish and Ian only narrowly escaped. And he plans to do more spear fishing here!

Back at Kosmos, we decided to invite the John and his family over to watch a movie. We thought it would be fun to make it as "authentic" of a movie going experience as possible. We had them watch it in the home theater in our bedroom, which has a big screen and surround sound. We also turned on the air conditioning and served buttered popcorn, both of which are a rare treat for them. We showed *Princess Bride*, which they hadn't seen and seemed to enjoy.

We enjoyed a nice sunset. As the sun dipped below the waterline, the eastern line of the horizon turned aquamarine blue. Above it, the sky was a subtle shade of lavender.

Monday, August 6

Today, we went diving by ourselves, jumping off *Kosmos* and staying in the anchorage. After our last dive, we were feeling fairly confident. More important, we knew that if we had an emergency, help was nearby.

Our first priority was getting the chain untangled. When the wind is strong, the chain is blown taught, making it difficult and dangerous to maneuver. But right now the wind was calm, and we figured that the chain would have some slack. We got into the water and swam down to the coral head. It looked like when we originally dropped anchor, the slack chain had gotten looped under a large coral formation. Then when the wind picked up and the chain got rigid, it must have wedged itself

154

deep into the coral formation. Now, it was tightly embedded. To make matters worse, the chain had broken off a big chunk of the coral, and the broken piece had collapsed onto the rest of the coral head, creating a ledge that trapped the chain. The broken piece was enormous; too heavy for us to lift. To get the chain free, we would have to figure out how to push the broken piece of coral out of the way and how to pry out the embedded chain. Words do not do justice to how bad the situation was.

We pulled and yanked on the chain to no avail. Then we rearranged the chain in other spots to create more slack and pulled again. The chain wasn't moving at all from under the ledge, so Eric went up and got the boat hook. Using the leverage of the hook, he yanked and yanked from every angle until it finally came out.

This is the second time our SCUBA gear has saved us; we never would have freed the chain without going into the water. And our boat hook gets equal credit. It's a good thing we didn't wait any longer to free the chain since it had been rapidly working its way deeper and deeper into the coral. Once it was free, we were able to relax and enjoy the underwater scenery.

We spent a lot of time examining all the little animals that live in the coral. There were several schools of tiny fish that were congregated around a spiky coral formation. They reminded me of butterflies hovering around a white rosebush ready to bud. Some of the tiny fish were aquamarine, some were kelly green, some had black and white zebra stripes, and some had black heads and navy blue bodies with little white tails. There were a ton of oysters, and enormously fat sea slugs. We also noticed a lot of small trigger fish, some grouper and huge butterfly fish, and lots of surgeon fish. We are proud to report that our first "real" dive all by ourselves was a success!

This morning, our cruiser friends Kip and Denise pulled into the anchorage. They announced that today is their wedding anniversary, so John decided to throw a party for them this evening. Veronica made Denise and Kip matching crowns out of palm fronds adorned with a single red flower. The special Polynesian hats added a festive touch to the atmosphere.

Veronica served several Cook Islander dishes, including three kinds of fish. One was battered and deep fried, one was in a curry sauce, and one was wrapped in aluminum and grilled on an Aussie-style grill. All were excellent. She also made delicious, sweet coconut pancakes, which were about an inch thick and deep fried, more like a fritter than a pancake. And she had a date cake for dessert. The bottom layer was made of dates (with pits) and the top layer was light custard. It was tasty, although we had to be careful of the pits.

For beverages, John served green drinking coconuts. When coconuts are green, the husks are full of liquid; as they ripen, they have less and less water inside as the meat forms. John opened the coconuts by hitting them against one another. After a couple strategic hits, the tops popped off, and *voila*, we had fresh coconut water. He made it look so easy.

After we finished eating, John pulled out his guitar and sang for us. He opened with "From This Moment" by Shania Twain for Denise and Kip. Then he played a few rock songs and a few Polynesian songs. The party was so much fun.

Tonight was the perfect example of why we decided to take this journey: We were sitting on an isolated tropical island around a campfire, with the warm wind rustling the coconut trees, the stars shining so brightly it looked like we could almost reach up and touch them, singing songs with a local family that has welcomed us with open arms.

156

It doesn't get any more magical than this.

Tuesday, August 7

Last night, John offered to take us all to a couple of islands farther down the reef, where we could see more birds and snorkel. This morning, almost all the cruisers met at 1000 and loaded into John's boat. It was low tide. We paralleled the reef around Suwarrow the entire ride, and we could see it was a solid land mass. John confirmed that it is possible to walk around the whole atoll on the reef (except for the passes).

We passed several small *motus* before John stopped at a larger one. As we approached, thousands of birds took to the sky. Unlike on Bird Island, these were all sooty stern birds. John explained to us that seafaring birds and their eggs are popular foods among islanders. Many of the species are vanishing from the other islands from over consumption, hence the need for a nature preserve. We walked the length of the *motu* and saw that any spot of ground with enough foliage to hide an egg under was covered with bird eggs.

Then we trudged through knee-deep water to the next *motu*, which is known for its coconut crabs. Coconut crab is a major delicacy in this part of the world and they are rapidly becoming an endangered species on many South Pacific islands. We didn't see any crabs, but a few cruisers in our group did. They said the crabs look like they are part lobster. Later, when John got Eric and I alone, he told us that he would have shown the two of us how to find the crabs, but didn't want to show the group because he was suspicious that certain people in our group would sneak back to catch and eat them.

While the adults were walking around, the four boys were fishing and caught four fish. They are great fishermen.

After we were done walking around the *motu*, John and Veronica surprised us with lunch. They had brought crackers, canned corned beef, and canned spaghetti. They put the corned beef on the crackers and topped it with a generous amount of spaghetti. We are constantly amazed by how generous this family is. They have so little, yet they happily share whatever they do have with all of us.

Once lunch was finished, we loaded into the boat and went to an excellent snorkel site. The coral heads were huge, and were covered in a plant that reminded us of pieces of thin cloth or tissue paper. We think it is the same plant that we saw in Moorea that we said looked like a flower glued to the rock, though in Moorea it was all pink and here it was green with a light pink spot. We saw an enormous napoleon fish, a black tipped reef shark, some parrotfish, a couple of purple pincushion starfish, along with the usual tiny fish that live in the branchy coral, and much more.

When we were done snorkeling, John took us all back to shore. As we were leaving the dock, he asked if Eric and I would like one of the fish. Without thinking, I said, "Sure." He pulled out a whole yellow snapper and handed it to me. Suddenly I realized I was going to have to clean this one all by myself. *It's okay,* I told myself as I held the slimy, scaly fish on the ride back to our boat. *You've done it before, and you can do it again.*

Back on board, I immediately got to work. This fish was bigger and harder to cut than the little squirrel fish we'd had in South Fakarava. I was standing in the cockpit, and as I worked, I threw the guts, scales, head, tail and fins overboard. Only a few minutes into the project, four large sharks began circling the back of the boat. They got so close and passed by so often that I got nervous, envisioning one of them leaping out of the water and landing on the deck to eat me whole, like in the movie *Jaws*. I was relieved when I was done and could retreat to safety inside the boat.

Tonight we had another party, this time to celebrate one of the cruiser's birthdays. We had an Italian themed meal, and the cruisers cooked for John and Veronica. Veronica later told us that it was the first time the cruisers had done all the cooking and that she appreciated the night off. The birthday girl got a crown similar to the one Kip and Denise received for their anniversary party. John played some rock songs for us, and we hung out and chatted.

It was a nice night in a fabulous setting. We can't believe we are really here. It is almost too good to be true.

Thursday, August 9

Yesterday, we went on another dive in the anchorage. It was even more fun the second time around. Last time we were nervous about getting lost, but this time we were more comfortable with our bearings and confident in our ability to navigate back to *Kosmos*. Last time, we were focused on all the new things to look at, this time we took closer looks at the more interesting things. And, we are becoming more confident in our diving skills, which helps us to relax and enjoy the scenery a little bit more.

Later that afternoon while I was taking a nap, Eric visited with some other cruisers. Eric told them that we planned to leave for Niue today, and they advised him to go to Puka Puka instead, since the most promiscuous women are there. When Eric told me about the conversation, I sarcastically said we should change our itinerary. Seriously, why would they say that to a married man traveling with his wife?

This morning I did a quick cleaning on the bottom and waterline before we pulled out. Growth on the sides and bottom slows the boat down, so ideally we like to start our long passages with a clean bottom. I only spent an hour on it, trying to get it "good enough." Neither the waterline nor bottom were too bad compared to last time, but they had enough growth that I will have to work on it some more in Niue.

We were sad as we pulled up anchor. Of all the places we have been to, Suwarrow was definitely the hardest to leave. We really enjoyed our time with John and Veronica and their wonderful four boys. It would have been nice to stay longer, but we need to keep to our schedule.

We were even more depressed when we exited the pass and got into the open ocean. The weather forecast had been five- to eight-foot seas. Eight-foot seas make for an uncomfortable but tolerable ride; we've realized it's about the most we can tolerate, so we were braced for a tough ride.

Unfortunately, the swells have turned out to be six to ten feet at rapid intervals, coming from the aft quarter, with frequent, large wind waves hitting us squarely on the port beam. The combination of seas from the back and from the side is making the ride miserable and the intervals between waves from both directions are painfully short, so we are being perpetually tossed, with no chance to physically and emotionally regroup in between each wave.

The beam waves are especially nasty. They often hit us with so much force that they make a huge thud on the hull. Most of them roll us between ten and twenty degrees to the starboard, and then an additional five to ten degrees to port as Kosmos rights herself. But we are also getting frequent waves that roll us a full thirty-five degrees to the starboard, plus twenty degrees to the port. And now and then we're even hit with a wave so big it rolls us thirty-five degrees starboard, thirty-five degrees port, and another twenty degrees starboard before *Kosmos* is able to correct herself. Those extra big ones are the worst we've ever experienced--truly horrendous.

160

When it is rough like this, we can't do anything. We only walk around the boat when it's absolutely necessary and then we have to hold on with both hands to avoid being thrown against the wall. We've spent most of the passage sitting or laying down. We can't read, use the computer, or watch movies. We tried to watch a movie once and we both got sick only a few minutes into it. On our watches, we sit and stare at the clock, willing the time to move faster. Off watch we lie in bed, whether we're sleeping or not, since that is the most comfortable and secure place to be.

Preparing and eating food is especially challenging. Food in the cabinets and refrigerator come flying at us when we open the cabinet/fridge doors, and I got a good head bonking from a can of soup. We've run out of frozen microwave food, which is by far the easiest thing to pull out (since the freezer is top loading) and prepare. When we do eat and drink, it is only in small quantities. We don't want too much in our stomachs in case it decides not to stay down!

Chapter 12: Niue

Saturday, August 11

After possibly the longest, most miserable forty-five hours of our lives, conditions began to ease up. The waves dropped to four-to-eight feet. The frequency and forcefulness of the nasty beam rolls lessened. The ride went from being unbelievably miserable to just uncomfortable.

One of the downsides of Niue is that it is difficult to anchor there. It is the world's largest raised coral island and stands two hundred feet above sea level, with no real shoreline. The anchorage is deep and rocky, so it is hard for the anchor to set, and you can't put a bunch of chain out to help it set better. There are sixteen moorings in the anchorage and we were advised not to stop in Niue if one was not available. If we arrive on Monday and we can't get a mooring, that means we'll have to keep going to Tonga, which is two days beyond Niue. We know of many yachts that are planning to stop in Niue right about now, so we're worried about being able to get a spot. I think I will have a nervous breakdown if we don't. Honestly, I don't think I can take two more days of this hell.

Sadly, Eric and I have been taking our misery out on one another and have been fighting most of this passage. Neither of us means to fight, but we've both been so absorbed in our own misery that we haven't had any energy to comfort each other, and we both desperately need comforting. The fighting has led to a serious discussion about selling the boat and cancelling our trip.

Before we left, we kept hearing stories about people who circumnavigated and never once hit rough seas thanks to careful weather planning. We thought we could do this, too, but we've come to realize there is a significant difference between us and them: These other people were cruising indefinitely and are not on a timeline. They could wait literally for months for good weather. We have a schedule to keep, so we can't wait for ideal—we have to go whenever the weather is good enough. We've done about 4,900 miles so far, and have about another twenty-four thousand to go. Worldwide, we will spend twenty-five to thirty percent of our time at sea. So far most of our days at sea have been uncomfortable, and I can't foresee it getting any better considering the pace we need to maintain.

I keep telling Eric that I don't want to live in such discomfort for such a big percentage of my life. I want to sell *Kosmos* as soon as possible. Eric is mad at me for wanting to give up the boat. He is just as miserable as I am, but he is more emotionally invested in *Kosmos* and our dream. I've been reminding him that we agreed to travel by boat as long as it was fun, and we are not having fun. Not even close. Of course, this discussion is only making the fighting worse.

Sunday, August 12

As forecasted, the weather slowly improved throughout the day. By mid-afternoon, the wind was down from twenty knots to twelve. The seas actually got bigger at six-to-ten feet, but the waves didn't come as frequently and thus didn't beat us up as badly. The nasty beam waves were less forceful. The ride actually isn't too bad right now. We hope that the improved weather means that a bunch of boats will leave Niue this afternoon, opening up mooring spots for us.

Our trip from Fatu Hiva to Manihi was three days of misery. This trip from Suwarrow to Niue was two days of complete misery, one day of heavy discomfort, and one day of moderate discomfort. We are debating which passage was worse. We're thankful we didn't get these super miserable seas on the twenty-one day passage. Had the seas been any worse, I may have acted on those suicidal thoughts.

With the better seas, we've stopped fighting and have both apologized. We have agreed to wait until Australia to make a decision one way or another about selling the boat. We're also back to our usual passage activities. Today we watched a movie called *The Descent*. Neither of us had heard of it before. It turns out that it is about people who go caving and get eaten by monsters. We can't believe that we happened to see this movie the day before arriving in a place famous for its caves!

Monday, August 13

At around 0400, we heard a boat calling the twenty-four-hour watch station for Niue, aptly named "Niue Radio," for assistance. It was a sailor trying to motor to the mooring area (conditions were poor for sailing). His engine was malfunctioning and was consuming many times the normal amount of fuel; he wasn't sure that he had enough fuel to make it in. The night was cloudy and moonless, making it pitch black with no visibility. What a scary night to have an emergency!

Niue Radio said everyone was still asleep and it would take a while to get help. Since we were only ten miles away from the distressed vessel, *Ragnar*, Eric called and offered to tow it in. Niue was relieved that there was someone close by to help. We increased our speed and changed course. Niue Yacht Club, which handles the moorings and also listens twenty-four hours a day, was monitoring the situation. While we communicated with the two groups regarding *Ragnar*, we were able to start the check-in process and found out that there were indeed moorings available for both our boats. What a relief!

When dawn broke, we were three miles away from the island, but we were still twelve miles south from the anchorage in the main town of

164

Alofi. Until the sun rose, the island had only been pixels on the radar screen. The coastline is comprised of sharp, jagged cliffs, but the tops of the cliffs are a verdant green. It looks like a giant cupcake with green icing. We knew that Niue is only two hundred feet high, but for some reason we were expecting it to be a majestic towering rock. It isn't. It's tall compared to an atoll, but low compared to fringing reef islands like Bora Bora or Tahaa. Maybe it was because we had just come off a rough passage, but the smell of rich, fertile soil was more powerful here than at any place since the Marquesas. I do think it may be the most beautiful smell in the world. How have we taken that smell for granted all our lives?

We reached *Ragnar* shortly after sunrise. The sailor told us he thought he could make it to the anchorage without a tow, but he wanted help getting attached to a mooring since he was unable to maneuver properly. He needed someone with a dinghy in the water to help him get attached. We were relieved we didn't need to tow him in because towing in the open seas can be dangerous, but we stayed alongside him until we got to the anchorage, just in case. At the anchorage, someone was waiting to help him with the mooring.

We had practiced tying to a mooring a couple times before we left, but this mooring was different and I was a little nervous. Moorings are underwater concrete blocks with a floating rope on them. In theory, by tying up to a concrete block, the boat will be securely parked. The end of the rope has a buoy on it. You are supposed to grab the buoy with the boat hook and pull it up to the deck, and then tie the rope to the boat.

I positioned myself at the front of the boat with the boat hook while Eric steered as close as he could to the buoy. After Eric's first pass, it was clear that the hook wasn't long enough for me to reach while standing up and leaning over the railing. So I laid on my stomach on the port side of the boat, with as much of my upper body hanging over the edge as possible to reach the hook closer to the buoy. It wasn't easy to maneuver in such an awkward position. Eric had to make several passes before I could finally grab the buoy with the hook. Pulling the buoy up onto the deck took more physical strength than I had anticipated, and I couldn't do it by myself. Eric had to come out and help me pull the buoy in. Once we were tied up, we were feeling celebratory, both about the passage and the mooring. Yay for us!

We called Niue Radio and told them we had moored and that *Ragnar* was taken care of. Then Niue told us they were ready for us to come to shore to do our customs clearance. That was fast.

There is a small wharf just to the north of the mooring area. From the wharf, there is a steep road leading up the hill to town. The top of the cliff is dotted with buildings. Desperate to get to land, we situated *Kosmos* and deployed the dinghy in record time. We knew we were in for a new experience with dinghy parking. Alofi is an "open roadstead," meaning there is no reef or bay to offer natural protection from the sea's big waves. If we were to simply tie our dinghy up to the quay and walk away, it would likely get damaged. Instead, we had to bring it onto the dock and put it in a dinghy parking lot.

First, we landed our dinghy on a set of steps set into the wharf's slab. After we got out, we pulled the dinghy over to a large crane hook dangling at the sea wall just beyond the stairs. We attached the crane's hook to the dinghy's lifting harness and walked over to the operating lever a few feet away. The crane is supposed to lift the dinghy out of the water onto the wharf so you can carry it to a parking spot. Fortunately, several men were there to help us operate the crane. The procedure was simple, but we would have puzzled through it without someone around to show us the ropes. As we carried the dinghy, we were glad we had opted for a lightweight model.

The customs office was at the top of the hill in a trailer-type building. We filled out some simple paperwork and were checked in within a few minutes. The next stop was immigration, located at the police station a few blocks down the main road. Once again, we filled out a couple of short, simple forms and were done.

The minute the legalities were completed, we went to a small café across from the police station to celebrate our arrival with a big meal. The cafe overlooks the water and has a beautiful view. The breakfast choices were mostly traditional New Zealand fare, such as spaghetti on toast or eggs, ham, sausage, and baked beans. In French Polynesia, the breakfast choices in restaurants are limited and the portions are ridiculously small, so we were thrilled to see hearty meal choices.

After breakfast, we headed to Niue Yacht Club, where we filled out another short, easy form. Keith, who helps to run the yacht club, told that there were only three moorings that weren't strong enough to support *Kosmos*' weight, and we were on one of them. Keith told us to move to mooring one, closest to the wharf, which was the strongest one. We had already been feeling somewhat uncomfortable about how fast we had left *Kosmos*, and this made us even more nervous.

Even so, after several miserable days at sea, we weren't emotionally ready to go back to the boat. So when Keith offered to give us a quick tour of Alofi, we jumped at the chance. While Alofi is bigger than many of the towns we've visited in the South Pacific, we could still walk from end to end in minutes. It reminded us of the main town in North Fakarava, with a nice, paved road lined with a mix of commercial and residential buildings. The inhabited buildings along the road are attractively landscaped, but in and amongst them are some severely damaged, uninhabited buildings, as well as a few lots with only foundation pads indicating where a building once stood.

Keith explained that in 2004, Cyclone Heta completely devastated Niue with three hundred kilometer per hour winds. The waterfront cliffs had been completely built up prior to the hurricane. Since the seaside structures were over one hundred feet above sea level, they were believed to be safe. But the waves managed to crash that high, destroying many of the buildings along the waterfront. The government isn't allowing new construction along the cliff edge. The rest of Niue is still being rebuilt.

After we finished our tour, we spent a few minutes wandering through the town's commercial center, which consists of a bank, a small grocery store, a telecom office, a post office, an Internet office, and a few retail shops that sell an odd variety of things. Eric and I were both so happy to be on shore. Having a few hours of solid ground to stand on more or less erased the misery of the last few days. I think it helps that Niue is difficult to get to by plane, which helps to justify what we had to endure to get here. We decided we were now emotionally ready to go back to *Kosmos*. We needed to move moorings and get properly situated, and hanging out on shore longer than necessary wasn't wise.

We carried our dinghy back to the crane and lowered it with no problems. Picking up the new mooring went smoother than the first time, though it still took a few tries. This time I laid on the starboard side, which worked better since I'm right handed. Once we were secured and situated, Eric deployed the paravanes, which were much needed to dampen the roll in the unprotected waters. Exhausted, we were in bed by 2000.

Tuesday, August 14

It rained all morning, so we weren't in a big hurry to go out. We love when it rains after a passage. Then we don't have to wash all the salt off the boat!

We left around noon, when the rain stopped. Our first mission was to find food. Eric and I checked out one of the cafés. The entire menu consisted of Hawaiian pizza slices, sausage rolls, quiche slices, chicken sandwiches, and ham sandwiches. I opted for the chicken sandwich. It was huge, with lettuce, sprouts, and grated carrot. Eric got some quiche and a sausage roll, essentially a long, thin sausage wrapped in a pastry. When we told the chef how good the food was, she said she had made everything herself that morning, including the bread. Nothing came from a package.

We've been told all the restaurants on Niue have extremely limited menus. There are a few reasons for this: One, since the island is so remote, it only gets deliveries once a month. The locals have to work with what they have on hand. Two, there aren't many people around, so it isn't cost effective to have a lot of choices. In fact, because the island has so few people and so many restaurants, most of the restaurants only open two days a week. By working together that way, each restaurant has two big days of business and five days off. If they all stayed open every day, they would experience seven days of slow business.

Our next stop was the police station to get driver's licenses so we could rent a car. The license is ten dollars (NZD) and they give it to you on the spot. It is an official license and ID card. It lists our address as the motor yacht *Kosmos* and makes a great memento.

Then we went to the main Internet store in the commercial center to check e-mail and load blog posts. The connection was painfully slow.

Shortly after we arrived, the clerk announced she was closing up for the day, so we headed out before we could finish.

In the evening, we went to Jenna's, a local restaurant with a traditional Niuean buffet. It was hands down the best Polynesian food we've had. Every single thing we tasted was good, and the number of dishes they prepared was unbelievable. We had already tried most of the dishes in French Polynesia, but there were some new ones, too,

Starting with the starchy dishes: the national signature dish is taro and papaya in a coconut sauce, which is on the sweet side and a new food for us. We also had boiled taro root, which was bland like boiled potatoes but with a slightly firmer and chewier texture. Next was a kumala salad. Kumala is a type of sweet potato. The dish is basically potato salad with eggs, but kumala tastes better than potatoes. There were breadfruit chips, which look like big potato chips, and are lighter and not quite as crisp as potato chips. For the less adventurous, the restaurant served regular French fries, white bread, and focaccia bread.

In the fruit and veggies category: We sampled a sweet coleslaw with crab, apple, and pineapple. I loved it, and I normally despise coleslaw. There were baked plantains, too, which tasted like bananas. Normally plantains have little flavor, so they must have been sweetened. There was also a cucumber salad.

In the seafood category: We had seared ahi with a pepper crust and accompanying sauce that were both out of this world. We got to try the infamous coconut crab, served in its shell, which was really darn good. There was also raw fish in coconut milk, fried fish, and baked fish.

In the meat category: We had chicken with taro leaves (much better than the ones we had in the Marquesas), small pork meatballs, and curry chicken.

After we had eaten so much we thought we would explode, the desserts came out. There were Tahitian cakes (called something different here) in both banana and pumpkin flavors. There was banana cake with a light creamy frosting. There was a cake that looked like it had a lemon filling, but the filling turned out to be more of a light papaya custard. There was fruit salad and three flavors of ice cream: Neapolitan, vanilla and orange chocolate chip.

We told the lady in charge that her food is the best we've had in Polynesia, and she began telling us how the various dishes are prepared. She said they make it all by hand, and she wasn't kidding. For example, rather than using canned coconut milk, she sends her husband to pick coconuts, grate them, and squeeze the coconut milk. Wow. Cooking is time-consuming enough with shortcuts like bread from the store and canned coconut milk. To make everything from raw ingredients is an overwhelming amount of work! We have no idea how they could possibly prepare so many dishes when each dish is so labor intensive. The most mind blowing thing of all, though, is the restaurant just has a regular house stove/oven combo unit, and only the smaller two burners work on the stove. We are so impressed with those chefs.

Wednesday, August 15

Today we rented a car and went on a tour of the island, heading north. Our first stop was the cave at Avaiki. There, we walked down a steep flight of stairs toward the ocean. At the bottom of the stairs is a large cave we had to walk through to get to the water. The cave is well lit, and we could see most of it from the mouth, but we still carefully checked the darker corners for monsters from the movie *The Descent*.

The cave has lots of interesting stalactite and stalagmite formations. It opens onto the "shoreline," which is actually a narrow limestone shelf.

There is no sand and the water is deep. The water looked turbulent, so we decided swimming was a bad idea.

We walked along the "shore" for a couple minutes, and then noticed another cave. This one had a shallow pool inside. The water was an amazing shade of blue, with small, bright blue demoiselle fish swimming inside. We contemplated getting in for a quick swim, but decided to hit the road instead.

Continuing north, we headed to Limu for snorkeling. We grabbed our gear and walked down a similar staircase to the shoreline. We were almost ready to get in the water at the bottom of the stairs when some tourists on their way out told us there was a better spot a little farther north.

We followed a path and came to a grotto of sorts—a stunningly beautiful pool surrounded by cliff walls on all sides, but with no ceiling. One wall had an arch that we saw people swim under, which led to a similar pool on the other side. In the far pool, ocean waves crashed in, filling it with seawater that flowed into the close pool. In the close pool, a freshwater waterfall of sorts filtered down through the rocky cliff, making the water brackish. The water was crystal clear and we could see the fish swimming inside.

We got in. The water was cold near the freshwater source, got progressively warmer the closer we got to the arch, and was pleasantly warm in the outer pool. We were surprised that under the water, everything looked blurry despite the incredible water clarity. While we could see fish, we couldn't tell what they were; it reminded me of the coating that is popular for shower doors that allows an onlooker to see that a person is in the shower, but blurs enough that the onlooker can't make out any specific body parts. We found out it was caused by the mixture of cold freshwater with warm ocean water. The swim was refreshing, despite the poor visibility, and the unique setting felt incredibly exotic.

Our last stop for the day was Matapa, where we were told we could find a swimming hole, a chasm, and a cave. We went to the swimming hole first. We walked down the stairs and out onto the ledge of the solid rock shoreline, where people were snorkeling nearby. At first we thought they were in the ocean, and were surprised when we realized they were swimming in a large hole in the rock that was probably thirty feet wide and thirty feet deep. We jumped in with them.

The plant life in the swimming hole was fascinating. The bottom was covered in a green plant, and there were some purple plants on the ground, too. On the sides were a different plant altogether that came in green and white. There were a few fish in the hole, including a large parrotfish, and a sea snake that came disconcertingly close to me. I didn't get too worried, though. Sea snakes are the most poisonous creatures on the planet, but they are not aggressive and their mouths are too small to bite humans.

Once we climbed out of the hole, we wandered the shore for a while, looking to see if we could find any more swimming pools. We didn't find any. It was an hour before dark, and we realized it was too late to see the other two sites in Matapa. We decided to keep the car for another day and finish our island tour tomorrow.

Thursday, August 16

This morning we stopped at the bakery and picked up some bread on our way out of town. They had several types of white breads. It was nice to have some choices. In most of French Polynesia, the only bread we could find was plain baguettes, although occasionally we would find coconut bread, which is on the sweet side and yummy.

We decided to head south this time. The first stop was the Ana Ana lookout. We climbed down a short staircase that led to a jagged coral ledge that hung one hundred feet over the water. Of course, we already knew that the island is made of coral and limestone, but the geological significance didn't hit home for us until right then. As we looked at the fossilized coral heads and sea creatures embedded in the ground, we knew there was absolutely no doubt that this ledge was once a healthy, thriving coral reef. Niue is a very, very old island. It started out as a volcanic island, then eroded into an atoll. Tectonic activity pushed the atoll up, transforming the underwater reefs into mountain peaks (which is similar to the way the Himalayas were formed). We clambered carefully over the sharp coral to the edge of the ledge. The wind was strong and the seas were rough. The waves smacked violently against the cliffs below, shooting sea spray high up in the air.

Next we went to Anapala Chasm. We knew the road was located along the backside of a school, but we couldn't find a road that connected to the road we needed. We wound up driving through the school's grass field (school wasn't in session so we didn't run over any children!) and found the dirt road.

The road was barely wide enough for one car. Overgrown bushes scraped the sides of the car, and the ground was rutted out and full of potholes. It was a long drive to the chasm (relatively, given the size of the island). If it weren't for a couple signs confirming we were on the right path, we probably would have turned around. We were relieved when we arrived.

We were expecting Anapala Chasm to be a lovely pool like the one we had swam in the day before at Matapa. As we descended the steep staircase, we were taken aback. Huge waves, probably more than twenty feet tall, were crashing onto the rock ledge. Because of the turbulent water, we couldn't actually see the large hole in the ledge, but we could tell it was at the bottom of the stairs by the abnormal water movement. On each side of the hole, huge amounts of sea spray went flying with each crash, but where the hole was, the water sort of dissipated. There was so much sea foam around the area that the water looked like milk. Swimming would be a death sentence, so we headed out, feeling a bit awed by the power of the seas.

The next stop was Togo, located in the Huvalu Forest Conservation Area. When we first got out of the car, we were in a forest that had a bit of dead coral strewn among the trees. The farther we walked, the larger and denser the coral formations became and the fewer trees there were. The coral formations all had bushes growing out of them, which was kind of strange.

The trees ended at the edge of the cliff, which had a steep staircase carved into it. After descending the staircase part way, we saw another ledge directly below us. This ledge looked just like a mini Bryce Canyon, except the rocky peaks were brown in color and there were some plants growing amongst the dramatic rock formations. Despite being seventy feet above the water and twenty feet from the edge of the cliff, we were consistently sprayed with seawater from the turbulent ocean below.

The staircase turned sharply to the right, so we didn't actually walk down to the Bryce Canyon-like ledge. Instead, the staircase took us another thirty feet or so to a chasm. Much to our surprise, it wasn't filled with water and had sand at the bottom. Someone had used coconuts and flip-flops to write "SOS NIUE." Leaning against the wall was a ladder. Climbing down it was a little intimidating, because it looked like a long way down, but it looked worse than it was. It is a fairly large space, and we quickly realized there was no other way out.

We headed back up the ladder, where we continued to follow the path down. It became more jagged and treacherous, ending at a ledge not far below the chasm entrance. Below us were three large rocks, two of them connected by an arch. It was hard to see the arch because the waves were so tumultuous. On days when the seas are calmer it is probably a lovely natural formation. The third rock had a large hole in the center. When waves crashed on the rock, some of the water would sink into the hole and slowly drain out the bottom.

We decided to cut sightseeing short so we could run a few errands in Alofi before all the stores closed. That night, the yacht club put on a barbecue for the cruisers. They grilled sausage and fish, and had sides of salad and "wedges." The wedges were a mix of fried taro root, kumala, and arrowroot (another potato like root). They tasted like potato wedges and were good.

Friday, August 17

Niue is a popular dive destination because of its incredible water clarity. Since the island is made of porous limestone, the rainwater simply seeps through the rock into the ocean rather than forming streams and rivers. Without rivers, there is no soil runoff to cloud the ocean water. It is the water running through the limestone that has carved out all the amazing caves and gullies around the island, both on land and underwater.

Eric signed up to go on two dives today. They only allowed certified divers, so I couldn't go. The first one was right off the coast. It was a leisurely, simple dive, but Eric said the scenery was actually a bit disappointing, without much coral or fish. Apparently, the coral used to be better, but it was destroyed in Cyclone Heta. Even before the cyclone, though, there weren't many fish. Without soil runoff to bring nutrients into the water, Niue can't support a robust sea life population.

Eric's first dive was a warm up for the second dive at Snake Gully. At first Eric thought the name meant the gully would be a narrow, winding shape. But the gully is so named because of its high concentration of sea snakes. The snakes go there to rest. They swim from the surface and back down every hour or so because they breathe air. Sea snakes are bolder than fish and will swim right next to you. They'll even let you touch them. At one point, Eric saw five snakes right in front of him, three heading up to the surface, and two heading down.

Eric was fine with the snakes, but he was worried about the next part of the dive, where the gully becomes two deep, dark caves. The dive master had assured Eric that this would be an easy introduction to cave diving, so Eric had decided to give it a try, but he was still leery. Remember, Eric gets nervous when there is not bright light and good visibility.

The first cave wasn't too bad. It had a few overhead holes that provided light, and he only needed the flashlight to see inside the crevices where lobster and small fished lived. It was a big cave and everyone went in it at the same time. The second cave was another story. It was small, completely enclosed, and pitch black. Only three people could go inside at a time, including the guide, and he needed flashlights to see anything at all. Eric was in there for about three minutes and saw large lobsters and a few fish. He found the small cave disconcerting and felt a bit panicky, but not enough that he needed to rush out. The dive concluded with a trip through some canyons near the shore. There were holes with bunches of sea snakes in them. Overall it was exciting and different than anything Eric had done before. While he was proud of himself for facing his fear, he said he's going to stick with well-lit, open water diving from now on.

Eric and Gisela arrived yesterday and this evening, the four of us went to Jenna's for fish and chips night. The lady in charge remembered our names and asked if we were still planning to leave on Monday afternoon. Wow, talk about making us feel special! Everyone here has been amazingly friendly and kind. Since only 1,200 people live in the country, they know who the tourists are, and the locals go out of their way to make us feel welcome. In fact, everyone, and I mean everyone, waves and smiles when they see us in passing. We think this may be the friendliest place we have ever visited.

Saturday, August 18

This morning we awoke early to go to a festival in the town of Lakepa on the other side of the island. Eric and Gisela joined us. Several people had told us to be at the festival by 0730 or 0800 to get good food, and that it would be over by noon. We have noticed that in Polynesia, they tend to get an early start on the day. All the farmer's markets begin at or before dawn and are over by 0800, which is why we have never gone to one.

The festival took place in a large grassy area. We noticed there was a tent with a group of chairs underneath. The front rows were occupied by what we assumed to be the island's elders. Each of them gave a long speech in Niuean. It looked to us like everyone in the crowd completely ignored the speeches. Since we didn't understand a word, we also focused on the other activities that were going on while the speeches were underway.

There were a dozen food booths spread around the perimeter. Most of the booths had similar food choices: barbequed meats accompanied by taro. Eric and I got a barbeque plate to share. It was piled high with sausage, steak, chicken, curried whole shrimp (including heads and little beady eyes pleading with us not eat them), fried fish, and large pieces of boiled taro. The fish was fishy, but everything else was good.

We found a booth that was selling coconut porridge, a traditional Niuean breakfast food, served in a coconut half shell. The broth was clear and had the consistency of egg drop soup. There were lots of chunks of cooked coconut and some chunks of cooked arrowroot. The arrowroot was chewier than the coconut. Not surprisingly, it tasted just like coconut. We got some banana cake and another dessert with a layer of white cake, a layer of custard, and a fruit topping. Neither was very sweet. We also saw a lady making coconut crab the traditional way, using an old fashioned stove. She wrapped the crab in coconut leaves and put it above a pot of boiling water to steam the crab.

Aside from the food, there were vendors selling produce, wooden carvings, embroidered bed and window coverings, and dried flower arrangements. We saw a truckload of baby pigs and several large coconut crabs tied up to the booths like pets. There were two carnival games as well. The first one consisted of throwing a metal ball into circles painted on the grass. The second one had participants use a golf club and a small wiffle ball to hit a mark roughly twenty yards away. This was especially tough since the wind was blowing the other way. For the kids, there was an astro jump.

After the elders were finally done speaking, a javelin throwing competition began, which also didn't garner much interest from the crowd. When that ended, the dancers came out, which seemed to be the main event everyone was waiting for. There were approximately ten dancers that ranged in age from about two to twenty; each did several dances. The Niuean dances are slower than the ones in French Polynesia, closer to the Hawaiian style of dancing. The music they played was more of an upbeat reggae than the pounding, rhythmic music we heard in French Polynesia.

After the dancing, the fair seemed to be over, so we went looking for more caves. We had heard that on Niue there is a guide named Tali that takes people on "amazing" cave tours. Tali only conducts tours on Wednesdays, so we had missed our opportunity to go with him. But our tourist map had marked the spots on Tali's tour, so we decided to go see these amazing caves on our own.

We drove up and down the main road three times before finding the small, unmarked turnoff. It was another overgrown road, but this time it was short. The road turned into a footpath that we followed for a good ways. The scenery was similar to Togo, beginning with dense trees and a little coral and ending with denser coral and fewer trees. The path let out at another Bryce Canyon-like cliff, though this one wasn't as dramatic as the one at Togo. Then the path just ended. We knew we were probably standing on top of the cave, but we couldn't find the entrance. Caves are harder to find than you'd think!

We gave up and went on to the next destination, Uluvehi, where the outrigger canoes landed in the old days. After getting lost on bad roads that probably significantly shortened the life of the rental car, we finally found it. Uluvehi was a bit of a letdown. In the side of a cliff were a couple of large caves that were similar to cave at Avaiki we'd seen on Wednesday. A few outrigger canoes were housed inside them.

Our next stop was Matapa. We had finally, after three days, had circled the island. The entrances to the two sites we wanted to visit were side by side, each one a footpath leading a different direction. We went to the arches first, since it was a longer walk. We figured we'd cool off after the hike in the water at the chasm.

The sign for the arch said it was an easy 15 to 30 minute walk, but we found the jagged rocks and uneven ground to be harder to traverse than advertised. The trail ended at the mouth of a cave where you could see a chasm below and three large arches gracing the shoreline in the distance. It was gorgeous. There were a couple more caves higher up in the cliff walls, so Gisela and I scaled up the rocks to one of them and explored inside. We could easily see a tribe of people happily living in these caves. Talk about a great view!

Once we emerged from the arches trail, we headed down the chasm trail. A short hike, it ended at what looked like a crack between two cliffs. The cliff walls were one hundred feet tall, and the gap was about fifty feet wide and a couple of hundred feet long. It looked as if we could swim beyond the chasm into another protected coral pool similar to the one at Lima. We had planned to go snorkeling, but at this point we were pooped. We had gotten up early and done a lot of hiking. There were a few locals there and they said it was a nice snorkel, but that there were better spots on other parts of the island, so we didn't feel bad about skipping this one. We sat at the chasm for a while, enjoying the view and relaxing before heading back to our respective boats for the night.

Monday, August 20th

Yesterday we went SCUBA diving with Eric and Gisela at a spot Keith told us about called the Chimney. Not far from the mooring field is an underwater cliff. The top of the cliff is thirty feet below sea level and it bottoms out at one hundred feet. In the middle of the cliff is a hole, or vertical cave. He told us it had a narrow opening at the top that widens at the bottom, with a mouth to exit from, hence the name. When he first mentioned it, we didn't think we could go. It is an advanced dive--totally out of our league. However, Eric and Gisela are certified rescue divers, so we talked them into going with us.

From the surface, the opening looked like nothing more than a small crack We wondered if a person could really fit through there. We all descended to thirty feet together, and the other Eric went in first to check it out. He disappeared into the hole, and the three of us intently watched the crack, expecting him to pop up and give us the all clear. We were all surprised when he snuck up behind us. He had gone down through the "chimney," out the mouth at the bottom, and come back to us from the outside.

Gisela and I descended into the chimney. I was having a tough time equalizing and made my way down extremely slowly while Gisela waited patiently at the bottom. This gave me an opportunity to examine the interesting purple plant growing on the walls, as well as the fish. Thanks to the amazing water clarity, there was plenty of light, even in such a narrow passage.

My Eric could not bring himself to go into another cave, so he and the other Eric descended on the outside and met us at the mouth. Just outside the mouth was an old Jeep that had been washed into the water during Heta. Of course, we all took turns pretending to drive it. We were 102 feet below, which is by far the deepest either Eric or I have ever gone.

Everything was fine until it was time to come up. I ascended way too fast, and I couldn't seem to control it. Coming up too fast can lead to serious medical problems, such as decompression sickness and lung damage—even death. A slow ascent, especially from such depths, is critical. Fortunately, the other three kept me out of danger by holding on to me and pulling me down.

After diving, the two of us went to dinner at Willy's Washaway Café, which is about the only thing open on Sundays. Our choices were a hamburger or a fish burger. We got one of each. The fish burger came on focaccia bread. The hamburger was topped with beet root and an egg fried over medium. Both were excellent.

We left Niue at sunset today, so we spent the day going through our usual "getting ready to go" routine. We took the computer to an Internet source to check email and send blog updates to Mike. We went to customs and immigration to check out. We checked out with the yacht club and paid for the mooring. And we went to the grocery store to stock up on food. The only premade frozen dinner choice was meat pies, so we loaded up on them. Meat pies are similar to chicken pot pies, but with thicker sauce and no vegetables. Then we headed back to *Kosmos* and got her ready to go.

The seas have been okay so far. The waves aren't very big, only three to four feet, but they are hitting at quick intervals, so it is still rocky. We're not getting any evil side waves, though, so as far as we are concerned, that makes life good.

We almost hit a buoy tonight that didn't show up on the radar screen. A buoy out in the middle of the ocean is unusual; we figured it must have been there for some research project. Thank goodness we actually scan the horizon every fifteen minutes. If we relied on the radar, we would have plowed into it. We also avoided some other debris in the water. Debris is usually harmless if hit, but there is a slim chance it might be something that could cause damage to the hull or propeller, such as fishing nets or shipping containers. So, we try to avoid it whenever we see it.

The meat pies have turned out to be good passage food. They are hearty but not too big, and we can eat them with just a fork and a small plate. I think it's funny that my definition of what constitutes "good food at sea" is radically different from "good food on land."

On another note, some of our friends are worried about our safety in Tonga because of the political unrest that occurred last year when the king died. Violence had broken out in the capitol city, Nuku'alofa, as people demanded that the new king give the people more say in the government. The unrest never spread to the other islands, and seems to have died down. Since there has never been any kind of unrest in Vava'u, where we are going, we believe it is safe.

Chapter 13: Vava'u, Vava'u Islands, Tonga

Thursday, August 23

Conditions weren't too bad during our passage to Vava'u. At some point last night we crossed the International Date Line. We had left Niue at 1400 (6:00 p.m.) on Monday, and 39.5 hours later, on Thursday at 0930, we arrived in Tonga. We skipped Wednesday altogether!

By the time the sun rose, we were already within view of two of the islands. (Yes, we like to arrive at sunrise whenever possible.) In Tonga, the islands are so close together that you can always see multiple islands at once. From the distance they look similar to Niue in terms of height and foliage, but these islands don't have nearly as many sheer cliffs.

We turned into the pass between the two islands and wove through a maze of small islands to Neiafu, the main town on Vava'u. As we came into view of Neiafu, we could see a large wharf lined with big commercial buildings of corrugated metal. We pulled up to the wharf and went into the customs office, which was located in one of the metal buildings. Customs then told us to wait at the boat. A few minutes later, four large Tongan men boarded from customs, quarantine, and health. The paperwork was simple and took only a few minutes.

While we were waiting for the immigration officer, an older man named Alofi came by in a small boat with an outboard motor. He was selling jewelry and invited us to a traditional Tongan feast he was putting on that evening. We had read about Tongan feasts; one of our guidebooks said they are incredible and to never turn one down. Alofi promised lots of food and was very pushy. Tired from the passage, we said yes before we found out the price: thirty dollars each! It seemed high, but he was relentless and promised so much that we agreed. Alofi asked for a soda and invited himself inside. After a quick look around, he told us he would meet us at the dinghy dock at 1700 and took off.

Shortly thereafter, the immigration officer arrived. He also had simple forms and was done in a few minutes. We left the dock and picked up a mooring in the mooring field/anchorage near the wharf. By the time we got *Kosmos* situated, it was time to go to the feast. When we went outside to get into our dinghy, we were shocked to see Alofi was waiting for us in a different boat altogether. He had sweet talked a cruiser into bringing him to us so he could make sure we were really coming. The fact that he had pushed his way inside *Kosmos* earlier and was so eager to make sure we left the boat made us nervous. Was he setting us up to be robbed? We made sure everything was locked tight.

We were under the impression that many people would be at this "feast," but when we got into the minivan, it was just the two of us. No one else was coming. We went to Alofi's house and were seated on a mat on the floor. We were given only a fork--no knife or napkins. His grown daughter brought out a plate of food for each of us with a piece of fried chicken, fried fish, a pork rib, two hot dogs, and some fried plantains. Since we didn't have a knife, we had to use our hands, which was messy with no napkins. She also served a big plate of whole lobster for us to share. Alofi cracked the lobster for us, and I was disgusted that he was handling my food with his unwashed hands. He also gave us the portion of the tail with the bladder gunk and expected us to eat it, saying it was good. For dessert, we received a small bowl of sliced papaya in coconut milk and a small bowl of bananas in coconut milk. The food was mediocre, and there was definitely not as much variety of food as Alofi had promised. He had also made it sound like there was going to be unlimited beer, but he provided only one each.

Alofi ate with us while his daughter watched. He spent the entire meal trying to sell us stuff: Jewelry. Clothing. Fruit. Bread. Powdered beer. Flags. Tapa art. Tours around the island. Laundry services. The church music that was playing on his CD player. Between the second-rate food and the pushy environment, it was a bad experience. We were eager to get out of there. Eric agreed to get the powdered beer to get Alofi off our backs. Alofi threw in two string necklaces with a little plastic turtle pendant for free.

We had to walk back to *Kosmos*, which really irked me since he'd said transportation was included in the price. There were a lot of dogs, pigs, and chickens roaming the streets. On the way, we stopped by the open air market, where locals sell both fresh produce and handicrafts. As it turned out, the powdered Tongan beer we'd purchased from Alofi was really kava. We had suspected as much, but Alofi had adamantly denied that it was kava. We were mad when we realized we had paid him quadruple the going price.

Kava is a popular beverage in most of the Pacific Islands, though you don't see much of it in French Polynesia. It is an anesthetic and analgesic, a mild tranquilizer, an antibacterial and antifungal agent, a diuretic, appetite suppressant, and a soporific. Needless to say, it has a drug-like effect when it is ingested. Kava is made by grinding up the roots of the kava plant (a species of the pepper family) and mixing the grounds with water.

Much to our joy, *Kosmos* was exactly as we left her. Phew! Eric tried the kava and didn't like it. I wouldn't touch it. It looked and smelled disgusting.

Friday, August 24

Last night on our walk back from Alofi's, we picked up a pamphlet specifically for cruisers. This morning we flipped through it, trying to figure out what to do today. The first thing it said was to beware of salesmen who approach your boat when you first arrive. Clearly, Alofi hangs around the wharf waiting for new arrivals so he can be the first to get hold of them. Too bad the customs guys didn't hand us this pamphlet when we checked in!

We decided to get breakfast and then wander around town. As we were walking out the door, Alofi rowed up in yet another boat. This time he had an entire stalk of bananas, some limes, and some bread to sell us. Eric told Alofi we were aware of his outrageously high prices and offered to trade him the kava he sold us for the bananas. We had seen the going price for bananas and knew the number of bananas he had matched what we had paid for the kava.

Eric handled the negotiation well, essentially tricking Alofi into admitting he had overcharged us for the kava, and then backing him into a corner. "Do you want to get rid of your perishable bananas and get your non-perishable kava back?" Eric pressured him. "Cause it's the kava or bananas. What will it be?"

Alofi reluctantly agreed, so now we have a five-gallon bucket of green bananas.

We found a place that serves American style breakfasts, which we enjoyed. After eating, we wandered up and down the town's main drag, which didn't take long. The streets were teeming with cars and pedestrians. Neiafu feels more third world than any place we've visited in French Polynesia. There is no graffiti or trash around, but it certainly doesn't feel clean and modern. There doesn't seem to be much in the way of nice landscaping. Many buildings are in need of serious repair.

While wandering around, we ran into a couple that we had met in Niue, and they invited us to join them for dinner. We went to an upscale restaurant. We ordered tuna, which came with salty green papaya slices, and taro hash browns, which taste like regular hash browns. For dessert we got a banana in a cinnamon sauce with vanilla ice cream. The food was great.

Sunday, August 26

Yesterday we spent much of the day doing boat chores. Eric changed the oils and fuel filters in the main engine and generator, and the air filter on the generator.

We did go out to lunch at a small café. On the menus here, hamburgers usually come with fried eggs and a choice of potato, kumala, or taro fries. Lunch was served with a citrus fruit called kola. Kola has green skin, is about the size of a lemon, and has orange meat. It is sour and tastes like a cross between a lemon and a lime. We also went to the Austrian bakery, which sells multigrain, whole wheat, and rye bread. After so many months of only white bread, it was exciting to have other choices. We got whole grain bread. It's so dense that we may use it as a secondary anchor!

Today we decided to hike to the top of Mt. Talau. The round-trip walk from the dinghy dock to the peak is about four miles. The top of the mountain is only 131 meters, so it didn't sound too strenuous. By law everything in Tonga is closed on Sundays, so the main drag was deserted.

We found the road that would take us to the hiking trail. The road was paved most of the way up. We passed six churches on the road, each with beautiful singing wafting from the windows. Most of the houses along the road looked small and weather beaten, with just one or two fenced yards. There were a lot of pigs roaming around.

The asphalt ended and we continued trudging up the dirt road. We could still hear the singing, making the walk seem somehow surreal. It felt like we were characters in a movie, and unbeknownst to the characters (us) there was going to be some crazy religious experience at the top of the mountain.

We found the hiking trail near where the road crested. The trail was steep, taking us over rock similar to the coral in the forest in Niue. There were a lot of trees and bushes at the top, but there wasn't the thick and tightly packed foliage that we had seen in French Polynesia. We could still hear small snatches of singing carried on the wind, but Jesus never descended from the sky to give us a prophetic message.

The guidebook said there were four viewpoints, but we only found three. They were all pretty. We could see the Neiafu harbor, several outlying islands, and the ocean in the distance. We could also see rain clouds coming, so we didn't linger. We hurried back to *Kosmos* and made it back just as the rain hit.

Tuesday, August 28

Yesterday while Eric visited with the other boaters in the anchorage, I started a SCUBA certification class. Vava'u is the perfect place for me to get certified. The water is warm and clear; the instructor is a native English speaker; and with the favorable exchange rate, the price is good. The first day of class consisted mostly of lecturing with a couple hours in shallow water practicing basic skills. The instructor chided me when he looked in my logbook and saw the dive in Suwarrow to seventy-two feet and the one in Niue through a cave to 102 feet. Even after I get this certification, I'm not supposed to go in a cave or go deeper than sixty feet. Both require an additional certification.

Last night we had another especially beautiful sunset. In all the islands, they burn trash and brush, so every day we see at least one small fire. Last night, there was an especially smoky fire that made the sky appear incredibly pink.

Today there was more lecture time and practice in the shallow water, followed by a dive in the harbor. The coral in the harbor was probably spectacular at one time, but now it is mostly dead, with only a few spots of color and few fish. We did see a lot of bright blue starfish and a few small versions of the puffy pink starfish Eric and I had seen in Suwarrow. We saw a manta ray, too.

Meanwhile, Eric did two dives with a local company. The first was Tonga's signature dive, known as Split Rock. The first stop was at a cave. Eric was a bit nervous going inside, but he made it in just fine. It was not completely dark inside, but flashlights did help. There were three sharks, each between two and three feet long, hovering at the bottom of the cave. Getting eaten alive by sharks in a dark cave is probably one of Eric's worst fears, but with several other divers in there with him, he managed to stay calm. After all, if the sharks got hungry, he could easily push a couple other people towards the sharks then swim away. From there, the group went through a massive underwater arch and around to a huge rock that was split down the center. Some of the group actually swam into the large crack to look around, but it was narrow and only a few people could fit inside. Since Eric is not comfortable going in tight spaces, he was happy to be part of the group that didn't go in. There were quite a few fish around the rock, including a massive napoleon fish.

The next dive was called Five Fingers, which followed the hand-shaped coastline along one of the islands. At the start of the dive, Eric saw a ghost coral—so named because the coral turns from dark brown to a ghostly white when you touch it. In two of the fingers, there were long tunnels within the reef, where they actually were surrounded on all sides by coral formations. The tunnels were just wide enough to fit a diver. Fortunately, the tunnels each had a crack in their ceiling that let in some light. It was a bit tight at times; at one point the dive master actually had to help the divers get through an especially narrow spot. Eric didn't care for the tight squeeze, but he still thought the tunnels were exciting since they are so different from his previous dive experiences.

Thursday, August 30

Eric spent the entire day yesterday doing boat chores. He changed the pre-filter on the water maker, cleaned the sea strainer, and changed the generator impellor. He did some general reorganizing and cleaning. He also secured the toaster oven and dish drainer so they wouldn't go flying when we get hit by a big wave; and re-ran some wires so we could move our computer gear to better locations.

Yesterday was my last SCUBA class. I took the written final exam and did three dives in other parts of the harbor. I passed with flying colors! After three days of being in the sun with my mask on, I'm now sporting mask tan lines that make me look like a raccoon.

Our friend Adrienne flew in this morning from San Diego, arriving a bit early to our rendezvous site. She was waiting patiently when a local man asked if she needed help. She said she was waiting for *Kosmos* to come and get her. He replied that he knew who we were and offered to give her a ride to our boat. Adrienne assumed we were famous in town. Of course, she didn't realize the man was my dive instructor!

192

Adrienne lucked out because she arrived just before the rain began. It poured most of the day. We braved the rain and went out to eat for both lunch and dinner. Interestingly, we've noticed that every restaurant we have been to except one has been run by *pelangi* (white people), rather than Tongans. The menu choices are almost the same as at home. The most exotic thing we've seen on the menus has been a lobster burger.

Adrienne's reaction to the food made us realize that we've been away from home so long that we now take the food for granted. She kept oohing and aahing over her burger, made with fish caught a few hours ago and freshly baked rolls. Food in the South Pacific tends to taste better than at home because the ingredients are fresher.

On a side note, I think I've been jinxed. Over the last few days, practically everything I've touched has broken, including two cameras, my electric toothbrush, and my SCUBA regulator. Fortunately, Eric thinks he fixed the regulator, and Adrienne brought us a new camera. We know that electronics don't have a long life on a boat—they can't take the heat, humidity, and rocking—but it's kind of crazy to have things die after only four months!

Friday, August 31

Today we went on a kart tour around the island. The karts are little open two-seater cars, sort of like dune buggies. We drove for quite awhile along paved roads, getting a good look at some of the villages around the island. The towns we passed through consisted of a shop or two, a few large churches, and several homes—some large, but most small, almost all in need of repairs.

Much of the land along the road was cleared, with little wild vegetation. The pavement abruptly ended, and suddenly we were off-roading on a dusty, narrow, overgrown road similar to the ones we'd been on in Niue. We zoomed through the dense forest for a bit before emerging at a viewpoint on the east side of the island. Standing at the top of a steep cliff, we looked down on the water. The cliff was dotted with jagged lava rock, similar to the coral rock on Niue. The shoreline also had a layer of flat rock that dropped off suddenly, though the shelf wasn't as large as it was in Niue.

We headed through the forest again. After a while, the forest abruptly gave way to a grass field with several coconut trees. We stopped at our second ocean viewpoint, also on the east side of the island, where a dramatic cliff jutted out into the water. It had a large oval hole in the middle of it.

We hopped back into the karts, passing some taro plantations before we were back in the jungle. The road was pretty rutted out, and the kart in front of us lost control a couple of times. Fortunately, Eric is an experienced off road driver and had no problems maintaining control.

Our third stop was at a beach in a small inlet. We parked on the grass and made our way to the shore where we saw the remains of a nightclub that was destroyed in a cyclone. Like most of the other sandy spots we've been to in the South Pacific, the sand was littered with small, sharp shells and coral pieces, so we didn't take off our shoes.

Our last stop at another viewpoint overlooking some small inlets. It was the prettiest lookout, with a view of several fingers of land sticking out into the ocean and many gradations of color to the water.

After the last stop we were only on dirt tracks for a couple of minutes before turning onto paved roads that took us through the town of Neiafu and back to the kart rental shop. As we were leaving, we noticed some cruiser friends having lunch at the restaurant next door. We went in to say hi and introduce Adrienne. Inside, I took off my sunglasses and the women at the table started giggling. I immediately knew that my face was completely covered in dirt except for the area protected by my sunglasses, exaggerating my already funny looking mask tan. Great.

Since we were all covered in dirt, we did the logical thing and walked across town to go to the market. The locals must have been appalled. As we were heading back, the rain began again, turning the dirt into mud. We took especially long showers after returning to *Kosmos*!

Saturday, September 1

Every winter, humpback whales visit both Tonga and Niue to mate and bear their young. Both countries allow people to swim with the whales if they are with a licensed professional whale watch company, but they strictly prohibit boaters from chasing after the whales alone. In Niue it is easy to control the boaters since there are so few visitors, but it is harder here in Tonga. Since we haven't had any luck seeing whales on our own, we decided to go out with the professionals today.

We woke up to gray skies and a weather forecast of eleven-foot seas at eight-second intervals and twenty-five knots of wind. We were disappointed, since we'd been told that the whales leave Vava'u when the weather is bad, returning when conditions are better. Had we not already paid, we may have cancelled since this seemed an unlikely day to see the whales.

Our whale watch boat picked us up from *Kosmos*. There were about a dozen passengers and three crew members. We headed through the maze of islands toward the sea. While we were still in the channel, the crew spotted a whale, so they stopped the boat for a few minutes. The whale seemed to be alone and traveling, so it didn't put on a good show for us. It was hard to see—we were impressed that the crew was able to spot him!

We continued out to the ocean, where the crew spotted a group of whales. This time there were three—two adults and a baby—and they seemed to just be hanging out. Much to everyone's surprise, one of the whales leaped out of the water, its entire body in the air. We watched this family for quite a while. The boat we were on was really fast, making it easy to follow the whales as they swam around the area. We saw at least seven or eight breachings and several nice views of the tails as the whales dove down. They put on an impressive show. I was hoping to get in and swim with the whales, but the captain said the water was too rough.

Since we were on a planing boat, we were bouncing along pretty hard. The captain decided to break for lunch and took us to a calm anchorage nearby to eat. As soon as we stopped, it began to pour. I doubted that we would be able to swim with the whales since the weather was rapidly worsening.

After a half hour or so we headed back out. This time the captain stayed within the maze of islands. It was still rough, but not as bad as in the ocean. The crew spotted some more whales—again two adults and a baby—though this trio didn't perform for us like the last family had. To my delight, the captain told us we could get in. I went for it, but Eric decided that swimming with whales was too much for him given his fear of sea monsters. As soon as the first swimmer got in the water, though, the mother and baby immediately dove deep and had disappeared by the time I got in, forty-five seconds later. Sometimes the whales will stay still and watch you watching them, but we didn't get so lucky. However, I did get a long look at the male.

Once the male dove deep, we all got back on the boat. The next time the family came up for air, the boat pulled up to them and the swimmers jumped back in. Adrienne hadn't gotten to go in last time, so she was one of the first in the water. Again, mama and baby immediately dove deep, and we both missed seeing them, but I got to watch the male as he floated directly underneath me for a long while. Unfortunately for Adrienne, one of the side effects of the scopolamine patch (seasickness medicine) that she's using is that it causes blurred vision. Whales are surprisingly hard to see underwater. With Adrienne's blurred version, she could hardly see the whale.

After a few minutes, the swimmers were called back to the boat. We repeated the process two more times. Since Adrienne couldn't see, she didn't get in again, but I went all four times. The last time we floated above the baby as it lingered in the water. During the last round, while most of the group was swimming, Eric, Adrienne, and the others still on board were treated to three more breaches right in front of the boat, so they were glad they didn't get in.

We came away with a much better understanding of how to find the whales. They are hard to spot both above and below water, and if you don't know what you are looking for you can easily miss a whale that is right next to you. We are hoping to see some on our passages now.

As soon as we got back to *Kosmos*, we took showers and got ready for the next exciting event of the day: a real Tongan feast. This time we used a booking agent. She told us that private families put on these feasts, so the quality varies based on who is hosting, but that the family she booked us with was usually good. She assured us that Alofi is an anomaly and no one else would try to sucker us.

It was still raining, cold, and gloomy. The taxi ride to Ano Bay took about ten minutes, and the taxi driver warned us the feast was outdoors. When the taxi pulled up, we saw a large lean-to on the beach, consisting of a metal roof held up by tree branches. Towards the back of it were a few picnic tables, and at the front, several women were selling handcrafts, mostly baskets and *tapa* cloth paintings. There was a similar, smaller hut nearby, where the cooking was going on. On a nice day it was probably a lovely setting with the hut, beach, and bay, but in the heavy rain it felt somewhat foreboding.

The festivities started out with three men singing Tongan songs. They were sitting on mats on the ground, with two playing guitars and one a banjo. Tongan music is slower and more melodic than what we heard in Niue or French Polynesia, and is closer in style to Hawaiian music. In front of them was a bowl of kava, which looked like muddy water. They instructed us to come forward one at a time for a drink. They used a half coconut shell as a ladle and scooped a small amount of kava into another half coconut shell for us to drink from. I thought it tasted like dirty sock water. Kava is an herbal drug, but we had such small amounts that we didn't feel any effects.

After everyone partook in the kava, the dancing began. The dancers were all schoolchildren—two boys and five girls. Their outfits looked Hawaiian, with grass skirts, flower leis, and flowers in their hair. The female dances were slow and gentle. In each dance, the girls told a story using arm and hand gestures, with few lower body movements. It was totally different from the French Polynesian dances with non-stop hip gyrations. The boys' dances were a subdued version of the ones we'd seen in French Polynesia--still mimicking hand to hand combat scenes, but without all the squats and jumping around. During the male dancers' routine, someone drummed a pounding beat on a steel piece of roofing, but the drumming was accompanied by soft guitar/banjo music instead of the fast, vibrant music that matched the pulsating beat. Even though it was still raining on and off, quite hard at times, the kids just danced away.

After the dancing, it was time to eat. The family had put down tablecloths of big banana tree leaves and covered almost the entire surface of the tables with assorted foods, with small quantities of each dish scattered up and down the tables. They explained that in the Tongan tradition, they eat on the floor without plates or silverware. They put the food on tables for our comfort, but weren't giving us regular plates, silverware, or napkins. Thank God Adrienne had some moist wipes with her!

All the food was apparently cooked in an *umu*, an oven inside the ground. The host led us in prayer and we dug in. Sitting directly on the banana leaves were chunks of beef; large pieces of breadfruit; green papaya halves stuffed with watermelon and banana; whole bananas; and slices of watermelon. A few items were served on individual-sized "plates"—rough containers made from natural plants and trees, such as a piece of bamboo cut about four inches long and split lengthwise. On the "plates" were fried fish; a seafood salad with cabbage and heavy mayonnaise; and a dish that looked like chopped suey with cabbage, carrot, and a mystery meat. I thought the mystery meat was lamb, Eric voted for chicken, and Adrienne believed it was chicken liver. None of us cared for the mystery meat. I didn't like the fried fish, but Adrienne and Eric thought it was okay.

There were a few half-coconut shells, all containing a papaya, banana, and pineapple dish. We expected the dish to be sweet, but it had a strong smoky flavor. There were also lots of small taro leaf packages on the table containing hot foods. They were fun to open because we had no idea what we would find inside; it was like opening a present. We tried spongy banana bread in coconut milk (that looked like fish); chicken wrapped in taro leaves with coconut milk; clams on the half shell; and a sweet dish similar to banana Tahitian cakes. I loved the spongy banana bread and the chicken in taro leaves, but Adrienne didn't like either of them and Eric wasn't crazy about the chicken. We all loved the clams, though.

We've noted the dishes that we liked most and least, and everything else that we didn't specifically mention got a good rating by all three of us. All in all, we were pretty impressed with the spread. Even after all our feasting, there was a ton of food left. Someone told us that the people from their village would come and finish off all the food—none of the leftovers would go to waste. This feast was half the price of Alofi's, with twenty times as much food, quadruple the variety, and most important, much better tasting!

Sunday, September 2

Over the last few days we have made banana-papaya-yogurt smoothies and banana-peanut butter smoothies for breakfast with the early ripening bananas. Today, our stalk of bananas are finally fully ripe. It is time for the banana-fest to begin. Adrienne and I made banana-pineapple pancakes for breakfast. Then we baked a batch of papaya-banana-pineapple muffins and a large pan of banana chocolate chip cookie bars.

Unfortunately, it is yet another day of gray skies, cool temperatures, and strong winds. The only days we've had good weather here in Tonga were the day Eric and I arrived and the three days I was in SCUBA class. While we've been eager to visit the anchorages in the Vava'u island group, we haven't wanted to leave the highly protected mooring in Neiafu harbor to go to a more exposed anchorage. We were told Point Maurell was one of the area's most protected anchorages, so we took a break from cooking and moved there for a change of scenery.

Point Maurell is near Neiafu harbor, so it was a short ride in a protected channel. Despite the twenty-five knot winds, we didn't get blown much. As promised, the anchorage was calm. Almost as soon as we were anchored it began to rain, so we opted to stay inside for the rest of the afternoon and I continued my banana mission. For lunch we had banana-papaya-pineapple-yogurt smoothies. I also made a couple desserts: I rolled banana chunks in finely chopped walnuts and brown sugar and baked them for a hot dessert today, and dipped banana slices in chocolate and froze them for a dessert for later. For dinner we had baked fish with a banana curry topping that was surprisingly tasty. The good news is we've made some serious progress on the bananas today and we only have three dozen left!

Monday, September 3

We awoke to more gray skies, so we headed out right away to go for a hike, knowing the rain would come later. We landed the dinghy on a tiny stretch of beach close to where we were anchored. This is actually one of the nicer beaches we've seen in the South Pacific.

The hiking trail that led from the beach inland was one person wide and well used. It tracked through a lovely forest. We followed it for a while when suddenly the forest ended and we came to a cute little village along the water. Like in Anaho and South Fakarava, there were no streets and no cars. We saw a few dozen small houses (one with an outhouse), two churches, a cemetery, a small concrete and rock dock with several boats tied to it, and a few boats that were beached. The "roads" were narrow dirt paths. The main one cut through the center of the village with a few offshoots heading to the shore, the churches, and so on. As with all the other towns we have been to in Tonga, pigs and chickens ran freely.

A group of kids were playing in the field in the center of the village. The kids were fascinated by us, following us and giggling. When we tried to talk to them, though, they got shy and scampered off, but still following us from a distance. Eventually, one of the braver, older boys talked to us a little bit in Tongan, but we had no clue what he was saying.

At the dock we chatted briefly with a resident. In French Polynesia, the locals usually waited for us to make the first move and responded in kind. So if we were smiley and chatty, they would smile and chat right back. But here, the people are more aloof (except, of course, Alofi). While Tongans are always incredibly polite, we find it takes them a long time to move from merely polite to openly friendly.

We headed out of the village, back the way we came. There was a fork in the road we hadn't noticed on the way in, so we took the other fork in hopes of seeing some new scenery. Oddly enough, there was a ton of cow dung in the forest, but we never saw any cows. And there were a lot of big spiders. Adrienne said she was afraid to step on them because they were big enough to eat her shoe! After about forty-five minutes of trekking through the forest, we turned around and headed back to *Kosmos*.

It started raining shortly after we returned and it poured for the rest of the afternoon and night. Eric had to go out and bail the dinghy twice. Of course, I continued my banana quest, making more papaya-banana-pineapple smoothies, banana bread, and bananas Foster. I threw the last of the bananas in the freezer and will use them in smoothies over the next few days. Project complete!

Thursday, September 6

On Tuesday, we awoke to gray skies, sporadic rain, and winds screaming at ten-to-twenty-seven knots. But as promised, the water was relatively calm in the protected anchorage. It was a lazy day on board. We spent the majority of the day reading and playing *Name That Tune*. We had some hilarious moments during the game. We'll always remember, "This is that girl band, Hansen!" and "I don't recognize this song. Oh wait… wasn't this the one we played for our first dance at our wedding?"

Yesterday, the sun finally came out. We were thrilled to see it after more than a week of gloom! We went snorkeling in Point Maurell bay. The snorkeling wasn't spectacular since a lot of the coral has died, but we still saw some pretty coral formations and a lot of mauve coral that almost looked like antlers. We saw yellow and white puffer fish, too. I think the white ones look like Chihuahuas. Eric saw a cuddlefish, a type of squid that changes color to match its background as it moves around. At one point, an enormous school of small fish swam right through us; for a couple of minutes we were surrounded by thousands of fish on all sides.

This morning we headed back to Neiafu for our usual "get ready to go" routine. Of course, in Tonga, there is absolutely no frozen microwave food in the grocery stores, but we found a restaurant that does catering, so we ordered a pan of lasagna and family-sized chicken pot pies and meat pies. We took the food back to *Kosmos*, cut them into individual servings, and froze them.

We also tried a soursop (cherimoya or custard apple) today. A citrus fruit, it is white and juicy inside. Much like an orange, the peel pulls off without a knife, you can pull it apart in sections, and it has seeds embedded in the meat. But unlike an orange, the meat is soft and custard-like in texture. It is both sweet and tangy, tasting like a combination of persimmon and pineapple, with a hint of banana. Adrienne and I liked it a lot, but Eric didn't.

After a few more errands in town, Adrienne and I went to war with *Kosmos*'s underwater ecosystem. Adrienne worked on the waterline while I did the bottom. Adrienne will attest that I am not exaggerating about how lush and thick the grass is and how much scrubbing it takes to remove it. Unfortunately, the bottom now has a new red algae type plant growing on it that takes a little extra scrubbing.

Much to our disappointment, we found out that shortly after we left, a mother and baby whale swam into Point Maurell Bay and hung out there. The people that happened to be in the anchorage swam with them and the whales didn't run off.

Sunday, September 9

On Friday morning, a fellow boater came by in his dinghy and told us the breaking news of the morning: Fiji has just declared martial law. Several countries, including the United States, have issued travel advisories warning that it is too dangerous to enter the country. He told us many other cruisers have decided to skip Fiji altogether and advised us to do the same.

Fiji has had several bouts of political unrest since 1987, but from what we can tell, there has never been any violence. After reading the news, we decided that the situation wasn't really that bad and that we would go as planned. Essentially, one of the country's leaders had been ousted in 2006 and exiled from Fiji. This leader returned from exile this week and now the current government is worried he will attempt to re-take power. Fijian government officials claim the martial law decree is solely for the purpose of keeping this ousted leader and his followers in check, and will not affect the general population.

At 0930, we pulled up to the customs dock to check out as we'd been told. Upon arrival, we were told pulling up to the dock was unnecessary and Eric just needed to take our passports to immigration.

We weren't too surprised by the sudden protocol change--other cruisers had warned us that the rules change frequently in Tonga.

Eric walked to the immigration office. There is only one immigration officer, and he was at the airport checking in a flight that had just arrived. He was expected back at 1230. Of course, lunch hour started at 1230, but by 1345, we were cleared and ready to head to sea.

We are happy to report that this is the smoothest long passage we've ever had. The seas have been (relatively) calm at only three feet, with an occasional bigger wave now and again. Even the bigger waves are not bad, though; we haven't had any dramatic rolling. The temperature is mild, which helps make the overall trip better. There is no moon right now and we've had a heavy cloud cover at night, so the nights are pitch black.

It turns out that Adrienne suffers from lethargy at sea, just like I do. She has completely lost her appetite and isn't eating at all, which worries me. She has spent every waking moment looking for whales, but she hasn't spotted one yet. She is also disappointed about the lack of stars and pretty sunsets.

We crossed over to the eastern hemisphere at 2156 (9:56 p.m.) today, another exciting milestone for us. At some unknown point, we also crossed from Polynesia to Melanesia.

Chapter 14: Viti Levu, Viti Levu Islands, Fiji

Monday, September 10

The wind completely died in the early morning, making the ride incredibly calm. Viti Levu was already in sight when the sun came up. It is a large, mountainous island with a reef, like Tahiti, and is surrounded by several other small islands. As we got closer, we started to see infrastructure. Suva, the first city we planned to visit, has 400,000 people and is by far the biggest city we have been to in the South Pacific. We could see a good-sized downtown area with quite a few buildings that are ten stories or more. To the left of downtown we spotted an industrial area; beyond that it looked residential.

The pass into Suva is wide and well marked, so entering it was a piece of cake. We pulled into the quarantine area of the harbor, right in front of the industrial area, a little before 1300 (1:00 p.m.). We dropped anchor and hoisted our yellow "Q" flag. (Every time a boat enters a new country, it is required to fly a yellow flag indicating "quarantine" status. After the boat and people on it are checked into the country, the flag can be taken down.)

We called the port master and let him know we had arrived. We were told the officials would be to the boat by 1430. At 1545 the officials still hadn't come, so we radioed port control to check status. They said their boat had broken down and they wouldn't be coming today. Since we didn't get cleared in, we weren't allowed to get off *Kosmos*. We were really disappointed that we couldn't go to a restaurant to celebrate the completion of our passage with a big meal.

Tuesday, September 11

The officials arrived at 0900 this morning. The customs boat pulled up and five Fijians boarded *Kosmos*, each with a battery of questions and forms to fill out. The whole process took an hour, and the officials were nice. Once they left, we moved from the quarantine area to the anchorage in front of the yacht club, then got *Kosmos* situated. Twenty-three hours after arriving in port, we could finally go to land. As we climbed into the dinghy, we saw that the grass had already grown back on the waterline. I thought Adrienne was going to cry. She had worked so hard to scrub it off and was incredulous that it could be back again so soon.

On shore, we ran a variety of errands: checking in with the yacht club, obtaining duty free fuel request forms, getting a permit to cruise in the islands, and going to the bank, produce market, and grocery store. Our errands took us all over downtown, so we saw a lot and got a good sense of the city. Suva has an eclectic feel. There are a wide variety of architectural styles, ranging from post modern offices to a Catholic church that looks like a castle to several French style buildings that look like they belong in New Orleans. The streets are bustling and crowded, with lots of cars, buses, and pedestrians. There are tons of shops, from department stores to mom and pop stores that sell everything that is normally available in a big city. It is clean, with no graffiti or trash. Of course, since it is a "real" city, there isn't much greenery around outside the parks.

The yacht club is in the industrial area, across from the prison. Not too far north from the yacht club is an enormous market, filled with vendors selling a wide variety of produce. It is a better selection than anything we have seen in the South Pacific. Across the street is a flea market of sorts. Going north toward the heart of downtown, the buildings and shops become progressively nicer. In the city center there are government offices, a department store and several expensive restaurants.

Everyone we've encountered is incredibly friendly and welcoming. Tons of people have said "hi" to us as they passed us in the street, although we did also run across a couple of people who hit us up for money, one man who offered to sell Eric weed, and another who offered to sell me either limes or lines. (I didn't stick around long enough for clarification!) There were a few people begging on the street, as is normally the case in cities. There were absolutely no signs of looming violence—no police patrolling the streets, no fliers being discreetly handed out. Everyone just went about their business.

One of the reasons we had wanted to stop in Suva was because we figured that we'd find a good selection of groceries. We wanted to stock up on frozen microwave dinners, as well as meat and dairy products, which have been hard to come by in most places. We also needed miscellaneous household supplies, like carpet cleaner and wood polish that we haven't been able to find. Much to our disappointment, the grocery store we went to had a limited selection; we couldn't get half the things on our shopping list. We were, however, able to stock up on the single most important food item: Tim Tams. Thank God! While we had bought several boxes in French Polynesia, we couldn't find them in Niue or Tonga. We were down to our last box and desperate for more. Not only were there a bunch of flavors, but the cookies were also on sale. Praise the Lord!

Back on board, Adrienne again reminded me about how different life is out here than in the U.S. After we unloaded the produce from the dinghy into the cockpit, she started to bring the bags inside and I screamed, "Nooooooo!" She looked at me in total confusion. I explained we needed to wash the produce before we could take it indoors. I pulled out a bucket, squirted a little bleach in the bottom, and filled it with water. Putting a few pieces of produce in the bucket at a time, I held all the produce under the water for a full five minutes. Adrienne's eyes practically bugged out of her head when she saw all the dirt and little critters float to the surface. In the U.S., even at farmer's markets, the produce is meticulously cleaned. We almost never see bugs!

Wednesday, September 12

Yesterday there was one errand we didn't get to. Almost every official that had come to *Kosmos* had charged a small entry fee for the department he represented. We were able to pay all but one of the fees on the spot. (While these may seem like bribes, the prices matched the guidebook's quotes and each person gave us an official written receipt.) The last fee needed to be paid at the health ministry office.

We headed to shore and hopped into a taxi, armed with an address the yacht club had given us. We were delivered to the four-story, official-looking Ministry of Health building. The receptionist told us we were at the wrong building and pointed to the fine print on the form the agent had given to us, which had the correct address. Oops.

We caught another taxi, and this time it took us to a building that didn't look at all like a government office. It turned out to be a vaccination clinic. We were confused until one of the nurses told us the cashier's office was upstairs. The health officials asked us where we going next. When we told them we were headed to Nadi, a city on the other side of Viti Levu, they informed us that the cruising permit we had gotten yesterday did not include Nadi. If we wanted to go to Nadi, we would have to check out of Suva and check back in at a city called Lautoka, also on the west side of Viti Levu. We found it bizarre that the cruising permit would let us go to other islands, but not other cities on the same island. This new bit of information frustrated us immensely. Lautoka was out of our way and supposedly not a nice place to visit. Had we realized we would have to go to Lautoka no matter what, we would have bypassed Suva altogether.

The clerk told us that all we needed to do to check out of Suva was to inform customs, so we took a taxi to customs. We were dropped off in front of a nice looking building with a big logo saying Fiji Customs. But it turned out to be the wrong office. Déjà vu. When we asked where the right office was located, the clerk pointed vaguely across the street. All we could see was a control tower peeking out from a vast field of highly stacked shipping containers, protected by a barbed wire fence. The fence stretched on as far as we could see, with no discernable gate. We followed the fence, and after a surprisingly long walk, we found the gate and went inside the compound. At the control tower office, we were warmly greeted by three of the same people who had boarded our boat yesterday.

We checked out, went back to *Kosmos,* and headed for sea. The ride started out windy but got better as we entered more sheltered waters. We were hit by occasional big side waves, but none were nearly as bad as what we've encountered on other passages. Adrienne asked if this was the roughest passage we had been on, and we laughed, telling her it was a relatively nice ride. She kept saying, "If you think this is nice, I can't imagine what you call rough!" It was déjà vu to our first passage with Richard.

In Retrospect

Over the next few weeks, we talked to many cruisers who all checked into Fiji somewhere other than Suva. All of them found the process to be easy and quick. In the other cities, the officials are housed in the same building, including the people who issue cruising permits and duty free fuel forms. The cruisers picked up the officials in their dinghy and brought them to their boats. What took us a full three days (thanks to initially waiting twenty-four hours because of the officials' broken boat and then adding all the time it took to visit the different offices around Suva) took them about an hour and a half. And they all paid less in fees than we did!

Thursday, September 13

We got to the pass that would take us into the lagoon near Nadi at 0400. It was pitch black outside, so we couldn't see anything other than a reef marker and two small flashing direction markers in the distance. Eric studied the radar, depth measurements, lights, and chart and saw that everything lined up perfectly, so he decided to enter. The pass is somewhat narrow and the seas were pushing the boat around a little while we were in there, which Eric found disconcerting. Staying perfectly lined up took careful steering. The charts were only medium resolution, too, and this only added to Eric's nervousness. Thankfully, everything went smoothly.

We pulled into Nadi this morning at 0630, ushered in by a lovely sunrise. The mainland area looks like Southern California, with rolling, dry mountains. There is quite a bit of construction on the flat land along the shore and virtually no buildings in the mountains. Around the mainland, several islands dot the horizon.

The reason we absolutely had to come here is because Nadi airport is where Adrienne is flying out of and my dad is flying into. My dad arrives tomorrow. We chose a rendezvous spot that would be easy for my dad to find and for us to get to: a well known resort on Denaru Island. Denaru is just off the coast of Nadi and attached to town by a bridge, so my dad could take a taxi from the airport. According to the charts, there was an anchorage close to the resort, which is why it seemed to be such an ideal meeting place. And, Denaru looked to be centrally located for sight seeing activities, so it seemed to be a good spot to base ourselves out of.

Our plan was to anchor at Denaru then take a bus into the city of Lautoka to notify the officials we had arrived. We didn't think we needed to take *Kosmos* to Lautoka since we already had an onboard inspection in Suva. As we approached the anchorage, we were delighted to see a marina that was not on our charts. A marina would certainly make life easier in terms of getting everyone's luggage on and off the boat.

We anchored, then dinghied over to the marina and inquired about a slip. The woman behind the counter asked if we had taken *Kosmos* to Lautoka yet. We said no; we were about to catch a bus there. She told us we absolutely had to take the boat there before we could bring the boat into the marina. We were really frustrated. Between getting the dinghy up and down multiple times, getting *Kosmos* situated in an anchorage and then ready for sea multiple times, and the transit time, a trip to Lautoka would take all day. In contrast, a round trip bus ride would have taken forty minutes.

After a quick breakfast at a café near the marina office, we went back to *Kosmos*, stowed the dinghy, and headed to Lautoka. It was a two-hour ride, but fortunately, we were in the lagoon the whole time, so it was a smooth ride.

Lautoka is an industrial city, with several wharfs and many commercial vessels. There is a factory in the center of town that spews out gobs of black smoke. It's the ugliest place we have been to, and it reeks with a foul stench. We anchored, got the dinghy down, and motored over to the government office. We were all grumpy about having to jump through more administrative hoops. In our minds, we should have been sightseeing and having fun since Monday afternoon. Instead, for the last four days, we have been trapped in red tape hell.

The customs officer was really nice and it was hard not to take our frustrations out on him. We filled out three forms to check *Kosmos* in—the very same ones we had completed in Suva—and one form to remove Adrienne as crew. They did not need to see the boat. Hearing that made us even crankier.

When we were done with the paperwork, we decided to go straight back to Denarau. Lautoka didn't seem like it was a nice place to visit. In the few minutes that we were at the customs office, *Kosmos* had gotten a coating of ash from the nearby factory. *Great,* I thought. *More to wash.*

We've had to move *Kosmos* four times in the last four days, which is tedious in and of itself. But to make matters worse, the ground here is sticky mud, and every time we pull up the anchor chain, it is completely caked in mud. We've had to use a ridiculous amount of precious fresh water (our salt water spigot isn't working right now) to rinse off the anchor chain. If we don't keep it clean, the mud will get caked in the anchor locker and start to smell bad. The whole front of the boat is splattered with mud and desperately needs a scrubbing.

At the marina, we chose a spot next to a seventy-eight foot Nordhavn, which looks like a giant version of *Kosmos*. We had to Mediterranean moor, which is still a learning process for us. I stood in the back and told Eric when we were centered between the two boats and when to start backing up. Unfortunately, I hadn't properly accounted for the current and wind, and as Eric backed up, we drifted too close to one of the boats. I told him to stop and to move forward again. This next time, *Kosmos* was off center when we started backing up, but it still wasn't enough. I told Eric to stop and that we needed to try again. Fortunately, some people on the dock gave us a few pointers, which helped. We had been nervous as all get out about hitting the boats on both sides of us, and were relieved when we got in our spot and tied up with no collisions. Side by side, the two Nordhavns look like a mama and baby whale.

Our foul moods improved dramatically once we got off the boat. First, we didn't need to deal with the dinghy. We just stepped off the boat onto land, which was quite a luxury. The tap water here is potable, so we could fill up our water tanks, which diffused my anger about the mud. (Since the day we left home, we have made all our own fresh water using a reverse osmosis filter. This is the first time we have been able to easily access potable tap water).

Once we were off *Kosmos*, we realized Denaru is the most upscale part of Fiji. The mall here at the marina has a small, high end grocery store, an ice cream shop, a bakery, and several clothing stores and restaurants. A sign in one of the windows says, "Hard Rock Café Coming Soon." All kinds of yacht services are available, including a fuel dock with modern, high speed pumps and boat washers/waxers. Normally, Eric and I are not interested in visiting places like this. We want to see the "real" local cultures, not replicas of America. But we have to admit that the convenience of Denaru is irresistible.

Ever since she arrived, Adrienne has been full of compliments about what a great team Eric and I make. She is impressed by the little things that are part of our everyday life now. For example, when we are getting the anchor up and down, I stand on the bow and watch the anchor while Eric drives the boat. We communicate via hand signals to tell each other when we are ready to drop or pick up, if the boat needs to be turned, if there is a problem and we need to stop, and so on. The way we communicated while backing into the spot today brought another round of compliments from Adrienne. I had viewed our mooring as mildly unsuccessful since I hadn't gauged the wind and current right and needed advice on how to get in. But she focused on the fact that we had no accidents and made it in by working together. I like her perspective. She's good for the ego!

Friday, September 14

This morning, Eric and I took a taxi over to the other side of Denaru to pick up my dad from the rendezvous spot. From what we understand, part of the island is natural, part reclaimed swampland, and part manmade land from the swamp dredging. There are several gated communities with fancy custom homes on finger cays that have private docks off their backyards. The taxi driver said the homes range from 750,000 to three million Fijian dollars. There is a golf course and a large number of exclusive resorts. It looks like Beverly Hills.

When we pulled up at the hotel, my dad, John, was waiting for us out front. He said he wasn't tired, despite the fact that he had just flown all night, so we decided to join a tour group heading to a nearby island with a private resort. The price included the ferry ride, lunch, and use of all the non-mechanical amenities the resort offered. It sounded nice. We stopped by *Kosmos* to drop off his luggage and pick up Adrienne, then were on our way.

The four of us loaded onto the ferry. It was a power catamaran that did forty miles per hour, and the ride was surprisingly smooth for the speed. In only twenty minutes we arrived at our destination. It would have taken *Kosmos* all day. The cat stopped near the island, and a small glass bottom boat pulled up alongside us. We offloaded into the little boat, which delivered us to a dock in front of the hotel.

Lunch was served right away. It was a buffet with fish, French fries, bok choy, green salad, and a pasta salad. Except for the fish, the food wasn't very good. The beach was nice, though. It is fairly obvious that the beach is man made, and that the resort has to regularly drag it to remove coral, shells, and other debris that washes up. We tried kayaking, but it was too windy, so we quickly came in, concerned about getting blown out farther than we could paddle in. Then we tried snorkeling, but the water clarity wasn't good. In fact, it was so bad that I didn't see a huge coral head until I collided with it. Also, the equipment was low quality and we couldn't breathe properly with the snorkels. After about ten minutes of snorkeling, we gave up and went in the pool. The water was cold, so we didn't stay in long. On a hot day, the cold pool would have been refreshing, but today it was gloomy, windy, and cool. Adrienne and I took a walk around the island while the guys relaxed in lounge chairs. The island is tiny, so the walk didn't take long. Outside the resort, the land is a forest of sorts, with a hiking trail that cuts through it. The walk was scenic, with peeks of the ocean here and there. We could see Viti Levu and several other small islands. Needless to say, we were all bored and happy when the ferry came to get us.

Back at *Kosmos,* however, we were met with disaster. I wanted my dad to have the more comfortable bed, so I was going to put him in the guest room and move Adrienne to the pull-out bed in the pilot house. As I was taking Adrienne's sheets off the guest bed to take them up to the pilot house bed, I noticed the sheets were wet. In fact, the whole mattress cover was wet. It turned out that Adrienne had not closed the porthole window over her bed tightly enough when we left Tonga, and water had leaked inside the boat while we were at sea. Only a small amount was getting in, but since it had been over several days, there could potentially be a lot of water damage.

There are two storage areas under that bed. I emptied out the upper storage area. Everything was wet. Feeling sick to my stomach, I opened the lower storage area and found that it was a pool of salt water. This was where I had stored all the photo albums. I had thought I was so clever when I picked this spot. It never occurred to me in my wildest dreams that it could get wet here. Fortunately, I had wrapped all the photos in plastic; none of them were destroyed.

By this time, my dad was exhausted and wanted to go to bed. Fortunately, marine mattresses don't absorb water, so I just took the cover off and put the sheets on the foam. He immediately passed out. Adrienne, Eric, and I all went to dinner at an Indian restaurant that came highly recommended. Fiji used to be a British colony, and the British had imported a lot of laborers from India to work the plantations. The British government strongly discouraged the Indians from mixing with the local Fijian population, so there weren't many interracial marriages. Today, the population of Fiji is half Indian, half indigenous Fijian Melanesians.

The Indians have maintained a strong cultural identity. We were expecting "authentic" Indian food. The three of us haven't eaten much Indian food, so most of the dishes on the menu were new to us. We were adventurous and only tried things we had never heard of: tandoori khazaha, a sampler of chicken, fish, shrimp, and veggies in a mint sauce called tikka; lamb chettinad, which was shredded lamb mixed with a coconut, curry and spice sauce; and kofta lababdar, pureed veggies and apricot in a curry sauce. We all got roti to accompany our food, which is a round, flat bread similar to flour tortillas. The food was excellent.

In Retrospect:

I firmly believe that everything happens for a reason. I think that sometimes bad things happen to stop you from doing something that would have been worse. Now I know that the leaking window was a warning from God to prevent what was yet to come almost exactly one year later. But we didn't clue in. If we had, it would have prevented the most terrifying night of our lives.

Saturday, September 15

Today, the three of us we went on a full day tour of the Coral Coast of Viti Levu, which is between Suva and Nadi. There were two other people on the tour. The drive was quite long. The scenery was mostly rolling hills with grass, scattered palm trees, and the occasional cow or horse. We also passed a pine tree forest and several farms, mostly sugar cane. We saw lots of cut sugar cane ready to be sent off to the factory for processing. (Sugar cane and pine timber are two of Fiji's major exports.)

Our first stop was Sagatoka Sand Dunes National Park. When we were told we would be taking a hike through sand dunes, my dad passed on the walk. He lives in Nevada, where he sees endless sand dunes on his way to and from work, so it didn't sound appealing to him. The tour guide stayed with my dad.

The hiking trail was well maintained. We walked up a steep hill offering scenic views of the surrounding countryside and a peek at the ocean. As we continued on the trail, we got to the sand dunes, which were small compared to the dunes in Nevada. After a short trek over the sand, we arrived at the beach. The trail followed the shoreline for a bit and then turned back inland into a forest. We were amused to see a couple pop art sculptures in the forest. The first one we passed was called *The Tree Huggers*, which had sculptures of people made out of sticks that were

218

literally hugging the tree trunks. The second was called *The Tree of Lost Soles*. It was an especially large tree that had shoes hanging off the branches like Christmas tree ornaments. Both were hilarious. The tour guide took my dad on a walk around the forest, so at least my dad got to enjoy part of the experience.

Each traditional Fijian village is known for some talent, and the next stop on our tour was a pottery village. It was tiny—a couple of rows of modest houses surrounded by farmland. After a quick tour, we went into the town hall for a pottery making demonstration and cultural experience.

It started with a traditional kava ceremony. One at a time, everyone was given a small bowl of kava to drink. The chief always gets the first cup, and my dad was elected our group's "chief." He was pleased with his new title, because in Fiji, chiefs are the only men allowed to have multiple wives. Before taking the kava bowl, and again after drinking it, each person had to say thank you and clap. Each time, everyone in the room then responded by saying thank you and clapping, as well. This kava was definitely stronger than what we had in Tonga, making it taste more like sock water than ever. We didn't drink enough to feel the drug-like effects, but it did make our tongues tingle.

After the kava ceremony, we watched the women make pottery. They mixed natural clay soil with sand and then began shaping. In just a few minutes, with no wheel and using only a rock, seashell, and stick, they created a vase, decorative bowl, and a figurine. They placed the pottery in an open fire. Then while it was still hot, they rubbed the pottery with tree sap, which made a waterproof glaze. Sculpting pottery is not easy, even with all the modern tools, and yet these women made it look simple. We couldn't believe how good the pottery looked.

Next, the ladies of the village danced for us. They all held fans and wore hot pink satin tops, long dark skirts, and short patterned brown skirts layered over the long skirt. The dancing was demure, with little motion. It seems the farther west we move, the less vibrant the dancing. The ladies looked like they were uncomfortable performing for us, so maybe the dancing is normally livelier. The dancers recruited us all to join in. We did a couples' dance that reminded us of square dancing in that someone would yell out commands and everyone would change direction in unison. That was followed by the popular Fijian snake dance, which was essentially a conga line.

After the village tour, we went to lunch. Food was included with the tour. We didn't have high hopes, expecting a stale buffet like we had gotten yesterday at the resort. Much to our surprise, it was a prepared to order meal with good food. While we were in the restaurant, it began to pour. It never let up, so we skipped our last stop, the beach. The Coral Coast apparently has great beaches, but this certainly wasn't beach weather.

Adrienne asked if we could go shopping in Nadi for the remainder of the time, and everyone agreed. The market was typical—venders in small booths hawking similar wares. All the wares were supposedly traditional items that were handmade in the local surrounding villages. Unfortunately, we were hassled by the pushy vendors, which kind of surprised us. The only high-pressure salesperson we have seen in the entire South Pacific until now has been Alofi.

Tonight we attended a Pacific Island dance show in the mall courtyard. The dances performed were from all over Polynesia and Micronesia, and the show was spectacular. There was a lot of fire dancing and they did all kinds of crazy stunts while twirling the flaming sticks. We found out that fire dancing is from Samoa, which is why we haven't seen much of it in our travels so far.

In Retrospect:

Several months later, while in Indonesia, we saw factory after factory cranking out these "locally made traditional artifacts" sold in the Fijian market. Since then, we have seen the same "locally made artifacts" in many countries. We have learned to be wary of "locally made" items that don't specify the village they were made in.

Sunday, September 16

Today I hit a wall, emotionally speaking. I think having overlapping guests has been too much for me. I feel stretched too thin. I know. . . I've been whining about how lonely I am, so I should be thrilled to have not one, but two guests. I do enjoy both Adrienne's and my dad's company, and I'm glad they're here. But as much as Eric and I enjoy having company, guests tire us out. We have slowed our pace of life drastically, and it's hard for us to keep up with people who are still going at that frenetic pace that accompanies life in America. I feel like we have been running at too fast a pace for too long. Plus, Adrienne and my dad didn't know each other before and they have zero common interests, so it has been stressful to find activities that they'll both enjoy. And, I think I simply haven't had enough time to myself over the last three weeks. I don't need a lot of alone time, but I do need some.

Basically, all day I was bitchy and grouchy and just wanted to be alone. It was one of those days where everything went wrong. In the morning, I put the bedding in the marina's washing machine. The machine filled with water, but the washing cycle never started. The marina office told me they were already aware that the agitator was broken, but hadn't bothered to put up a sign. I had to drag the heavy, sopping wet laundry back to the boat, wash it by hand, then hang it to dry (the bedding was too big to fit into our tiny washer/dryer on board). Putting the bed back together was also a nightmare. It took three people to wrestle the mattress back inside the cover. I swear that the mattress had arms, because it managed to knock me around good.

Needless to say, I didn't do anything fun today. Adrienne went sightseeing without us. I don't even know what Eric and my dad did all day, but I felt really guilty that my dad wasn't out sightseeing, too.

Monday, September 17

Today I was feeling better, but still not feeling like myself. Trying to make it up to my dad for not doing anything fun yesterday, we scheduled another busy day of activities. First we went to downtown Nadi to run some errands. Nadi is a much smaller city that Suva, but it offers all the basics, with restaurants, grocery stores, a nice hardware store, clothes stores, a five and dime, and several souvenir shops. The produce market in Nadi is similar to the one in Suva, with stall after stall of vendors selling raw ingredients, including fish and spices. Between the various shops, we were able to get everything we needed, including more Tim Tams.

Like Suva, Nadi is clean, with no graffiti or litter. But while Suva has some charm, Nadi has none. Except for the Hindu temple, the architecture is utilitarian. The biggest difference from Suva, however, is the people. In both places, many people approached us, but here literally everyone who approached us was looking for money. Some were panhandling, some were trying to pull us into their stores, some were trying to pull us away from the store we were at and into a different store. Yes, a few people approached us in Suva for money, but the vast majority of Suvans were nice just for the sake of being nice. We still think that

222

Fijian people are some of the friendliest people around, but had our only impression of Fiji been Nadi, we would not have had as many good things to say about Fijian people.

After hitting the shops in Nadi, we went to see the Hindu temple, which is beautiful and amazingly ornate. The entire exterior is a giant relief (style of carved art intricate images) painted with bright colors. Virtually every inch of the interior is painted with large, colorful images similar to the ones on the exterior. There were several altars around the temple where people lined up to worship, many offering sacrifices of food. The altars are small kiosk-type structures, each housing a statue of some sort. Some of the statues are animals, some people. We wandered around and looked at each of the altars and admired the artwork.

In the afternoon, we went on a helicopter ride, which was an incredible experience. We flew over a couple of the islands, up into the mountains above Lautoka, and through a scenic narrow gorge in between the mountains. Then the pilot flew us to another section of mountains where we spotted a stunning waterfall. At the end, we went over the valley where Nadi is located. We could see *Kosmos* from the air as we approached Denaru for the landing. The scenery around here is spectacular, particularly over the islands.

For dinner we went to a five star French/Fijian fusion restaurant in Nadi. The food and service were absolutely incredible and the portion sizes were generous, yet the average price for a main course was only twenty-five dollars (U.S.). We had already agreed that it was the best value for the money of any restaurant we've ever been to when we experienced the icing on the cake. Earlier in the meal, we had mentioned to the waitress that Adrienne was on her way to the airport. While we were eating dessert, all the waitresses gathered around our table and sang

Adrienne a Fijian song that would bring her safe travels. After dinner we said good-bye to Adrienne. As it turned out, she did have a safe flight back to California, so the song must have worked.

Oh, and this morning we also hired a crew of people come to wash and wax Kosmos (yippee! I don't have to do it!).

In Retrospect:

Denaru/Nadi is the biggest tourist area in Fiji. After visiting several more countries, we figured out that the more touristy the area, the less friendly the locals are. In areas where they don't see a lot of tourists, like Suva, the locals are genuinely excited to have you in their town. But in places where the tourists flock, foreigners are seen as nothing more than a walking wallet and are treated as such. In some places, it goes beyond panhandling and pushy sales tactics to actually targeting tourists for crime. Nowadays, we believe that the less touristy the area, the safer we are, which goes against American conventional wisdom. We find that most Americans feel like they are safer when they stay in large groups in tourism centers.

Thursday, September 20

On Tuesday, my dad, Eric, and I took a ferry to another resort island called Malolo Lailai. It looks like a stereotypical South Sea island: low and flat with a big sandy beach and lots of palm trees. The weather was nice. We spent the day snorkeling, walking around the island, and lounging by the pool. We also had lunch there. We ordered fish in coconut milk and were surprised that the fish was cooked.

When we got back from Malolo Lailai, saw the waxing was completed. We are so glad we hired them. We had been dreading waxing the boat ourselves because we know what a big job it is. It took four professionals two days. Imagine how long it would have taken the two of us!

Here at the marina, there is a fairly decent Internet connection but no Wi-Fi. You can only use the Internet in the marina office between 0800 and 1600 (4:00 p.m.), Monday thru Saturday. Eric and I had a lot of online chores to take care of, like loading our blog, paying bills, and responding to emails, so yesterday we decided to take the day off from sightseeing to attend to responsibilities. Eric and I took turns working on the computer. The person not online hung out with my dad on board.

My dad flew back home last night. I was sad to see him go; I'd hoped he would stay longer. Despite my meltdown on Sunday, I really did enjoy having him with us. I have always been a "daddy's girl" and value my time with my dad. In a perfect world, we would have had a week between Adrienne leaving and my dad arriving, and my dad would have extended his trip. But I have to admit that I was a bit relieved that it was back to being only me and Eric again. Eric is overjoyed about having total privacy again.

We're also glad we can finally leave Denaru. Being in Denaru is just like being in America, which made it a good place to stay with guests. Our guests got to enjoy a nice vacation with all the comforts of home. If it weren't for our guests, though, we would never have come here. So first thing this morning, we filled up with fuel and headed out to see some rural islands.

In Suva, we were told we could get duty free fuel as long as we met the minimum quantity requirements, so we were frustrated and disappointed when it came time to pay and we found out that we really didn't qualify after all. In Suva, they neglected to tell us that your boat also has to weigh one hundred tons or more. (*Kosmos* is "only" twenty-one tons.) Even at the higher price, though, we're glad we got fuel here. All the ferries fuel up at this dock and they go through a ton of fuel, so chances are it is good.

This is an important point. "Dirty" diesel—contaminated with dirt, rust, water, and/or organisms—could basically stop our engine from working and leave us stranded, so we have to be careful about getting clean fuel. Believe it or not, organic species live and grow in diesel. The longer that fuel sits in a container, the more likely it is to absorb rust from the container, or for dirt and water to get in the container, or for microscopic critters to grow into giant colonies of monsters out to destroy your fuel injectors. As a precaution, our fuel system is equipped with multiple filters to to help ensure the fuel is really clean by the time it hits the engine.

Our next destination was an anchorage located between the islands of Nevadra and Vanua Levu, and was a relatively short day run. It was 1600 when we approached the pass. The sky was dark gray and ominous. With no sunshine at all, it was incredibly hard to see what might be lurking under the surface. To make matters worse, the charts were not much help because they were low resolution. In fact, we don't have any high resolution charts of Fiji. But we do have a cruising guide, which had supplemental information about boating in Fiji intended to supplement the charts. The cruising guide helps, but is no replacement for a high resolution chart.

I went outside and stood on the front deck, leaning over the bow as far as I could in an effort to spot any dangers in the water. At one point, the depth sounder went instantly from sixty feet to fourteen feet, which made us nervous. We were clearly above a reef. Would it get shallow enough for us to hit it? Fortunately, we made it in okay.

Once in the lagoon, we had a similar challenge with dropping the anchor. How could we avoid anchoring in a reef when we couldn't see the coral? There were no other boats in the anchorage, so there was no one to ask for advice. Eric did his best to guess where a sand patch described in the cruising guide was. We crossed our fingers and lowered the anchor.

From the odd way the boat is swinging now, we're pretty sure we are stuck on some coral. Oh well. The SCUBA gear has definitely paid for itself!

This anchorage is absolutely beautiful, though surprisingly rocky. Even with the paravanes out, it feels like we are at sea; we thought we'd have better shelter in this bay. Navadra Island, a big hill with a sandy beach along part of it, is directly to our northeast. Just a few hundred yards from Navadra's southern tip is Vanua Levu. It's hilly at one end. Along the other end is a big beach, and at the edge of the beach is an enormous rock. Between the islands is a reef, and together, the three form a protective semi-circle.

We were under the impression these islands are uninhabited, so we were surprised to see two coconut palm structures on the shore of Vanua Levu. We watched the shore the rest of the evenings to see if any villagers appeared, but the only signs of life were the goats.

Chapter 15: Vanua Levu, Mamanuca Islands, Fiji

Saturday, September 22

When we woke up yesterday, the sun was brighter than it had been when we arrived. We looked in the water and could see all sorts of spectacular coral formations. Guess we missed the sand patch. "At least it'll be a pretty dive when we free the anchor," I said to Eric.

We stayed on board all and did absolutely nothing. It was wonderful having the anchorage to ourselves. We relished the total peace, quiet, and privacy.

Today we felt recharged, ready to explore the islands. Since they are small, we figured it wouldn't take long. This bay was an ideal spot to go kayaking, being both remote and sheltered, so we got the kayaks down instead of the dinghy.

Curious about the huts on the shore, we went to Vanua Levu first. We landed on a small beach with fine white sand on the mountainous part of the island. It was the nicest beach we'd seen since leaving San Diego. We started clambering up the hill. After a while, we found a well used hiking trail, which surprised us. Who would have thought we'd find such a nice trail on an uninhabited island? Was it really uninhabited?

We followed the trail to the summit, where the views of Navadra and other islands in the distance were nothing short of spectacular. We walked around the summit for a while. The foliage on the island is diverse, with lots of different plants, but it isn't dense, so it was easy to wander between the trees and look around. We noted an especially large amount of young trees, saw a lot of lizards, and a half dozen goats. We found an area that looked like it had been recently cleared for use as a campsite, with

228

campfire ashes in the center and enough room for several tents. We were appalled to see the site littered with discarded water bottles and soda cans.

Then we followed the trail all the way back down. As we suspected, it led to the two huts. The huts baffled us. Connected by a small single deck, each consisted of a single room with three sets of bunk bed frames, but no mattresses. They were full of trash. They looked like they were relatively new, yet they were in disrepair and seemed to be abandoned. The huts were set on platforms that looked like Western style construction. Near the huts were little walkways along the shore that had been dragged of debris and lined with coconuts. Clearly someone had spent a lot of time and energy creating these walkways, and with none of the coconuts showing signs of rot, we guessed that it had been done recently.

We headed down the shore toward the enormous rock and circled its base. The ground at this end was rugged, with large black rocks scattered about. In between and around the bigger rocks there were pretty, multicolored, hand size rocks, making it a unique and aesthetically pleasing shoreline. We were surprised at the diversity on this tiny little island.

There were lots of crabs along the rocks, which were dark in color like the rocks and hard to see. Once back on the sand, we noticed a lot of little white crabs against the white sand. Mother Nature is so smart.

When we finally got back to the kayaks, we realized we had gotten lucky on our timing. The tide was coming in and it looked like the kayaks would be washed to sea soon. While we were gone, six boats had pulled in. We saw some people swimming and went to say hi. It turns out they knew the answer to the mystery huts. The television show *Survivor Kids* had just finished recording here the day we arrived, and the kids had stayed in the huts. Apparently, while the show was being recorded, no boats were allowed in the anchorage. All the boats that arrived today have been waiting for the camera crew to leave.

We counted our blessings. Had the film crew still been on the island when we pulled in, they would have shooed us away, too. We wouldn't have had enough time to get to another anchorage before dark, and with the low resolution charts for this area, we would not have made a night entry into an anchorage. We would have spent the whole night doing circles in deep water. That would have been no fun!

Sunday, September 23

Shortly after we woke up this morning, we saw that a small cruise ship had pulled into the anchorage, shuttling people to the two islands in their tenders. Then we realized that there were more than a dozen people snorkeling behind *Kosmos*. We picked an interesting place to anchor!

We decided to go diving first, then to Navadra. We put on our SCUBA gear and jumped in. The coral wasn't especially colorful—mostly browns with some yellows—but the formations were absolutely incredible. We've seen big coral before, but these were terraces upon terraces of huge, delicately shaped coral. There were a lot of fish, but not nearly as many or as big as we would have expected on this vast amount of coral. Fortunately, it didn't look like our anchor and chain was stuck on anything.

We took showers when we were finished with our dive, and were just about to make lunch when the people we had met yesterday stopped by to tell us the wind was changing. It was going to come from the north, a direction from which we had zero protection. They were leaving right away to go to a more suitable anchorage ten miles north. We instantly decided to follow them. It was already rocky and uncomfortable here, and we couldn't take it getting worse. A third boat also said they'd join us.

It was 1330. We immediately went to work on getting *Kosmos* ready to go. As predicted, the wind steadily picked up as we prepared the boat. At 16:10 (4:10 p.m.), we finally pulled up anchor. Even though everything looked okay below, we were still nervous about the anchor or chain getting snagged on something on its way up, and we were relieved when it came up with no problems.

Because it was so late in the day, we needed to get to the next anchorage immediately. There were several coral hazards along the way, and the later it got, the harder it would become to see the coral. To maximize speed, we ran at 2000 to 2250 rpm (we normally cruise at 1600 to 1750). We were going into the wind the whole way, which slowed us down even more. We were a little worried about our safety, as well as the safety of the two sailboats. They may have left before us, but they had a longer transit time, and sunset was rapidly approaching. An hour and a half later, we were safely in the Yalobi lagoon off Waya Island. One sailboat was already there, and the other arrived just as dark began to fall.

The lagoon is horseshoe shaped, with one side appearing to be longer than the other. In reality, what looks like the longer portion is actually a separate island altogether, called Wayasewa, but it is situated close enough to Waya that from here it looks attached. With its dry, rolling hills, the islands look like a tiny version of western Viti Levu. The rounded part of the lagoon has a nice beach, with several small, low buildings visible a few hundred feet back from the shoreline. The rest of the shoreline has little or no beach—the mountains plunge right into the sea.

It was too late in the day to get the dinghy down and go to shore, but we assumed the whole town was in church anyway. Hymns were floating in the wind to us. After a few minutes, the hymns turned to zealous preaching, and after another hour everything was quiet.

The wind was blowing at fifteen knots inside the protected anchorage, and later it started to rain. We are happy to report that even with the strong wind, the anchorage is calm and we haven't had to put out the paravanes. It was a wise choice to move.

Chapter 16: Waya Island, Yasawa Islands, Fiji

Monday, September 24

In Fiji most of the land outside the cities is owned by individual villages. These villages not only own the land, but they also lay claim to the surrounding water. In Fijian culture, it is extremely important to obtain permission to be in a village's territory, and there is a special ritual involved in asking for permission. The importance of carefully following this custom was stressed to us by our cruising guide, the office that issues cruising permits, and other cruisers. Needless to say, the first thing on our agenda today was to visit the village chief and ask permission to be anchored in his water.

It was sprinkling when we woke up. Our experience in Fiji is that light rain usually precedes a big downpour, so we decided to wait until after the big rain to go into the village. By almost 1100, though, the downpour still hadn't come, so we decided to head in—we had probably let too much time elapse as it was.

Villagers are conservative people, and risqué dress is considered offensive. I chose a shirt that covered my chest and shoulders, along with a skirt that hung past my knees. Then we grabbed our gift for the village: a bundle of kava. In Fiji, you must come bearing a gift of whole kava root, not ground kava. We had gotten different advice about the appropriate quantity to bring, so we picked a number in the middle of the range, a quarter kilo. You can't just hand the chief a bunch of loose roots, either; the kava must be properly wrapped. When we bought the kava in the produce market in Nadi, we had asked the vendor to wrap it appropriately. He covered it in newspaper and tied it with string, similar to a flower arrangement.

We landed the dinghy on the beach. As instructed, we did not wear hats or sunglasses, and we held our backpacks in our hands. Someone greeted us as soon as we pulled up. We asked to see the chief, and he led us to the bungalow.

When the chief invited us in, we were careful to remove our shoes, which is the custom when entering a home both here and in Tonga. His home was simple and modest. There was no furniture in the living room, just mats on the floor. The chief introduced himself and told us to call him by his first name, Tom. He invited us to sit on a mat and then sat across from us. We were careful to sit cross-legged. What we assume are his wife and grown son came out from other rooms and perched quietly behind him.

We set the wrapped kava on the floor in front of the chief, but we realized we'd forgotten to write down the special wording that we were supposed to say at that point. Fumbling, we admitted to Tom that this was the first village we had ever visited and we weren't sure what we were supposed to say. Much to our relief, he waved off our faux pas and picked up the bundle. This meant he would let us stay. Phew.

In accepting us as guests, the chief was saying he was willing to watch over us and keep us safe. Likewise, we were expected to follow the village's customs to make sure we didn't wear out our welcome. Tom asked us where we are from and then told us he was going to say a blessing. He chanted in Fijian for several minutes, and we heard "San Diego, California" in there somewhere. Once he was done with the prayer, we talked for a few minutes. It turns out that this village sees a lot of tourists. There is a small backpacker hotel here, and a cruise ship comes in every Monday. The villagers put on a dance show for the cruise ship and sell locally made handicrafts. The chief invited us to tonight's show. He told us that we were free to walk around the village, which we took as our cue that it was time to go. He sent us off with a couple of ripe papayas.

Just after we walked out of his house, the anticipated downpour began. A woman in a house a couple doors down called to us to get out of the rain and come inside her place. We were grateful for her invitation. From the outside, her home looked similar to the chief's, but inside it had more furniture. Three comfy chairs stood in a row along one of the walls and a table near the kitchen. There were several different types of linoleum patterns on the floor. We could see a bed in the next room.

She urged us to sit in the chairs. Her husband, Lai, sat in the third chair, and she sat on the floor amid three big piles of fiber, which she was using to weave a mat. We chatted with them for about forty-five minutes, until the rain died down, asking her question after question about their lives. She told us that she has lived in this village her entire life, but that all their children are grown and have moved to cities, one of them in California. We also found out that the chief had recently died and Tom is only the acting chief until a new one is chosen.

The tour guide on our Coral Coast tour had explained how chiefs are chosen. We had assumed that, like most monarchies, the title gets passed to the eldest son. In reality, all of the chief's sons and all of the chief's brother's sons are groomed to be future chiefs, including a higher education. When a chief dies, the village elders choose the person in the candidate pool that they believe has the best character. We think this is a brilliant system. While there are some blood line requirements, the chief actually has to earn the title. It isn't just handed to him.

Our hostess worked nonstop while she talked. To make the mats, she takes long, wide strips of fiber from a certain plant and puts them out in the sun to dry for several days. At the moment, she was cutting each strip lengthwise into about a dozen narrow strips, which she would weave together later. Eric and I enjoyed the talk. As we were leaving, we bought a couple of shell bracelets she had made, and she gave us a couple more ripe papayas.

From there, we wandered the village. The heart of the village consists of three neat rows of homes. Most are bungalows like Tom's, with a few grass huts in between. There is a church on one end of the middle row. On the other end is a covered patio where the villagers can gather. The rows are separated by plant-lined, narrow dirt paths. There are a few homes scattered behind the main area of the village. Just beyond the edge of town is the backpacker's resort (youth hostel), set back a bit from the beach. Further down the shoreline is the school. We always find villages with no roads for cars to be charming.

Near the backpacker's resort we found a footpath that led inland, so we decided to see where it went. Within a few hundred yards we got to a mangrove swamp, where there were millions of crab holes in the thick mud surrounding the marshy water. As we followed the trail around the swamp, Eric commented that this is the ideal movie setting for a horror flick *Attack of the Killer Crabs*.

Beyond the swamp, we came to farmland. We passed by several acres of neat rows of what we thought was *cassava* (tapioca). As we walked, we noticed it was starting to smell. We assumed the plants must have been recently fertilized, but at the end of the cultivated land we found the source of the smell: pigs! There was a pigpen full of them, including several adorable newborns. We had to hold our breath as we walked by because the pigs seriously stank.

Beyond the pigs, the landscape turned into forest. The path began to ascend steeply, so we turned around. I was wearing girly shoes that matched my skirt, and there was no way I could do a serious hike in them.

Back at the shore we met a local named Tooey. It turns out that he has been to San Diego! When his daughter was small, she had a medical problem that was too complicated for the local doctors to treat. Some American tourists came through town and took an interest in the girl. They brought her and Tooey to Los Angeles, where specialists operated on her. The tourists paid for all the medical expenses. They also took Tooey and his daughter sightseeing along the California coast. Tooey loves Americans, especially people from Southern California.

Tooey offered to take us on a hike. We asked for a rain check for tomorrow, since it looked as if another big rain was coming. In the dinghy, instead of heading straight for *Kosmos*, we took a tour of the bay. We scoped out the coral, looking for a nice dive/snorkeling site. We cruised by neighboring Wayasewa Island, checking out the village from the dinghy. (We didn't actually go to shore since we didn't have any kava with us.)

Afterward, we went back to *Kosmos* and had dinner. It started to pour again right before it was time to leave for the show. Since chances were that the show was outdoors, we decided to skip it. Not going turned out to be a good call, because within a few minutes it started raining so hard it felt like a monsoon. Eric had to bail out the dinghy after forty-five minutes, then again forty-five minutes later. Fortunately, after a couple of hours the rain lightened from monsoon-heavy to merely pouring, so we relaxed and went to bed.

Tuesday, September 25

We had a hard time sleeping last night; it was windy, rocky, and uncomfortable. So when we awoke to clear skies and bright sunshine, we were pleasantly surprised. We couldn't have ordered a better day for a hike. We met Tooey on the shore in front of the school at 1000, bringing two of the sailors who had made the exodus with us from Navadra. They were also Americans from Southern California, which seemed to please Tooey.

We hadn't explored the school yesterday because we had been afraid to trespass, so Tooey took us there today. There is a large field in the center, lined with buildings on all sides. Some of the buildings are classrooms, some are housing for the teachers, and some are dorms for the kids. Tooey explained that the children from all four villages on Waya attend this school, staying on campus during the week and going home on the weekends. The school goes through eighth grade, which is compulsory for all children. High school is optional, and high schools are usually only located in big towns.

Tooey walked us through the school's field to a small footpath between two of the dormitory buildings. At the edge of the school, we came to the forest. We followed the path through the forest for about a half hour. Some stretches were quite steep. We walked by a few patches of farmland, but the area was mostly uncultivated. The surroundings were green and pretty; we were surprised at the variety of foliage around. There were points along the trail where we couldn't see the path through the brush. We're sure we would have gotten lost if Tooey weren't guiding us. Tooey was armed with a machete, cutting down overgrown brush as he led us along. The soil smelled rich and fertile.

We came to a stunning viewpoint where we could see the bay we are anchored in and the islands we had come from in the distance. After taking a few photos, we continued on. The farther we walked, the sparser the foliage became. Soon it was replaced altogether with overgrown, dry grass. Tooey took us to another viewpoint. Below was another village along a different shore. The view of the ocean and the horizon beyond the village was beautiful. We headed back to the school and said good-bye to Tooey. Tooey gave each of us a drinking coconut, which was nice. Everyone we meet in this village sends us off with food!

Afterward, we had planned to go snorkeling, but the weather had suddenly turned ugly. Big clouds had moved in and it looked like rain was a certainty. Eric doesn't like to go diving or snorkeling when it is cloudy, since visibility isn't as good, so we stayed on *Kosmos*. Boarding the boat, we noticed the soles of our shoes were caked with a gummy mud that wouldn't come off. We scrubbed the shoes for a long, long time before they were clean enough to bring inside. In the evening, the rain came.

Chapter 17: Viti Levu, Viti Levu Islands, Fiji

Thursday, September 27

Yesterday afternoon we left the anchorage, intending to go back to Lautoka. It was still raining heavily when we left, but it had rained all night and all morning, so we figured it couldn't possibly last much longer. Local custom requires that you tell the chief in person when you are leaving, but we thought Tom would understand why we didn't trek out in the rain to say good-bye.

We planned to anchor in Lautoka for the night. In the morning we would run some errands, check out of the country, and leave for Vanuatu in the afternoon. As we neared Viti Levu, though, we decided to change course. The heavy rain wasn't letting up and the seas were fairly big. Anchoring in the Lautoka harbor was already unappealing; even on a good day it is rocky from all the commercial vessel traffic. With the bad sea conditions thrown into the mix, we knew we would have an uncomfortable night.

We've learned the hard way that it is important to get a good night of sleep before heading off on passage, so we decided to go to a marina located between Lautoka and Denaru. But, the winds were screaming at thirty knots, visibility was terrible, and the charts weren't high enough resolution for us to navigate the small channel without being able to see clearly. At that point, we determined that the safest thing possible was to go back to Denaru, where we could follow our previously plotted course in to the marina. Surprisingly, the ride back to Denaru wasn't too bad, considering the conditions.

This morning we took a taxi to Lautoka to check out. We knew we were supposed to bring *Kosmos* there, but taking a taxi would save us literally six hours of time between the transit, getting the dinghy up and down, situating *Kosmos* in the anchorage, and washing the anchor chain. We didn't think it would matter since no one has ever asked to see the boat upon checkout, only check in.

We were under the impression it would only take twenty minutes to get to Lautoka by car. It was actually a forty-five minute drive, and our taxi driver was really slow, so it took closer to an hour. The road was set inland, but we frequently saw glimpses of the ocean along the way. We passed by several farms and villages along the way. The ride north was much greener than the ride south to the Coral Coast had been just eleven days prior. We mentioned it to the taxi driver, who told us that there had been very little rainfall prior to our arrival. Apparently, things green up fast in Fiji with the rain.

When the landscape went from farming to industrial, we knew we had arrived. Lautoka is a blue-collar town with several factories, a brewery, a sugar mill, and a couple of wood mills. One of the wood mills had a small mountain of pine chips. There were also several car dealerships. We could see the wharf in the distance, littered with containers.

The taxi dropped us off at the wharf entrance. We were surprised by the tight security there. We had to present our passports and prove we had official business before they let us in. We went into customs and filled out the same forms that we had at check in. Just as the customs agent was about to stamp our passports, he asked us where the boat was. Our plan was to lie and tell him it was in the Lautoka harbor, but Eric just couldn't do it. He admitted the boat was at Denarau.

The customs agent refused to check us out and insisted that we bring the boat to Lautoka. Sigh. Since there was no way we could get *Kosmos* to

Lautoka before the office closed, that meant we couldn't leave until tomorrow. And the problem is that we were supposed to meet a friend in Port Vila, Vanuatu on Sunday, and now he is going to be stuck waiting on us.

Friday, September 28

We arrived in Lautoka shortly before 1000. Last night we had lucked out. We met a sailor who was also going to Lautoka to check out today. He offered to buddy boat over with us and give us a dinghy ride to and from customs, which would save us a ton of time.

Since we had filled out all the forms yesterday, we were done with customs in minutes. The officials never asked to see the boat; they just took our word for it that *Kosmos* was really in the harbor. The other boat's checkout paperwork took a little longer, but *Kosmos* was on her way out of the harbor by 1100.

Since we left, the sea conditions have been our usual fare—twenty knots of wind from the port aft, which creates uncomfortable beam seas. The weather forecast said there would be five- to six-foot (two meters) seas, but these are more like eight to ten feet (three meters). We're getting hit by nasty big side waves on a fairly regular basis. The worst part, though, is that we seem to have a current running against us, so we're making poor time. From Suva to Nadi, we were doing seven knots at 1500 rpm. Today, we're doing six and a half knots at 1825 rpm. If we can't get our speed up to over seven knots, there's no way we'll make it to Port Vila before dark on Monday, which means our friend, Jaime, has to wait yet another day for our arrival.

Saturday, September 29

Day two at sea was exactly the same as day one: slow, rocky, and not fun. We have accepted that it's impossible to make it to Port Vila before sunset on Monday, but we are still going to try to make a night entry. The only catch is that the moon is rising at around 2300 right now, and at the speed we were doing, we were on target to come in during the darkest hours. So we have slowed down to 1700 rpm (closer to what we like to cruise at, anyway), hoping to get in late enough that the moon will give us some visibility.

Chapter 18: Efate, Vanuatu Archipelago, Vanuatu

Tuesday, October 2

The sea conditions started to improve on Sunday. By Monday afternoon, they were actually fairly decent. Still, I couldn't wait to get off the boat. I've come to the realization that if a passage starts off nice and gets progressively worse, I can cope with it better than when a passage starts off bad and gets progressively better. Once the seas have become miserable and I get into a funk, only going to shore snaps me out of that funk.

Port Vila is located on the island of Efate, and is the capital of Vanuatu. The port is protected by a double bay. The outer bay, Mele Bay, has no reef. But Port Vila Bay, which lies within Mele Bay, has a reef that separates it from the outer bay. Within Port Vila Bay are two islands, which add another layer of protection between the city of Port Vila and the open ocean.

Eric and I don't usually make our approach in the dark. But we knew the moon was going to be three quarters full and bright, and the charts had indicated that there were navigational markers. We approached Mele Bay at about 2300 on Monday night, the same time as the moon rose. The promised navigation light marking the bay's entrance wasn't there, but we didn't worry as the charts seemed to be good enough resolution, the depth and radar all matched the charts, and there seemed to be no real hazards lurking about.

As we neared the pass into Port Vila Bay, we were again disappointed to find that the lights that mark the center of the pass were gone. Fortunately, the more important red and green lights that mark the

244

outer edges of the channel were working. Using the channel markers, radar and depth gauge, we were able to enter safely.

When we dropped anchor in the quarantine area in between the two islands at around 0100, I was pretty darn thrilled. Even though we didn't go to shore until after daybreak, knowing we'd be able to sleep for more than four consecutive hours and that we would be on shore soon cheered me up. As soon as we'd gotten *Kosmos* situated, we passed out.

We were up again at 0700. Cruising guides are incredibly useful for boaters. One of the many things they cover is how check-in works for each country. We've had a cruising guide for every country we've visited to, up until now. Unfortunately, we were unable to locate one for Vanuatu, so we were feeling a little lost. While in Denaru, we had looked up some information about Vanuatu on-line, and one of the things we read was that there was a yachting service that would help cruisers with check-in. With fingers crossed, we radioed the yachting service and asked what we were supposed to do. They told us to sit tight; they would bring the quarantine officer to our boat.

While we waited, we checked out our surroundings. We were closest to Irikiki Island, which is low and lushly green. Neat rows of cute little hotel bungalows line the shore. What we could see of the mainland is also very green, with some rolling hills.

The yacht agent arrived with the quarantine officer around 1030. The officer was a nice guy, and the paperwork was simple. After a quick look around, he was done. The yacht agent told us he was going to drop off the quarantine officer on shore, and then he would return and take us to the mooring area.

Within a half hour, he was back. We followed the agent around Iririki and into the most protected part of the bay, between the mainland

and Irikiki Island. It is tricky to get in there as the water is shallow and the channel is narrow. He guided us into the mooring field—located smack in the center of downtown Vila—and helped us attach to one of the moorings. After our last mooring disaster, I was grateful for his help. Interestingly enough, we were moored catty corner to a Nordhavn 46 named *Suprr*. (The 46 is the original Nordhavn ocean crossing trawler that was eventually replaced by the 43.)

We quickly got *Kosmos* situated and the dinghy down. While we were working, the couple from *Suprr* came by to say hello, and we made plans to go out to dinner with them tonight. We headed to shore to find Jaime, who was waiting for us at the dinghy dock. The first thing on the to-do list was to have our celebratory arrival meal, which we ate at the burger place that adjoined the dinghy dock.

Our next stop was customs, on the south edge of town. We caught a taxi, which dropped us off at the edge of a commercial wharf. We wandered down the wharf until we found the customs office. We were handed a large stack of paperwork to fill out. While there was a lot of paperwork, it was the most organized package we'd seen yet. All in all we were only there for a few minutes before we headed back downtown to immigration.

Downtown Vila can be walked from end to end in about a half hour. Most of the buildings are two stories, although there is one six-story hotel. While there are a few colonial style and 1960's-style buildings, most of them are blocky, with little character. There is a big open air produce market similar to what we saw in Fiji. Next to the market is a large, beautiful park that parallels the waterfront. The streets buzzed with activity, with a lot of people out and about. We noticed most of the

246

women were wearing enormously large moo-moos with short puffy sleeves. (Jaime called them Mother Hubbard dresses.)

We had a hard time finding the immigration office, which was no wonder: It turned out to be up an unmarked staircase above some shops. After going into a wrong building, a kind local walked us to the correct staircase. Thank goodness he did, because we would have never guessed it would be the entrance to official government offices. The paperwork was simple and we were done quickly. Afterward we made a detour at a French bakery. We decided we absolutely needed dessert right then and there—and it was heavenly. The last stop was to officially check in with the yacht agent, who also runs the moorings. We took Jaime back to *Kosmos* and rested until dinnertime.

The Nordhavn 78 that we had parked next to in Fiji also arrived today. Much to our delight, the crew was able to join us for dinner. This is the first time we have seen three Nordies in one place. We all went to a French restaurant on the water near the dinghy dock. They were out of most of the menu items, so after several attempts at ordering other types of food, everyone wound up with steaks. Eric and I are not big steak eaters, but we thought the steaks were phenomenal. One of Vanuatu's major exports is beef, which is known for its excellent quality.

When we got back, we were dismayed to find that the boat next to us was having a loud party. Eric and I were still tired from the passage and had been looking forward to a full night of sleep, so we irked about being kept up late by their noise. We seriously considered going over there and asking them to quiet down, but we didn't.

Wednesday, October 3

Today, Eric, Jaime, and I took a guided tour of Efate. While Eric and Jaime were paying, I loaded into the minivan with the others and introduced myself. One of the couples mentioned they were tired because they had been up late partying with their friends on a yacht. *Aha!* I thought ruefully. *These are the people that kept us up last night!* I mentioned that we are moored next to them, but I didn't complain about their party. Then Eric and Jaime climbed in and we took off.

We headed south. On our way out of town, the guide pointed out assorted buildings, including government offices, some schools, the university, and the jail. The road was paved in Vila, but as soon as we were beyond town, the surface became crushed coral—bumpy and full of potholes. The landscape was a seemingly endless expanse of gently rolling green hills dotted with trees, similar to rural New Zealand. These turned out to be cattle farms. Here and there we saw small herds of large cattle lazing around in the fields. Almost all the cattle here are organically grown, and all of it is green grass fed.

When the cattle ranches ended, the landscape changed quickly from cultivated pastures to the indigenous jungle-like landscape, which is also like New Zealand. From time to time we passed a plot of land that was cleared and cultivated, including several large coconut plantations, but the majority of the land was au natural for the rest of the ride. Eventually, the road began to parallel the coast. To our right was the ocean, dotted with the occasional scenic island, and to our left were lush rolling hills. It was beautiful.

Our first stop was at a beach on the southeast side of the island. It had an inviting looking swimming area, but it was cool outside and looked like it might rain, so no one in our group opted to swim. Instead, we wandered the beach taking photos. There was quite a bit of plant life around the beach. We also found a lot of pumice stones. As we walked, we chatted with the couple from the other boat. At one point, Eric

248

yawned and started to complain about the obnoxious people who kept us up late with their partying. I cringed. I hadn't had a chance to tell Eric that they were the partiers! The couple sheepishly admitted to Eric they were the culprits.

After a few minutes, we loaded back into the minivan and kept going. We passed a fairly large bamboo and palm frond building with a tree growing through the middle of it. Someone had literally built a structure around the tree!

The next stop was at Epule Village on the northeast side of the island. We turned onto an even rougher dirt road, driving past a number of small structures. Some were made of modern materials like cinder block and metal, some were made of traditional materials like coconut fronds, and most were a mix of the two. The minivan stopped at a small quad area. The guide ushered us out of the van and handed us all headbands made of woven leaves. He told us to continue down the relatively short road on foot.

Halfway down the road, the guide told us to stop and wait. A man appeared at the end of the road wearing a woven mat wrapped around his waist like a skirt. The skirt was fringed, and the man had several different kinds of leaves and flowers adorning his body. His face and chest were painted with black lines. He began blowing into a large seashell.

Our guide nudged us forward. We all moved slowly, sensing something ominous. As we got closer to the chief, several male villagers of all ages (including small children) wearing similar attire jumped out from nowhere, brandishing spears. We were completely surrounded. Each of us tourists had several weapons pointed at our necks and chests. After a very long minute, the villagers spontaneously ran off down the road--all except one precious little three-year old that had bonked his head during the ambush. He looked as dazed and confused about the villagers running off as we did.

The guide explained that just like the majority of the South Pacific, in the pre-colonial days, Ni-vans (what people from Vanuatu call themselves) were cannibalistic. Today, most Ni-vans still live in villages that continue to practice traditional customs. While cannibalism is a thing of the past, these villagers still pride themselves on their hunting prowess, particularly ambush skills.

We sat on a nearby bench, and the villagers reappeared and danced for us. Musicians played rhythmical percussion instruments while the dancers all sang along in a deep bass. It was powerful. Most of the dancers stood in neat rows and danced in place, using their weapon as a prop. They all wore ankle bracelets of toasted nuts in the shell, making a maracas-like rattling sound in time to the music. There were a few leads who danced all around and through the group, mimicking animal movements. Each dance was devoted to a particular animal, so for example, in the bird dance the leads were all flapping their arms like birds wings.

After the dancing, the villagers led us to a nearby covered patio. They fed us a delicious appetizer of cabbage and sweet potato in coconut milk. They also served drinking coconuts and kava—the most powerful kava we have tried yet. While we ate, a few of the villagers sang for us. This time the music was happy and lyrical, using mostly string instruments and falsetto tones. When it was time to go, we climbed into an outrigger canoe adorned with flowers and two men paddled us down the river where our van awaited. The ride was peaceful and the scenery beautiful.

We hopped into the van and went a few kilometers to a small restaurant right on the water in Sara Beach for lunch. The view was absolutely spectacular. It was a low bungalow similar to most of the homes we have seen in the South Pacific. To our surprise, there were no interior walls, and the floor was made up of the coral fragments that wash up on shore. The food—fried chicken and beef stew—wasn't very good.

After eating, we watched a demonstration of how to open and shred coconuts that was similar to the one we had seen in our tour of Tahaa. Although, we did learn some new information--toilet paper is a waste of money; coconut husks and tree leaves do the trick just fine. The guide was quite emphatic about that.

We continued north. The northeast tip of the island was an important U.S. military base during World War II. The American presence during the war had a huge, lasting impact on the people of Vanuatu. Because the Americans saved them from a Japanese occupation, the Ni-vans absolutely love America and Americans. (From the warm welcome we've received here, we can attest to this!) We drove over to the old base, and the guide pointed out where the buildings and facilities used to be. Apparently there was a lot of infrastructure then, but now only the airstrip is left.

We continued up the road, and not too far away we came to some military vehicles poking out of the water near the shore. Sadly, when the Americans left Efate, they tore down everything they had built, and buried or sank everything they had brought. Eric and I cannot understand why the Americans would sink the vehicles instead of bringing them back to the States.

Our next stop was at the Port Havannah markets, a series of small stalls along the side of the road in the middle of nowhere. They sell a variety of souvenirs, including seashells and World War II trinkets, especially old glass Coca-Cola bottles. One of the stalls had a couple of kiddy pools with a mama turtle and a half dozen babies. We even got to hold the turtles.

Our last stop, just a few miles from the market, was a scenic campground where the TV show *Survivor* was recorded a few years ago. This is the third *Survivor* site we have been to since leaving home. The water was calm here—two islands across the way offer protection from the ocean—but none of us wanted to swim because of the cool and rainy weather.

The road turned inland only a few miles beyond the last beach stop. The northern outskirts of Vila are certainly more developed than the southern side. We passed several suburban looking areas, an industrial area, and some high dollar resorts. All in all, it was a great tour. Not only did we get to see the island, we got a taste of the local culture.

Thursday, October 4

One of the biggest tourist attractions in Port Vila is the Mele Cascades Waterfall, located a few miles outside of town. We caught a bus there. The local bus system is very different than what we are used to—there's no regular route. You simply hail a minivan with a "B" license plate, tell the driver where you want to go, and wait patiently. The driver eventually takes you there… after a few stops along the way (and out of the way) to deliver other passengers.

The "bus" dropped us off at a nice, park-like area. From the entrance, we could see a footpath paralleling a stream. We walked up a gentle slope that was attractively landscaped, passing quite a few tiny waterfalls. Birds were chirping. It was really serene. At one point on the trail we saw a spectacular view of the ocean and a small island just off the coast.

At the end of the footpath, we came to some slightly bigger waterfalls. It took a minute to register, but we realized that the path continued inside the stream. There were ropes mounted in the water that acted as a handrail of sorts, leading up the little falls like a staircase. *Wow, I thought, we'd never see this in the United States!*

The "staircase" was actually short, but it was weird to be walking along in the rushing water. At the top were a couple clear, small pools that were filled by an enormous waterfall above. It was gorgeous. Several people were swimming in the main pool that got the most rushing water from above, so Eric, Jaime, and I went to the smaller one, which we had all to ourselves. The water was cool, clear and fresh. The guys swam and I waded, as the water was a little too cold for my liking. After a few minutes, the group left, so we went over to the other pool, too. Eric liked sitting directly underneath the torrent of water.

We couldn't lounge in the pools too long, though. We still needed to run errands. Tomorrow is Constitution Day, the twenty-seventh anniversary of when Vanuatu became an independent nation. All the government offices and some stores will be closed for the holiday. We reluctantly headed out and caught a cab back to town.

First, we went to customs to let them know we planned to move the boat to the island of Espiritu Santo over the weekend. The officials gave us a sealed envelope and instructed us to take it to the Espiritu Santo customs office on Monday. It was odd being asked to play courier! Next, we booked a tour to the island of Tanna for tomorrow afternoon. Tanna is famous for having the most accessible active volcano in the world, and we all wanted to see it. But since Tanna is off our planned route and doesn't have a very good anchorage, we decided to fly there. We would take *Kosmos* to Espiritu Santo when we got back.

Then we went to the grocery store. The beef there was gorgeous—high quality and organic. Even though we're not big beef eaters, I still wanted to stock up. The reason we hadn't so far was because all raw meat products get confiscated in Australia (the next country on our route), so stocking up seemed ridiculous. But yesterday we realized we could cook all the meat before leaving for Aus and freeze it. Then we would have loads of food for the next few passages.

As we were leaving the grocery store, we noticed there was a fair going on in the big park, so we went over there to check it out. There was a small city of white tents filled with assorted venders. Many of the tents were still being set up and stocked, but some were already open for business, selling everything from clothes to carvings to cleaning products to furniture to pre-fabricated houses. At the end of the park there was a big stage where it looked like bands would be playing.

Friday, October 5

We had been told there would be a big parade this morning at 0800, so we arrived on shore early so we could see the festivities from the beginning. It turned out to be a ceremony, not a parade. Across from the produce market, in front of one of the government buildings, was a small podium. A dozen official looking people were seated behind the podium, and in the middle of the street there was a small squad of soldiers. The spectators mostly stayed on the sidewalk by the market. The whole area was surrounded by police.

The ceremony began with the usual formalities: a flag salute, the reading of a portion of the constitution, and so on. Everything was in French, English, and Bislama (the local language), so it took a while with the three translations. Then the president of Vanuatu gave a long speech. We were a little in awe about how close we were to the president of a nation. This is the second time we have been unbelievably close to a president, though granted, French Polynesia is a territory, not a nation.

Not long after the president started speaking, it began to pour. All the spectators took shelter in the market, where it was hard to see, but everyone could hear just fine. We felt sorry for the soldiers that had to stand in the rain. We listened to the speech for a while, but we realized we were running out of time. Eric had broken his glasses last night and we wanted to find an optometrist to fix them before we flew out. Eric did have a spare pair, but he didn't care for them much and really wanted his primary pair fixed Fortunately, there was one open at the other end of downtown and he was able to fix the glasses immediately. We walked back through the park, where the vendors were all open for business. There was already a fairly large crowd there even though it was early.

We headed back to *Kosmos* to grab our overnight bags. Buzzing with nervous anticipation, we got her ready to be left alone for the night. We were concerned that the batteries would get low, which would cause the refrigerator and freezer to shut off. Normally, we only need to run the generator once a day, so in theory, we should be okay going away for only twenty-four hours. Beyond the fear of the batteries, we were also feeling uncomfortable leaving our baby--we hadn't spent a night away from *Kosmos* since leaving San Diego. And, we have to admit that we were also worried that the volcano would be a dud. The trip was kind of expensive--would it be worth the money?

The tour operator was waiting for us at the dinghy dock when we returned. She whisked us off to the domestic terminal of the airport—a tiny, low, single story building. When it was time to board, all the passengers were instructed to walk across the tarmac in a single file line and then climb the stairs into the small plane. No security check, no confiscating liquids, no interrogation, no hassle. The flight itself was only forty minutes. We could see whitecaps in the ocean below, which just confirmed we had made the right choice by flying.

The airport is on the west side of Tanna, and consists of a runway with a single small terminal building. A man named Phillip met us there. He owns the bungalows we would be staying in and would be our tour guide up the volcano. Phillip took us to a four-wheel-drive truck where a driver was waiting. Eric, Jaime, and I climbed into the cab, while Phillip, his wife, four kids, two other hotel guests, and another gentleman all loaded into the bed of the truck. Nine people in the bed of a truck is another thing you won't ever see in the U.S.!

We took a dirt road through the interior of the island to the east side. The road was bumpy and hilly, cutting through dense, fertile jungle and offering stunning views from all the peaks. It reminded us of our tour of Nuka Hiva. It was a long drive, and with such a heavy load, the truck was moving slowly. I was surprised the tires didn't pop from the weight, especially with the bad roads. We passed a few villages with a handful of small homes. Like Epule Village, most of them were built with an odd combination of modern and traditional materials. Along the way, we also passed several vehicles, all of them pickups with just as many people crammed into the bed of the truck, if not more.

We came to an area that looked almost like moonscape. It was a giant, empty expanse of ash hills and some scattered rocks at the base of a big mountain. It looked like Dumont Dunes in California, except with dark ash instead of light sand. Philip later explained that the mountain is the volcano and that the area devoid of foliage used to be a lake that mysteriously drained away in April of 2000 after unusually heavy rains.

We cut through the ash and picked up the road at the other side of the dry lakebed, arriving at the hotel a couple minutes later. The hotel was adorable. Someone had clearly put a lot of love into it. The main house, with the kitchen and eating area, was near the road, and there were several walkways lined with plants that led to the individual huts. All the buildings were made of traditional materials, giving the grounds a rustic feel. In between the walkways were neatly kept gardens that somewhat shelter the bungalows from view, giving visitors a sense of being in a private place out in the wilderness.

It was about 1700. We were told we needed to quickly set our stuff down in our bungalows so we could make our way up the volcano before dark. As we scurried to our hut, we noticed the ground was ash, which isn't as smooshy as sand, but it was still gentle on our feet—like walking on carpet.

Just a few hundred yards from the bungalows, we came to a poorly maintained, very steep dirt road that led almost to the peak of the volcano. The truck dropped us off at the end of the road. We were amused to see a mailbox there--the only mail box on a volcano in the world. Too bad we didn't bring any postcards. Like with the waterfall hike, there was a rope handrail to guides visitors up to the crest. It was a steep but surprisingly short walk to the peak. We could hear the volcano rumbling as we approached. It was a deep, almost anguished, groan that reverberated through us.

As we got to the crest, we could see a huge hole in the ground. Glowing red sparks and smoke were coming up from the depths of the hole and landing on a ledge on the opposite side from where we stood. From the scattered rocks on the ground around us, we could tell that sometimes the lava lands where we were standing, which shocked us. We had thought we'd be at a viewing station a safe distance from the fallout, but we weren't. We were literally standing *on the rim of an active volcano!* Even more surprising was that there were no barriers of any kind. We could have jumped into the volcano if we wanted to. This definitely tops the list of things you would never be allowed to do in the U.S.

The volcano consistently growled, spewing forth red rock and smoke. The rumbling grew steadily louder and more pained, and the lava spurts became thicker and taller. After about ten minutes, the volcano let out a tremendous roar and an enormous amount of lava shot up at least fifty feet over our heads. Fortunately, even in the bigger blow, the lava sparks all landed on the other side. After the big blow, both the rumbling and lava immediately quieted back down, but then steadily built up again for about twenty minutes. Then there was another huge blow. We realized it was a pattern--consistent small eruptions interspersed with a big eruption every ten to twenty minutes.

After the first big blow, I realized that if the wind changed and one of those rocks hit me, I'd die. If there was an especially large eruption, those red rocks would completely cover the ground around us in seconds and every one of us would be dead. Wow. I couldn't believe we were really here.

We were completely mesmerized as we watched the volcano, feeling like the abilities of humans were insignificant and feeble compared to the raw power of Mother Nature. This volcano created this large island all by itself, and probably also created the surrounding islands. Its might was almost inconceivable. But for some reason it wasn't scary. It was simply awe-inspiring.

As the sun began to set, the molten red rocks began to glow vividly. Soon it was pitch black outside, but the entire top of the volcano was brightly illuminated by the glow of the red rocks. The volcano's power was even more evident in the dark. We watched the red spots fly up and then ever so slowly float down, land, and slowly slide back into the hole.

The volcano put on an impressive display for us. We were expecting to see a hole with little activity, not a powerful show that was a million times more spectacular than any fireworks we've ever seen.

On another note, after examining the lava rock up close, it suddenly makes sense to us why the lava islands eventually shrink back into the sea. The rocks are light and airy, and can be ground up with little effort. With so much air in them, it is clear that as time goes on they eventually compact down under the normal pressures of nature, thus eroding away.

Shortly after sunset, Phillip told us it was time to go. We didn't want to tear ourselves away; we probably could have sat there all night. We stalled him for a couple minutes and finally, reluctantly, followed him down to the road.

The truck did not belong to Phillip. He had hired the driver to pick us up from the airport and take us to the volcano, so we had to walk back down. The hike down was pleasant. The ash is soft to walk on, making it easy on the knees. It rained a little, and Phillip told us we were lucky to see the volcano. He said that often the rain clouds completely block the view.

Dinner was waiting for us back at the bungalows. It was a simple meal of fish, rice, and vegetables, but the portions were huge and the food was delicious. We pigged out. The other two hotel guests—Australian volunteers who teach at a high school in Tanna—were already eating when we came in. They were on their way to the John Frum villages to watch the Friday sing-along. We asked if we could tag along.

In 1936, a boater named John Frum came to Tanna. At that point, Vanuatu was a European colony (then named New Hebrides). Frum told the locals that if the Europeans left, there would be an abundance of wealth. This sparked a neo-pagan uprising, with followers going back to their traditional ways (except cannibalism). Only a few years later, World War II began. The Japanese seized New Hebrides and kicked the Europeans out. The Americans conquered the Japanese and set up bases in Efate and Tanna. Many Tannese went to work on the military bases and were amazed at the wealth the Americans had brought with them. John Frum was right! John Frum is still idolized almost as a god by a couple of villages on Tanna. Every Friday night, the villagers sing songs and dance in hopes that he will return, as he had promised.

Two of Phillip's brothers escorted us to the village, about a four-mile trek each way through the dry lakebed. The volcano smoked and rumbled as we walked. Whenever there was an especially loud rumble, glowing red sparks were visible at the top. It was pitch black outside, so we couldn't see what the village looked like as we entered, but we could hear the music. We followed our ears to a group of people sitting on the ground under a gazebo, heartily singing. A few men were strumming guitars, and several people were standing in a circle around the perimeter of the gazebo. The music was melodious and happy.

We were directed to sit on a nearby bench, and told we were welcome to join the dancing if we wanted to. Ah, the people on the outskirts were dancers. Most simply swayed back and forth in time to the music, but a couple of women were doing what looked like a line dance. The whole atmosphere was casual. Between the style of music and the setting, we felt like we were at a campout. The only things missing were the fire and the s'mores.

The chief sat down next to Eric and told him about a trip he had taken to America in the 1980s. Our escorts must have told him we were Americans. Talking to a chief is always an honor of sorts, even if it is a small village. We stayed for about an hour.

As we trudged back through the soft soil, I reflected on the day. I saw the president of a country speak. I flew to a beautiful island. I stood on the rim of a volcano. I saw lava shoot up over my head. I got to partake in the customs of a village that hasn't been Westernized. This may very well have been the most amazing day of my life! Today embodies exactly why we are traveling.

Saturday, October 6

The bungalows don't have electricity. Our room was lit only by a small oil lamp, and we couldn't see much last night. When we got up this morning, we took a better look at our accommodations. The beds had mosquito netting over them that protected us from bug bites. The floor was covered in woven mats, the kind that we watched the lady make on Waya Island. The hut's frame was made of large bamboo rods, and the walls had two layers. The interior layer was thin bamboo stalks lashed together, and the exterior layer appeared similar to the woven mats on the floor. We've been told these kinds of walls hold up well in cyclones. Since the wind blows through the weaving/rods, there is little wind resistance.

The roof was made of palm fronds with a relatively tall pitch. It fit snugly on the wall frame at the corners, but in the middle there was a big gap between the wall and the ceiling to provide air ventilation. The eaves extended far enough out that there is no exposure to rain, despite the gap. This style of roof that is popular in the South Pacific, even in buildings using modern materials.

We found the restrooms to be entertaining. They were communal, in a separate building. There was a stall with a toilet, a second stall with a shower, and a basin with soap and water. There wasn't running water, but Phillip and his family tried to make it appear as if there was. For example, after one a guest would use the toilet, someone brought in a bucket of water to fill the toilet tank so the next person could flush. Someone looking for first world luxuries probably wouldn't like this place, but we absolutely loved it.

Breakfast was coconut pancakes, eggs, bread, peanut butter, and bananas. We were expecting a meager continental breakfast, so we were delighted to be served such hearty, good food. We were hungry after so much walking last night.

After breakfast, we went on a "cultural tour." We were expecting Phillip to take us to his village, a five-minute walk south, for a quick tour and maybe a dance or two. We knew something was up when we walked north. We turned off the road onto a narrow footpath leading into the jungle. After a couple minutes on this path, we were suddenly completely surrounded by men of all ages brandishing weapons. Déjà vu.

After our last experience, we were kind of expecting the ambush and had been looking for potential attackers, but we did not see these men at all. It was unbelievable how seamlessly they could blend into their surroundings. This group was wearing full skirts made of dried leaves. Most had on hats of dried leaves or twigs.

To drive home how skilled they are at the art of camouflage, we were ambushed a second time by guys lying on the footpath. They had their skirts draped around them so they appeared to be nothing more than a pile of leaves. We looked right at them and didn't realize they were people. When we got close, they jumped up and screamed. It's a good thing none of us have weak hearts!

The villagers showed us all kinds of interesting things that are integral to their life. They proudly demonstrated the various traps they make for different kinds of animals. The traps are simple, yet highly effective. Then they showed us how to make a stretcher out of leaves and how to make fire by rubbing a stick against a log. They also showed us a few of their medicinal tricks.

The cultural tour was quick, but informative and fun. Just like at Epule, the villagers are proud of their way of life and seem to be happy to show off their culture and traditions. We sensed these exhibits weren't only a way for them to make a quick buck—they genuinely wanted to bring us into their world. They are kind people who are quick to flash a big smile, which you wouldn't expect from a "warrior" culture.

As we were leaving, they sang us a farewell song using string instruments in the same happy, melodic style we had heard in Epule. We read somewhere that the Americans brought this style of music during World War II and it became popular with the locals. We were loaded into the bed of a different pickup truck along with three other people. The ride was actually kind of fun—bouncing along on the bumpy road, enjoying the fresh air, sunshine, and unlimited views. It wasn't quite as fun for our backs and buttocks, though.

The flight back to Efate was quick and uneventful. The tour company picked us up at the airport and delivered us back to the dinghy dock. Our dinghy was still there. Good sign. *Kosmos* was still floating. Another good sign. Back on board, we were pleased to see that the solar panels had kicked in and we hadn't used up much battery juice in the twenty-four hours we were gone. What a relief! Now that we know we can safely go away for a night, we may do more trips.

In Retrospect:

At the time, we knew that trip to Mt. Yasur would be one of the highlights of our world journey, and in looking back, we both rank it as probably the most incredible experience of our lives. But we had no idea how much that twenty-four hours on Tanna would ultimately help to shape the course of our future, in more ways than one. Had we not gone to Tanna, our lives may have been very different.

Chapter 19: Espiritu Santo, Vanuatu Archipelago, Vanuatu

Monday, October 8

We headed out to sea yesterday morning. The other islands in the area often protected us during the 120-nm ride, so overall the passage was calm and smooth, but we did hit rough patches now and again. It was a scenic ride with the islands on the horizon. We saw a good-sized pod of spinner dolphins, which was exciting, especially when they jumped for us. We were still going against the current, though, with slow speeds considering the engine's rpm.

Months ago, during our twenty-one day passage, we had posted a blog about how the food in the refrigerator had jumped out and attacked us while at sea. Jaime had commented on it, saying it was hilarious. His comment must have angered the refrigerator gods, because as soon as we got to a rocky stretch, Jaime opened the refrigerator and a pile of food fell on the floor in front of him. A bottle of teriyaki sauce broke, which he quickly cleaned up.

A few hours later, I did an engine room check. My heart just about stopped when I saw big brown spots all over the engine. *Holy crap, the oil must have exploded!* I thought. I quickly looked for the source of the explosion. Seeing nothing obvious, I went upstairs and approached Eric.

Swallowing my panic and trying to sound casual, I said "Hey, what are those huge brown spots all over the engine?"

Eric's eyes almost popped out of his head, and he bolted downstairs. For the first thirty seconds he also thought it was oil. But after touching it, he realized it wasn't oil at all—it was teriyaki sauce that had dripped through the floor!

The island of Espiritu Santo became visible around noon today. Much like Efate, it is very green, with low hills near the shoreline and higher mountains in the distance. Directly across from the southwest corner of Santo is another small island called Aore, which is flat and green. The two islands create a relatively narrow channel.

As we headed through the channel, we could see that Santo had lots of grassland, presumably for cattle farming. Aore is dotted with small homes along the waterfront, with big stretches of foliage between the houses. About three quarters of the way up the channel we arrived at Aore Resort, supposedly the most comfortable anchorage in the area. The hotel gave us permission to use one of their moorings. Getting attached to the mooring was something of a nightmare. The current was super strong and Eric had a hard time getting us properly positioned next to the buoy. The buoy was not very big and I couldn't quite reach it with the hook, so Jaime tried. Jaime was able to grab the buoy, but because of the swift current, Eric wasn't able to hold position long enough for Jaime to pull the line all the way up to the deck. Jaime wound up dropping both the line and the hook. We both ran to the back of the boat as fast as we could and managed to retrieve the hook as it floated past the cockpit, which was a huge relief. Jaime and I both unsuccessfully tried again to catch the buoy, and we managed to drop the hook a second time. Again we caught the hook as it floated past the cockpit. Eventually, though, we did manage to get attached.

Once we were situated, we surveyed our surroundings. Aore Resort looks much like all the other hotels in the area, with a row of tiny bungalows facing the water. Across the way on Santo is downtown Luganville, a former U.S. military base and now the biggest city on the island. From where we were, it just looked like a smattering of low, small buildings.

Instead of celebrating our arrival by eating out, Jaime made us a big meal onboard. He cooked up a wonderful beef stew, with plenty of leftovers to freeze for passage food. We also made arrangements to do several dives over the next couple of days.

Tuesday, October 9

At 0800 this morning, the dive company picked us up from *Kosmos*. We were going to dive the famous *USS President Coolidge*, a luxury liner that was commandeered by the American military during World War II. She sunk in 1941 after hitting one of several mines that had been planted in the bay near Luganville by the Americans. Unfortunately, the Americans neglected to inform the *Coolidge's* captain about the mines. He had been doing eighteen knots when it exploded and the ship sank in only thirty minutes. Fortunately, only two lives were lost.

The *Coolidge* is two hundred meters (six hundred feet) long and twenty-five meters (seventy-five feet) wide. She sits mostly intact on her port side, leaning against a reef. Her bow is twenty meters (sixty feet) below the water line, while her stern is sixty meters (180 feet) below. Many artifacts are still in place. Jaime and I were excited about going, but Eric was hesitant. The idea of diving into a small, confined space didn't appeal to him, especially knowing it was dark, there were hazards, and it was possible (though unlikely) to get trapped inside.

It was just the three of us with the local dive guide. The boat ride over was short. We tied to a mooring and prepared to descend by holding on to the mooring line until we reached the bottom. After months in the South Pacific, we've gotten used to clear water with at least one-hundred-foot visibility, so we were surprised when we couldn't see the ship from the surface. The lack of clarity pushed Eric over the edge; he decided to sit this one out.

Jaime and I had descended most of the way before the front of the ship came into view. I was struck by its massive size. There were lots of fish around, in many varieties, but we didn't stop to look at them. Instead, we followed the guide as he swam over the foredeck, which still had equipment laying around, ready for use, such as gas masks and rifles. There was also an anti-aircraft gun with a pile of large shells stacked up next to it.

We swam up to the promenade deck (a long covered walkway), which was now on its side. The area was closed in on three sides and the escape route was down, not up. *It's a good thing Eric didn't come*, I thought as we swam through the deck. *He definitely wouldn't have liked it.* From there, we entered some of the cargo holds below the promenade deck. The cargo area was fully enclosed and relatively dark, with little natural light filtering in. The guide shined a flashlight around so we could see the treasures below. It was still full of supplies for the base, and we saw trucks and ammunition. We were 120 feet (forty meters) below, my deepest dive yet.

Getting in and out of the holds was a bit tricky. We were actually swimming through the support beams of what used to be walls, and the spaces we had to swim through were not much bigger than a person. Jaime, who is a highly experienced dive master, was aghast that the guide would take an inexperienced diver like me—who has only a general certification to sixty feet—into such small, dark spaces. Jaime was surprised that I was not intimidated or freaked out.

We exited the wreck through some more of these tight squeezes and ascended to the safety stop. A safety stop is a place somewhere between ten and twenty feet deep (three to seven meters) where you sit for a few minutes to let your body adjust from the lower depths before going back to sea level. Once again, I had been coming up too fast. Thank God that the place we stopped had something for me to hold onto so I didn't float away. This was the second deep dive in which I'd gotten dangerously close to harming myself.

After the dive, we headed to Luganville to look around and deliver the envelope to customs. The shoreline was littered with rusted out mechanical parts and hardened bags of cement. Like in Efate, when the American military vacated Luganville, they had thrown most of their supplies into the ocean, and we are sure the junk along the shore was the Americans' trash washing back up. The dock was in serious disrepair, almost to the point of dangerous. We were eagerly greeted by a couple of locals having lunch on the beach. They welcomed us and chatted for a while, telling us some of the fun things to do in the area.

On our way over to the main highway, we passed several rusted-out half-dome metal buildings. San Diego has six major military bases and they all have these same metal buildings, so we are sure these are remnants from the war. We were glad to see that the Americans had left something intact. The main road was six lanes wide, with two lanes of traffic and a parking lane on each side. Where we come from, all the main roads are at least this big, so it took Eric and me a while to realize that this is by far the widest road we have seen in the South Pacific. (Although Jaime noticed right away!) The road was also made of asphalt, which is standard in the U.S., but unusual for the South Pacific. Concrete holds up better in the heat. Clearly the Americans had built the road, too.

As we had surmised from the boat, downtown Luganville is small. There is a nice park in the center and a produce market at the south end.

Most of the buildings look like they are left over from the war. There were a few more metal domes and several low, blocky buildings identical to the ones that adorn the bases in San Diego. The tallest building is a bizarre four-story structure. The bottom story is a petrol (gas) station; the story above it looks like office space; and the third and fourth stories look like apartments. We've never seen businesses or housing above a petrol station before! There are quite a few shops, too, most selling a strange assortment of random goods. It looks like they stock whatever they can get their hands on, mostly things the first world countries reject.

We walked the length of town. It was hot outside, and the tar road radiated heat, making the walk uncomfortable. We stopped for burgers at a small café, then caught a cab to customs, located at the commercial wharf just north of where we landed the dinghy. They checked our ID and made sure we had official business before letting us in. We found customs, handed over the envelope, and filled out a form. A couple minutes later, we headed back to *Kosmos*.

For dinner, we went to a Ni-van buffet and show at the Aore Resort. The show started with a string band that played cheerful, lively music for about an hour while weak kava and fried coconut appetizers were served. When the band finished, the buffet opened. Several dishes were new to us, including the national dish, lap lap. There were two varieties of lap lap: banana and taro. It was starchy, dense, and heavy. It didn't take much to fill you up, and it wasn't very good. We did like a roasted pumpkin and kumala dish. We also tried tuluk, which looked like a sushi roll without the external layer of rice over the seaweed. It was actually made of a cassava and beef filling wrapped in fried spinach and topped with a coconut cream sauce. It was pretty good. There was a whole poulet fish out on the table; we could pick off as much of it as we wanted. The fish was excellent, and so was the curry sauce that accompanied it. The rest of the food was more familiar—whole prawns in garlic sauce, beef curry, chicken in soy sauce, potato salad, green salad, rolls.

After dinner the main performance started, featuring dancers from the Banks Islands, which is the northern part of Vanuatu. The Banks Islanders are known for their flamboyant costumes. In Santo and the surrounding islands, the traditional attire for the villagers is simply a leaf strategically placed over the private parts. We guessed that the resort had imported dancers with outfits that would be less offensive to the tourists. One of the amazing things about Vanuatu is the diversity of culture. In Polynesia we saw lots of dancing, and most of it was fairly similar from island to island. In Vanuatu, each island's dance style is extremely different.

This show started with an assortment of animal sounds coming from the darkness around the gazebo dining area. The dancers were making the animal noises, and they sounded remarkably real. They mimicked sheep, chicken, birds, goats, and pigs. If we weren't sitting in the middle of a resort, we might have thought there were really animals out in the bushes.

Then the performers—males of all ages, including kids as young as four—came out of the darkness and into the center of the dining area. All had bare chests and feet, and wore several strings of the noisemaker nuts around their ankles. Some wore dry grass skirts; some wore two woven mats, one over their crotch and one over their buttocks, leaving their thighs exposed. They all had big branches of assorted foliage tucked into the back of their waistbands, and the foliage covered most of their backs. They had white lines painted on their faces, chest, and thighs, and they wore funny little hats with wigs attached to the hats. The wigs were made of dry grass. Some were natural color, some were dyed a darker brown

271

that was closer to the locals' hair color, and one wig was striped with natural, red, and blue hues. Some of the hats were pointy and some were round; most of them painted bright colors.

Two drummers stood in the center of the group while everyone else danced around them. The music came solely from the drums, ankle rattles, and low grunting noises the dancers made. The dances involved a lot of hopping and squats, and must have taken a lot of energy. The dancers tended to move in unison with someone yelling out commands. With each command, the dancers changed direction, body motion or dance steps. In between dances, the dancers would lean forward and grunt for a minute or two before starting the next sequence. We were impressed with the show!

Wednesday, October 10

This morning we were surprised to see a couple more people in the boat when the dive company picked us up, one a dive guide and one a regular diver. Jaime and I were going to go deeper inside the *Coolidge* with the same guide as last time to see the famous "Painted Lady," a sculpture that adorns the first class dining room in the center of the ship, thirty-six meters down (one hundred thirty feet). Eric was going to dive around the exterior with the other two guys.

Eric's group did a beach entry instead of going down the mooring line. Eric was more comfortable starting from shallow water and getting deeper than he was starting in deep water. Nevertheless, the descent was still scary for him since the visibility wasn't good. For much of the descent, he saw an empty expanse of nothingness, which freaked him out. He was relieved when the ship came into sight. They followed the same route Jaime and I had the day before, except they didn't go into any of the cargo holds.

272

Jaime and I descended the mooring line again. We went over the starboard side of the boat, which is now the top since it is leaning on its side. We passed over a long series of portholes with the glass long gone. Each porthole was adorned with an assorted cluster of colorful, pretty corals. There were quite a few more small clusters of coral scattered over the metal. I spotted a lionfish, which are neat to watch.

We entered a blast hole in the hull, then descended straight down into the relatively dark interior. Once again, only the guide had a light. We followed several narrow, enclosed corridors with few areas to escape from should anything go wrong. We came to a pitch black shaft, which was the dining room (remember the ship is on its side). We descended the long room to the opposite end where the sculpture hung, still intact. Honestly, it was anti-climatic. The sculpture was small and ugly, a woman in Victorian attire standing in front of a white horse. The room was gloomy and eerie, with a small amount of light coming in from what used to be a skylight.

We headed back up the shaft, getting ready to exit the wreck. We took a different route out, exploring more cargo holds as we headed toward the bow. The cargo holds were quite dark and the spaces we were passing through were very small. At one point, I kicked a steel bar with the tip of my fin and my fin flew off. Thank God Jaime was able to catch it before it floated away. Still, Jaime was growing more and more worried about my safety. After all, this was my deepest dive; we had been at concerning depths for longer than was prudent; we were swimming amongst serious potential hazards; and there weren't many escape routes. When Jaime realized that the dive guide planned to take us all the way forward to the chain locker, he put his foot down and insisted we all go up immediately. We exited from the next opening, ascending into the brightness of the open water, where a school of colorful fusilier fish greeted us. As we made our way to the safety stop spot, we passed Eric's group.

I had added six more pounds of weight today (2.75k) to make sure I didn't float away. It didn't work. I still had to hold on for dear life to stay down. I couldn't believe it—I had on eighteen pounds (eight kilos) total and it still wasn't enough!

The dive company took us to a nearby beach and served us lunch. After lunch, all of us did a shore descent into Million Dollar Point, the biggest military junkyard in the world. The Americans had set up ramps and literally drove jeeps, tanks, trucks and tons of other stuff into the sea one right after another, creating walls of discarded vehicles. The top of the junk pile was only a few feet below the surface, making it a popular snorkeling site. It was longer than I expected it to be, stretching for what seemed like forever. We went down ninety feet and still could not see the bottom of the heap.

Seeing the extent of the junk upset me for two completely unrelated reasons. First, millions of American taxpayer dollars were literally thrown into the trash. We could have used all this stuff again back in the States and in subsequent wars, for scrap metal if nothing else. I wondered *How could they justify this obscene wastefulness? Does this kind of wastefulness still go on?* Second was the obvious toxicity of the debris. It has been sitting there for sixty years, so we were expecting a lot of coral growth. There wasn't much coral all, which was disappointing and disturbing.

We did see a little bit of sea life: four species of nudibranch (sea slugs, Jaime's favorite). We also saw a crocodile fish, a cuttlefish, a couple of long fin lionfish, and a shrimp hiding in some coral. One of the guides poked at a sea cucumber. When attacked, sea cucumbers spew long white strands of guts out of their rear and then grow new innards. He wanted us to see what it looked like. This horrified Jaime, who strongly believes in leaving the underwater environment untouched.

After the dive, the guys went and hung out at the resort pool while I started cooking the food that would otherwise be confiscated in Australia. I froze it all in individual serving size containers and now we are all set for passage food.

Chapter 20: From Vanuatu to Australia

Saturday, October 13

This morning we left for a nine-day passage to Cairns, Australia. Being that it is such a long trip, we had to do some serious preparations. We spent all day Thursday and most of the day Friday doing chores. Jaime volunteered to scrub the waterline, which delighted me. I think that the waterline is by far my hardest job duty. I did the bottom.

Because of the two-knot current, we could only work during slack tide. Since we didn't have much time before the current picked back up, it took us three rounds of scrubbing over two days. Jaime is planning on buying a Nordhavn and is trying to decide between a 43 and a 47. After finally completing the waterline, he announced that he had decided on the 43–he couldn't possibly take doing the waterline of the 47. For my part, I was horrified by the amount of growth on the bottom. It was totally covered in fine green grass, with some patches of red grass, and tons of little red spots that looked like chewing gum. I had to scrub harder than ever. I don't know what I would have done had Jaime not scrubbed the waterline. There is no way I could have done the whole boat alone.

In between scrubbings, Eric and Jaime plotted the course to Cairns, changed the main engine oil, rearranged the lazarette, cleaned the sea strainers, changed the water maker filter, checked all the anti-siphon valves on board, and checked to make sure all the systems were working properly. I finished cooking everything on board likely to get confiscated in Australia and did some cleaning. On Friday afternoon we went to shore to check out of the country and run some errands.

When we untied from the mooring this morning, *Kosmos* was struggling against the powerful current; we were doing only two-and-a-half knots at 1700 rpm through the channel. Once we were out from between the islands, it got a little better, but our speeds were still unbelievably slow.

As expected, the seas were calm while we were in the lee of the islands. Much to our surprise, though, it was still relatively calm even after we arrived in the open ocean. So far today is one of the best days we've had at sea. Our speeds have picked up some, but we are still creeping along.

The most exciting news of all is that Jaime caught a tuna! We think it is approximately eight pounds. He made us a fabulous tuna steak dinner.

Thursday, October 18

Today is day five. To celebrate our making it to the halfway mark, a pod of dolphins did a show for us. Eric and Jaime spotted the dolphins at about 14:30 (2:30 p.m.), and we went outside to get a better look. There was a big group of them surfing the waves around us. Many of them stuck their noses up and then dove down, arching their backs out of the water. A couple of them even rolled over as they were diving so their bellies arched, which was exciting because we haven't seen them do that before.

Then out of nowhere, one of the dolphins jumped several feet out of the water, vertical to the sea. We were stunned. After that initial breach, the dolphins put on quite the show for us, including several more full body breaches. They also did several partial body breaches where they seemed to stick their heads up out of the water to say hi. Sometimes they even dove forward off the top of a cresting wave, which sent them flying up about a foot above the descending water level before they plunged back into the ocean.

They seemed to be having a lot of fun playing in the waves and showing off for us. The other dolphins we've seen appear to enjoy playing at the bow, but these dolphins took it to a whole new level. The seas were following, so the waves were coming from behind. The dolphins would surf the waves alongside us, then leap toward the bow as the wave neared it. At times there were five or six of them jostling for position at the bow, and newcomers would sometimes jump over the others to get in. They didn't seem to stay at the bow for long—they tended to swim toward the front of the boat, and then drop behind it to repeat the surfing process all over again.

Many of the dolphins were especially large, some of the largest we have seen to date. Many had distinctive scars, and one even had a big chunk taken out of his back. After the initial burst of rapid activity, they slowed down the intensity of the show, but were still performing. The pod stayed with us for more than half an hour, and then vanished. It is the best dolphin show we have seen yet and we absolutely loved it.

Unfortunately, the nice seas were too good to be true. They only lasted for thirty hours. Then it went back to "normal" for us, with twenty-knot winds at our aft beam and confused seas that made for an overall uncomfortable ride. From there it kept getting progressively worse, going from uncomfortable to really uncomfortable. Now we are consistently getting hit with huge, awful side rollers as well as corkscrews. The bad news is there is a big storm to the south of us that is sending up these big swells, and it is only going to get worse. Sigh.

Eric has been struggling with seasickness the last few days, and he and I have been fighting a lot, so it has been emotionally miserable as well as physically miserable. We're trying not to fight in front of Jaime, but we're sure he hears it. Mostly, the fighting is simply us taking our misery out on one another, but sooner or later every argument goes back to the same issue: whether we should sell *Kosmos* or not. We have to decide soon,

278

because if we are going to put her on the market, Australia is the best place to do it. Neither of us really wants to sell her, but neither of us wants to spend another year and a half in miserable seas either.

Jamie seems to have no seasickness or lethargy issues, but I sense he is having a hard time with the sedentary life at sea. He seems to be almost anxious to find things to do. I haven't said anything, but inside I am laughing because I know how hard it is to relax. Actually, now that I think about it, sitting still doesn't bother me anymore. I no longer feel wracked with guilt if I'm not productive every minute of the day. I wonder when that change happened?

Saturday, October 20

As expected, the seas went from really uncomfortable to miserable. Seas were ten-to-twelve feet and confused, with lots of those nasty big beam waves. While Eric was in the shower we were hit by one of them. He said the boat rolled over so far on its side that the porthole was completely underwater.

Jaime said one of the most memorable moments of his time with us was standing at the back of the boat watching waves much taller than *Kosmos* gunning straight for us, and thinking that the waves were going to crash on us and we'd all die. He was astounded that our little *Kosmos* contentedly rode the waves up and down, seeming oblivious to the fact they were bigger than her.

We are all so ready to get off this boat, and it seems like an eternity before we will reach Cairns. I am literally counting the hours until we are supposed to arrive.

Yesterday, we got an updated report from our professional weather routing service. They told us there is a tropical depression in the area that looks like it may turn into a full blown cyclone. It doesn't affect us at all, directly speaking. But the fact that there is a hurricane a full six weeks before hurricane season is supposed to begin is disturbing. We need every minute of those six weeks to clear the hurricane zone, and knowing we could get caught in an early storm is frightening. It also makes us count our blessings. If we had left a few days later from Vanuatu, we would be caught in it right now.

Today we had a couple of birds stop by for a visit. Both stayed for a surprisingly long time and left us gifts to remember them by.

Monday, October 22

Thankfully, the seas improved yesterday, dropping down to merely uncomfortable with six-to-eight foot seas. Uncomfortable is a big step up from miserable. Yesterday we rolled up 10,000 nm on the odometer. An astounding 8,200 of those miles have been done in the last six months. We also had a few more bird friends stop by, including one with lime green feet.

At 0400 this morning, we approached the entrance of the Great Barrier Reef. Praise God! Even though it would be several more hours until we got to land, at least we would be in protected waters and out of our misery. It was still dark, but since the pass is about a mile wide, we felt like it was safe to enter it. The charts seemed to be accurate and there was a lot of room to maneuver. We were so, so happy when we got inside and it was suddenly flat and calm. Ahh!

As the sun came up, we could see the mainland in the distance ahead and a few islands dotting the horizon to our north and south. The main land was hilly and green, with parts of it enshrouded in clouds. The water was an emerald green, which is new for us. All the deep water we've seen until now has always been a sapphire blue. As we got closer, we could see the city of Cairns in the distance. The coastline appears to be built up, but the mountains behind it look untouched.

We pulled into the marina at around 0900. The marina is located in the heart of downtown. In front of the marina is a fancy hotel with an attractive, almost Cape Cod architectural style and a pedestrian boardwalk between the hotel and the marina entrance. The ground floor of the hotel is lined with restaurants. There is a new-looking tall building directly to the left of the hotel, and to the right there is a construction zone.

We can't even begin to tell you how exuberant we felt as we tied up to the dock. We just crossed the entire Pacific Ocean from end to end. The whole thing! Do you know how darn big that ocean is? And *we* crossed it!

This is day 176 of our journey. Fifty-eight days—33 percent of our time—have been at sea. A few of those days at sea were nice, but the vast majority of the time, the conditions ranged from uncomfortable to miserable. Getting as far as we have is a huge accomplishment. In my mind it is a big enough accomplishment that we can sell the boat without feeling like failures for not completing an ocean circumnavigation.

We've already decided that if we sell *Kosmos*, we'll still complete our round-the-world journey. We'll just switch to more conventional modes of transportation. Through the South Pacific, we really did need a private boat to easily get from island to island, but a private boat isn't necessary in the rest of the world. Why stay on the boat and be miserable when we don't need to be?

But, did we really want to sell her? Both of us were so conflicted…

In Retrospect:

We are going to spoil the ending and tell you we decided to continue traveling by boat. We are so glad we didn't give up. Now we know that the South Pacific has the most consistently big seas in the world. While we did hit our worst weather later in the journey (including a couple very scary times!), overall we had a mix of good and bad throughout the last three-quarters of the world.

Just like in the South Pacific, there are places throughout the rest of the world that are off the beaten path and difficult to get to without a private boat. Several of these remote places became our most treasured stops along the way.

2390 Shelter Island Drive, Suite 216 - San Diego, CA 92106

Call Henry at (619) 226-8661

MARINER'S GENERAL

INSURANCE GROUP

Randy & Rebecca Tisch 734-446-0095

Kosmos Diagrams and Description

Kosmos is a Nordhavn brand 43 foot boat built in 2006 in Taiwan by the company Pacific Asian Enterprises. It is not a sailboat. It is a powerboat, specially designed for long range voyages. Powerboats capable of crossing oceans are sometimes called "passagemakers". Also the style of the boat can be called a trawler. Trawlers are commonly used as commercial fishing boats, so many people mistake her for a commercial fishing vessel.

Overall it is like a tiny 2 bedroom, 3 story apartment with all the comforts of a land based home. The salon (living room) is mid level, the pilothouse is top level, and the staterooms and engine room are on the lower level. Here are various drawings:

Exterior Profile:

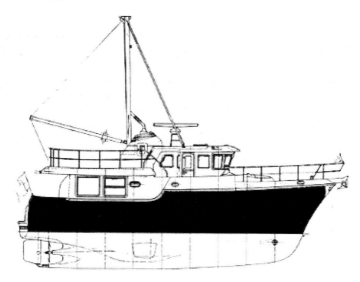

Interior Plan:

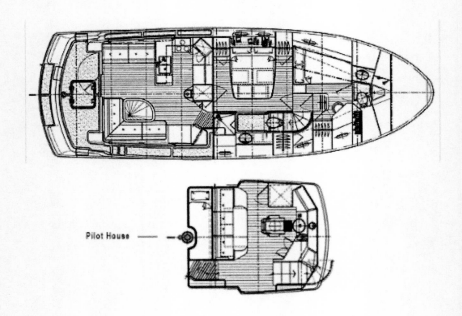

Pilot House

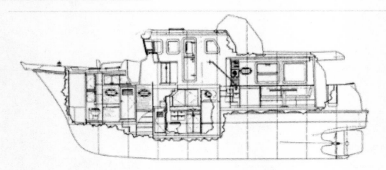

Starboard Inboard Profile:

Port Inboard Profile

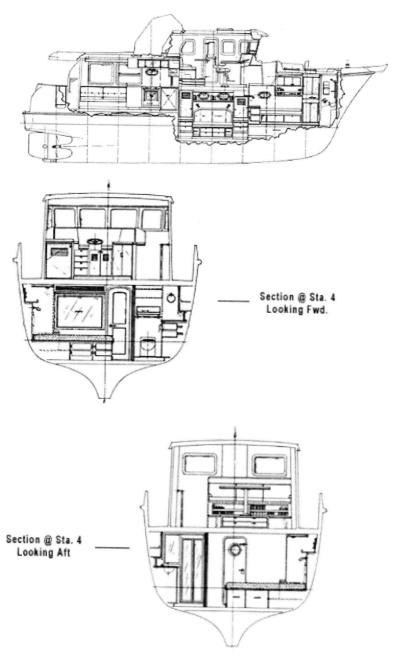

Section @ Sta. 4
Looking Fwd.

Section @ Sta. 4
Looking Aft

Some facts and equipment aboard *Kosmos*:

- 43 feet long (45 including anchor).
- 14 feet 10 inches wide
- 5 feet 3 inches draft (depth below water line).
- 54,540 pounds at full load of water and fuel (that is very heavy/stout for a boat this size).
- 2 staterooms (bedrooms).
- 2 heads (2 bathrooms with toilet/sink/shower).
- 120 volt power.
- Full air conditioning/heat.
- Washer/dryer (combo unit).
- Trash compactor.
- 2 refrigerators and 1 deep freezer.
- About 3,000 nm range on one load of diesel fuel.
- 5 to 7 knot cruising speed (6 knot average, ~2.7 nm/US gallons, ~2.1 US gallons/hour).
- 1250 US gallons of fuel capacity.
- 300 US gallons of water.
- 105hp diesel main engine. Lugger LP668D (6 cylinder, 6.8 liter) main engine (naturally aspirated, as opposed to turbo).
- 27hp diesel Yanmar wing engine and propulsion system (emergency back up propulsion system).
- American Bow Thruster (ABT) TRAC active fin stabilizers.
- Paravane stabilizers with two 40 lbs. "fish".
- 8kw Northern Lights generator.
- 400 gallon per day AC watermaker (Village Marine Squirt 400).
- 160 gallon per day DC watermaker (Village Marine Stowaway 160).
- Radar (x2): Furuno 1944C (6kw, 4 foot open array) radar and chart plotter, NavNet2 version. Furuno 1744 (4kw closed array), networked with Furuno Ethernet hub.

- Furuno GP32 GPS (x2).

- MaxSea Commander (software for PC).

- Simrad AP26 autopilot system (AC40 computer, RP300 pump) (x2).

- Furuno BBFF1 depth sounder.

- Icom 602 VHF/hailer.

- Icom 802 SSB.

- Pactor Modem (for SSB e-mail and weather fax).

- Seacas 100 AIS Reciever.

- Iridium Satellite Phone with Applied Satellite Docking Station.

- EPIRB (emergency satellite beacon) with GPS.

- Belkin wireless USB hub to allow wireless sat phone connection and MaxSea dongle connection/sharing.

- Winslow Offshore Rescue Maxi-4 (6 person life raft, includes watermaker and EPRIB).

- Delta 88 pound anchor primary anchor with 400 feet of high tensile 3/8 inch chain.

- Florentino Parachute Anchor (18 feet).

- Galerider Drogue (42×48 inches).

- 400 feet of line nylon deployment rode for Para anchor or drogue.

- Fortress 55 anchor (big stern anchor, or secondary anchor to 88 pound Delta).

- Danforth High Tensile 20lbs (stern anchor) mounted in lazarette.

- 50 feet of G4 HT chain attached to 150 5/8 three braided nylon (stern line or secondary anchor rode).

- Water tight floating "ditch bag" loaded with flares, first aid, and misc. survival and safety goodies.

- Gig Harbor Navigator (10 foot sailing/rowing/power hard shell) with Honda 2hp 4-stroke motor.

- Achilles 10.4 LSI (10.4 foot all inflatable Hypalon) with Nissan 6hp 4-stroke motor.

- Two 125 watt solar panels.

- Solar charge controller (Blue Sky Energy 2000E)

- Xantrex 2512 pure sine wave inverter/charger (DC to AC power converter).

- 50 amp Mastervolt multi-phase, multi-voltage battery charger.

- Bauer Jr. Air Compressor (110v) for filling SCUBA tanks (3200 psi).

Glossary

Boaters have a special language all their own. When Eric and I started this endeavor, we didn't speak "boat" and often had no clue what people were talking about. I wrote this glossary myself because I had trouble understanding the standard boating glossaries. Hopefully, it will help non-boaters better understand our book. Some of the definitions are overly simplistic, but give enough information to follow the story:

Aft: The back of the boat. Used interchangeably with "stern."

Anchor (noun): Weight on a chain that is attached to the boat. The weight is thrown overboard in an anchorage and keeps the boat from drifting away.

Anchor (verb): Essentially parking your boat in the water by dropping the anchor.

Anchorage: A designated and favorable place where boaters are allowed to anchor. In most places, boaters can't simply drop anchor anywhere they want.

Anemometer: A device that measures how many degrees the boat rolls.

Beam Seas: When the waves are hitting the side of the boat. Normally, boaters will say, "port beam" or "starboard beam" to distinguish which side.

Bilge Pump: A pump that removes sea water that may leak into the boat.

Boat Hook: A large hook on a long pole.

Bow: The front of the boat. Used interchangeably with "forward."

Buoy: A floating object that is a marker for something, such as a mooring or a channel.

Chain: In addition to the usual definition, "chain" can also mean extra weight above and beyond the anchor. Since chain is heavy, the more chain that is put out, the less likely the anchor is to move.

Cleat: a piece of metal attached to a dock that you tie the lines to.

Cockpit: Back deck, where the aft entrance to the boat is.

Confused Seas: Waves hitting from multiple directions at once.

Course made good (CMG): Sailboats often have to make zigzag patterns to catch the wind right. CMG refers to how many straight-line miles a boat has done, as opposed to how many miles it really did by zigzagging. Sometimes, if the wind is coming from a bad direction, a boat will do fifty real miles, but only ten CMG miles.

Decks: Outside areas meant to walk around on.

Dinghy: A small boat used to get cruisers from the boat over to the shore. It is the boater's equivalent of a car. Also called a skiff or tender.

Dock (noun): A walkway that goes from the shore out to water that is deep enough to park a boat in. Boats can be tied up to the dock, allowing the boaters to walk to shore.

Dock (verb): Parking a boat along a dock or a sea wall (quay). Each dock/quay has its own system for how boats must be parked. Sometimes getting "docked" can be tricky.

Dorade Vents: Special vents for boats. They have a water trap so that fresh air can get inside without water also getting in.

Drag (noun): a special kind of rake for sand.

Drag (verb): When the anchor fails to keep the boat in place. Dragging is really, really bad.

Eddy: a pocket of still water in an area of flowing water. Eddies present potential hazards to small boats, particularly kayaks and canoes.

Fish: Besides the obvious, the nickname for the paravane weights, also sometimes called birds.

Flopper Stoppers: Similar to paravanes, but for use only when the boat is at anchor. Often people mistakenly use the terms interchangeably.

Fly Bridge: A second place to drive the boat from, located outside, on top of the pilot house. It is an optional feature on the Nordhavn 43 that we decided against.

Following seas: Waves hitting the boat from the back.

Forward: Front of the boat, used interchangeably with "bow".

Full Displacement Boat: A heavy boat with a deep keel that pushes through the water as it moves. Since it actually pushes the water, it can't go fast, but is stable in big seas. This type of boat tends to have a rolling motion. Most powerboats are planing boats and people are always surprised that ours is full displacement.

GPS: Global Positioning System. A magical device connected to a satellite that tells the user exactly where in the world they are.

Hail: Call, usually on the VHF radio

Head seas: When the waves are hitting the boat from the front.

ITCZ: Inter Tropical Convergence Zone. In the northern hemisphere winds and current dependably move one way and in the southern hemisphere they dependably move another. Near the equator, weather is less dependable because you get caught between the two weather patterns. It is nicknamed "the doldrums" by sailors because the trade winds often completely die here.

Keel: A fin under a boat that usually extends between three and ten feet deep. It is weighted and prevents the boat from flipping over when hit by a big wave.

Knot: The amount of time it takes to go one nautical mile in one hour. We report all our distances in nautical miles, and all our speeds in knots (nautical miles per hour).

Lazarette: Storage space under the cockpit.

Lee: Protected. For example, "lee side of the island" means there are no big waves that crash on that part of the island. Opposite of "windward".

Marina: Essentially a parking lot for boats with docks or a sea wall where cruisers can tie their boats.

Mast: Pole that holds up the sails and other various equipment.

Mediterranean Mooring (med-moor): One of many ways to tie a boat to a dock. First, the boat is positioned several feet in front of the desired parking space. Then the anchor is dropped and the boat is backed into the parking space. The back of the boat is tied to the dock and the front is held in place by the anchor. What makes this intimidating is that you usually have to slide into a space between two other boats, and backing into tight spots takes skill.

Mooring: Usually sunken blocks of concrete with ropes that are used to secure a boat.

Nautical Mile (nm): The Earth is divided up into 180 degrees of latitude (east to west measurement). One degree is then further divided into sixty minutes. One nautical mile is equal to the distance of one minute. This measurement system is very logical, unlike the random statute mile used in the USA. A nautical mile is about 1.15 statute miles or 1.85 kilometers. We report all our distances in nautical miles.

Paravanes: A stabilization system used when the boat is in motion. These poles stick out from the sides and drag weights, called "birds" or "fish," in the water. The weights retard the boat's ability to roll from side to side. They also prevent motion at anchor.

Planing Boat: A boat that skims the top of the water as it moves. It can go quite fast, but it needs a lot of power to lift up out of the water. These boats bounce up and down on the surface of the water, creating a pounding sensation in big waves.

Port: Left side of boat (facing forward)

Porthole: A strong window that can be sealed tight. If shut properly, it will keep water out.

Resolution (for charts): How detailed the chart is. High resolution is extremely detailed (shows each curve in the shore, no matter how sleight, every rock, etc). Low resolution shows only the major features and leaves out the minute details. When using medium and low resolution charts, one must keep a careful watch for uncharted potential hazards.

Rigging: Ropes and cables that usually hold things to masts. *Kosmos* has rigging for Paravanes and the crane to raise and lower the dinghy.

Quarter: Corner. Examples: "port aft quarter" means "back left corner" or "starboard forward quarter" means "front right corner".

Quay: A sea wall, usually concrete.

Sacrificial Zincs: Replaceable zinc pieces are attached to any metal that is under the water line, and the zincs corrode instead of the other metal.

Sextant: Mechanical device that helps cruisers figure out their coordinates by using a triangulation between the boat, the sun or a star, and the horizon. It is one way sailors navigated before GPS was invented.

Slip: Parking space in a marina

Snubber: A rope that you attach to the anchor chain. The rope acts as a shock absorber and keeps the chain from making noise while at anchor.

SSB: Single Side Band. Short for SSB Radio. A long range marine radio that can go hundreds of miles.

Starboard: Right side of the boat (facing forward)

Stern: Back of the boat, used interchangeably with "aft".

Stern anchor: A secondary anchor that is attached to the back of the boat, used to minimize the boat's movement in tight anchorages or to minimize rolling in anchorages with an unusual swell/wind pattern.

Trade Winds: Predictable wind patterns for a region.

VHF Radio: Very High Frequency Radio. A short range marine radio, with about a twenty mile reception range.

Windlass: A mechanical device that deploys and brings in the anchor and chain.

Windward: Unprotected. For example, "windward side of the island" means the side that gets pummeled by big waves. Opposite of "lee".